ACUTE MYOCARDIAL INFARCTION
reaction and recovery

ACUTE MYOCARDIAL INFARCTION
reaction and recovery

Rue L. Cromwell, Ph.D.
Professor of Psychiatry, Pediatrics, and Psychology,
Director of Research Division, Department of Psychiatry, University of Rochester,
Rochester, New York

Earl C. Butterfield, Ph.D.
Professor of Pediatrics and Psychology, University of Kansas Medical Center,
Kansas City, Kansas

Frances M. Brayfield, M.A.
Director, Career Planning Office, Scripps College,
Claremont, California

John J. Curry, M.D.
Formerly Director, Coronary Care Unit, Holy Cross Hospital,
and Associate Professor of Medicine,
Georgetown University Medical Center,
Silver Spring, Maryland

In collaboration with:
James V. Dingell, Ph.D.
Mary Headrick Haynes, Ph.D.
Carol Raff Tarica, M.A.
Barbara E. Siebelt, R.N.

with 24 illustrations

The C. V. Mosby Company
Saint Louis   1977

Copyright © 1977 by The C. V. Mosby Company

All rights reserved. No part of this book may be reproduced in any manner without written permission of the publisher.

Printed in the United States of America

Distributed in Great Britain by Henry Kimpton, London

The C. V. Mosby Company
11830 Westline Industrial Drive, St. Louis, Missouri 63141

Library of Congress Cataloging in Publication Data

Main entry under title:

Acute myocardial infarction.

    Bibliography: p.
    Includes index.
    1. Heart—Infarction—Psychological aspects.
2. Cardiovascular disease nursing—Psychological aspects. 3. Stress (Psychology). I. Cromwell, Rue L. [DNLM: 1. Myocardial infarct—Nursing.
2. Myocardial infarct—Rehabilitation. 3. Stress.
WG300 A188]
RC685.I6A24   616.1'2   76-49883
ISBN 0-8016-1079-6

GW/CB/B 9 8 7 6 5 4 3 2 1

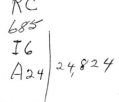

PREFACE

This book is many things. It begins with a major study of stress, personality, and nursing care factors involved in recovery from acute myocardial infarction. To do justice to these factors, routine medical and coronary care unit factors are also studied. The book then builds a bridge from the individual research fact to the way facts are applied. The psychological understanding and treatment of coronary patients and the prevention of coronaries are discussed in the final chapters.

It is a book for nurses and, in a subtle way, about the life nurses experience on a coronary care unit. It is an assertion that nurses, like those of other professions, can understand research procedures and can interpret results. It is a recognition of the emerging responsibility of nurses. It is a book about questions that coronary nurses often ask but seldom find answered in textbooks or with real data. It is a message to nurses—a plea, if you will—that the future development of their profession and the future understanding about patients in general must be greatly based on controlled research. It is a message that encouragement of controlled research by nurses and participation in it are among the highest of their professional functions and in no way contradictory to the humanitarian interest in care of the individual patient.

It is a book for physicians. It attempts to present research data clearly in order to bear directly upon the decisions about coronary patients that only physicians must make. It is a book that did not spring from a point of view; it sprung from a commitment to collect facts carefully and to point to ways the practitioner can translate facts into his own actions.

It is a book for the research scientist. It presents at times the tables and detail for evaluating this project or for setting up another project. Some passages will give the scientific reviewer a basis to judge the acceptability of the research and its design, and the physician and nurse in practice may wish to skim these passages briefly. Some tables and figures are basic references. The scientist and practitioner will wish to return to them, as to a dictionary, to locate a particular piece of information, but the specific facts are not necessarily crucial to understand the project, the book, and its implications. It is a message to those who believe that clinical research must always be descriptive, naturalistic, and uncontrolled. It is an argument that research projects must begin with a mindfulness to data management and precise statistical analysis rather than wander in this direction as an afterthought. As a research monograph (Part One), it departs from the practice of fragmenting research results into several publications. The results will presumably be more valuable as an integrated whole. But, then, after the monograph some leave is taken of the research scientist to return in Part Two to the practitioner.

It is a book for all those in the health professions who deal with life-threatening illnesses. Centers for medical training have traditionally taken on the bias that the issues of diagnosis and treatment of the severely ill patient are strictly biological, that the behavioral scientist has no place in coronary units or cancer wards. Here is a monograph that not only challenges this notion but places the psychological data alongside the biological data for the reader to compare. It is a psychosomatic approach.

It is a book for psychologists. It cuts across environmental control, physiological psychology, psychometrics, perception, social psychology, personality, behavior modification, and clinical psychology. It recognizes and draws upon the body of data from each of these and then illustrates how many levels of description should be considered in approaching complex problems. It is especially important for the psychologist working in medical schools and general hospital consultation.

It is a book for the educated layman who wants to know more about heart attacks. While not written for this purpose, it is inevitable that the prevalence of heart disease in our society will lead many to seek out how to prevent a coronary or what to anticipate if a coronary has been experienced.

It is a romantic book about a small group of people I was privileged to know, who wanted to make a contribution that would benefit people, and who were determined to forebear the frustration, uncertainty, and rejection often imposed on those today who advance knowledge through controlled research on human subjects.

Rue L. Cromwell

CONTENTS

APPENDIXES

INTRODUCTION
an odyssey in conducting coronary care research

In October of 1964 Dr. John J. Curry, a cardiologist and then forthcoming director of the coronary care unit being constructed in Holy Cross Hospital at Silver Spring, Maryland, approached the National Institute of Mental Health for assistance. He was interested in planning research on stress factors in recovery from myocardial infarction. Through referral from Drs. William C. Rhodes and Caroline Chandler of this agency, I was asked to consult with Dr. Curry, and the present project was subsequently designed and conducted.

With the approval and funding of NIMH Special Project MH-09220, we began our activities at Holy Cross Hospital on June 1, 1965. The first seven months of the project had been scheduled to develop research instruments and to gain sophistication in the literature and the subject matter of our task. Then, the first patients were examined in our subject sample. After 26½ consecutive months of data collection, we began data reduction, computer analysis, and preparation of results.

The problems and challenges . . .

In this project, psychologists worked with a cardiologist and the nursing staff of his coronary unit to examine the role of stress in the recovery of acutely ill heart patients. We expected and encountered resistance, obstacles, insecurities, and other grim realities from the beginning to the end of the project. It is clear now that success of the project rested greatly upon a devoted research team. Its members patiently endured these pressures and kept the faith that what they were doing was substantively important.

. . . within the research team

First, the issues and content of the research led to insecurities and pressures within the research team itself. Fortunately, these conflicts were on a professional rather than personal level, and all of them were resolved by open and unreserved discussion with no loss of teamwork, rationality, or esprit de corps. The psychologists on the team did not know how much psychological testing and environmental manipulation could be exercised without causing greater illness or death to the already acutely ill patients. The proposal by the cardiologist to investigate exercise was shocking to laymen-psychologists and to some physicians, too. The research review committees were concerned about the amount of blood to be drawn from the patients. In each of these cases, Dr. Curry's informed leadership, knowledge of literature, and careful explanations based on his clinical experience led us to resolve each of the methodological questions and personal hesitations. Even so, the insecurities persisted.

Although we had developed our procedures carefully and were committed to their value, there was the possibility, as in every truly good research project, that the particular factors examined would be found irrelevant. In addition, there was the continuing fear that a patient might die or become more seriously ill as a result of our research activities.

Another conflict, a true godsend, was the difference in approach to problems by Dr. Butterfield and me. I greatly needed to see the daily operations a success—to see cooperation excellent, spirits high, and all problems solvable. Dr. Butterfield became the pessimistic troubleshooter. He continually called to my attention potential lapses of cooperation within the coronary care unit. He pointed to other obstacles that could reduce or destroy the validity of the project. The interplay of my optimism and his pessimism broadened and prolonged our thoughtful discussions. Consequently, many problems were anticipated and successfully handled that each one of us alone may not have handled as adequately. This check-and-balance dialogue, a most rewarding research relationship, contributed greatly to the success of the project.

Also, as expected, problems arose from doing research in three locations. The data were collected by Frances Throne Brayfield and the staff at Silver Spring. Statistical planning and library research took place with Butterfield at Yale. The fiscal, administrative, and computer work took place with me at Vanderbilt University. Since Holy Cross Hospital had no wet research laboratory facilities, plasma samples were frozen and transported for analysis to Dr. James V. Dingell's and Dr. Murray Heimberg's laboratories at Vanderbilt University. Shipping the frozen plasma by air freight was unsuccessful, and the airlines raised many objections before finally allowing our technicians to bring freezer chests on board. The problems of having our laboratory technician working as a guest and adapting to the routine of someone else's laboratory are perhaps obvious. However, with the very kind help of my colleagues at Vanderbilt and a substantial telephone and travel budget, each of these obstacles was overcome.

Finally, there was the conflict about when to stop collecting data and to begin analyzing it. We were scheduled to complete data collection on January 1, 1968. However, at that time the sample size was just short of what we had hoped. Frances

Throne Brayfield, an uncommonly capable problem-solver, decided to continue collecting data on newly admitted patients and to delay the computer analyses as long as she could. Her arguments were unchallengable, and we continued data collection until March, 1968. After March came the race toward data reduction, computer analysis, interpretation of results, preparation of slides, and preparation of results for initial reporting. It was clear that the time for these activities had been sacrificed in favor of collecting the additional data. Carol Raff Tarica, in charge of the computer analyses, withstood my anxieties, the installation of a new computer at Vanderbilt University, and all the accompanying hardware and software problems that interfered with our good intentions. Thanks to her, much was accomplished before the fiscal end of the project in May, 1968.

After the project termination, data analyses and writing continued without attempts for further funding. Unfortunately, however, these final steps have gone slowly because all of us moved on to new responsibilities.

. . . on the coronary care unit

The investigation demanded that the three shifts of coronary care nurses carry out nursing and other procedures in a prescribed and structured fashion. It also depended upon a reasonable number of private practitioners who were willing to cooperate in our study of their patients. The vast majority of those who were asked granted cooperation. When it was not granted and when criticism and hostility were aimed at the project, it simply fell to the project research staff at Holy Cross Hospital to bear the burden. Besides the leadership and responsibility assumed by Dr. Curry in handling these problems, Barbara E. Siebelt, the head nurse and active collaborator on the research team, became an indispensable liaison with the nursing staff and physicians. Being a consultant on the project from the beginning, she remained a prime resource in understanding and investigating nursing care.

The resistance to psychological research with heart patients was contributed to by the newness of the coronary unit concept itself. Physicians and house staff were unaccustomed to and insecure with the new cardiac monitoring equipment and emergency treatment procedures. The cardiac nurses were assuming a new role of responsibility. They maintained surveillance of the patient's physical condition, applied emergency treatment procedures, and diplomatically instructed the less experienced physicians in coronary care. All this was new to coronary nurses at that time. With their traditional prime goal of patient care it is no wonder that the nurses would display anxiety and hostility when research workers administered various procedures daily to the patients. These procedures did not appear at the time to have any immediate value in getting the patient well and back home.

Another problem arose from the fact that nurses and general practitioners are traditionally not trained in research design. Thus, the need for strict scientific controls had to be explained often. For example, the need to assign randomly the incoming patients to nursing care procedures without any prior judgment about the patient's personal needs seemed highly objectionable to some. It was an insight for some to learn that selective rather than random assignment of patients would prevent the results from being fully interpretable.

As another example, some nurses had not realized that high diversional stimulation need not be considered beneficial simply because patients wanted it. While patients are often made unhappy by depriving them of smoking or by drawing blood, it is often assumed by some in nursing that psychological aspects of nursing care should always be oriented to the patient's immediate happiness. To question objectively the benefit or detriment of these aspects was a new idea. The clinical staff discovered that preconceived opinions about what was right and wrong could be questioned. While criticisms, logical and emotional, were frequent, cooperation was always received. The clinical and research staff grew together to realize the importance of answering research questions within the context of clinical care. Research and clinical care came to represent a common high goal rather than competitive territories of endeavor.

When physicians (fortunately very few in number) refused to cooperate, the solution was simple. Their patients were not included in the project. When nurses were resistant to cooperation, the matter was more serious. The quality of the research data was at stake. To augment the personal diplomacy of John Curry, Barbara Siebelt, and Frances Throne Brayfield, I flew to Washington occasionally for special meetings to discuss with the nurses their special questions of concern. We discussed the relation of the research to the welfare of specific patients, the government's financial research investment, which could so easily be wasted, and the possible changes in care for future cardiac patients depending on our findings. In addition, the research staff wrote and distributed regularly to the nursing staff bulletins on the progress of the research. Since the head nurse could both conceptualize research well and also understand how the questioning of long-held nursing practices could be upsetting, all such endeavors ultimately met with success. Although this kind of research on human subjects can never have machine-like precision and although the feelings of hesitation and objection were sincerely voiced by various nurses, we continued to receive ample evidence from patients and nurses that the different nursing care procedures we studied were being carried out as prescribed for the different groups. The nurses did not enjoy the idea of limiting visitors, television, and reading for certain patients. They did not enjoy staying away from pleasant conversation with certain ones in order to give them a more quiet atmosphere. But, they gave their cooperation anyway and saw the importance of doing so.

One incident occurred that could have terminated the project. A patient on the coronary care unit broke a window in an attempted suicide. The incident was immediately blamed on the research staff for conducting psychological tests and interviews on personal topics. Shortly, however, it was learned that this particular patient was not eligible for our study and had not been seen by the project staff.

The outcome of this incident, ironically, seemed to reduce tension and provide, thereafter, a closer mutual working relationship between the research and the clinical staffs. Even though such ominous threats to the research progress continued to occur, the vast and increasing majority of doctors and nurses gave congenial cooperation and support.

. . . in the committees and agencies

Besides the problems in planning and conducting the research, other problems arose. Two of these involved the acceptance of our project by the research committees that evaluated human rights and risks. Another concerned a reorganization of NIMH.

The committee responsible for evaluating human rights at Vanderbilt University School of Medicine, the sponsoring institution, disclaimed the project and declared that all responsibility had to lie with Holy Cross Hospital. The Vanderbilt committee felt that some of the procedures would endanger the lives of the patients and that it was unwise for psychologists (nonmedically trained) to conduct research with seriously ill patients. There were also similar objections by the comparable research committee at Holy Cross Hospital. These objections were conscientiously and successfully countered through the efforts of Dr. Curry.

Strong and sound safeguards for the welfare of research subjects are unquestionably vital and must be the first priority in clinical research operations. The rights and welfare of patients in research would be violated often unless there were clear and strong ethical guidelines and controls. However, it became evident that the decisions of committees depend on the expertise among their members. The particular committees evaluating our project were poorly represented in both cardiology and behavioral science. Physicians in general are trained in psychological research either inadequately or not at all. Such being the case, sociometric considerations tend to play an undue role in decision making. Any truly conscientious committee with less than intimate knowledge of a research area can retard the advancement of knowledge more often than it can discern how to safeguard human welfare. The present project became a reality with the eventual approval by the Holy Cross research committee, and no death or even minimal complication occurred as a function of the two years of conducting research procedures.

We soon discovered that half the admissions to our coronary unit were retrospectively found to have insufficient evidence of myocardial infarction (MI). While the disconfirmed MIs provided a fairly ideal control group, the limited number of MIs meant that we had to apply to NIMH to extend the project from two to three years. NIMH was being reorganized at this time, and the project was transferred to a new branch. Consequently, the "special project" status (MH-09220) was discontinued. This meant that the project had to be resubmitted as a new grant request (MH-13614) and had to be reviewed by individuals who had no knowledge of its ongoing history and progress. This was done. The site visit, competitive reapproval, and refunding attempts were successful. However, to our team of investigators there was the obvious threat that the project would be interrupted prematurely, the findings never realized, and their jobs abruptly lost.

The mortality

With the problems and threats associated with this type of research, it is understandable that we should breathe a sigh of relief and satisfaction when data collection was over. During the period of this study the commonly reported mortality rate was 30% for heart patients admitted to regular hospital wards and 18% for those admitted to coronary care units. Of the 229 patients who participated in this study, none (0%) died on the coronary care unit, four (1.7%) died after being transferred away from our study to a regular hospital ward, and four (1.7%) died within 12 weeks of their attack but after returning home. Our mortality rate was below and not comparable to the former data for two reasons. Patients over 60 years of age were not a part of the study. Of the group under 60 years of age, we judged 7% too seriously ill to take part in the research. Even so, the mortality of patients in our study was lower than we had initially expected. Even if the mortality rate had come close to normative expectancy, suspicion would have been cast on the unique investigations we were conducting.

Our thanks are offered to the 229 patients who participated in our study. We hope our findings have made some contribution to the understanding of myocardial infarction and its psychological treatment. We also hope we have presented an example of the role behavioral science can play in research on heart patients and other severely ill people. As with any other study, our findings must stand the test of scrutiny by future investigators before a proper and final evaluation can be made.

Who did what

The authorships of a study do not always communicate the contribution that each person made. Therefore, a summary of these contributions is presented here.

I, as principal investigator, formulated the basic research design, prepared the original proposal, hired the initial staff, served as head of the research team in conducting the project, administered the budget, supervised the computer analysis, and played the primary role in interpreting and presenting the findings in oral and written form.

Earl C. Butterfield, the executive consultant, played a major role in supervision and policy decisions. He refined the detailed aspects of the research design, planned the statistical analysis, developed various instruments, troubleshot the weak spots in the project, worked with the group at Holy Cross in my absence, helped prepare the extension proposal, reviewed the literature, helped interpret the results, and participated in the writing of the project. During many segments of the project his commitment and contribution were tantamount to being in the role of principal investigator and senior author.

Frances ("Frankie") M. Brayfield, the research associate and field director, was in charge of the research staff and operations at Holy Cross Hospital. She participated in the final research design planning, the instrument development, the pilot work, the hiring of research assistants for her staff, the equipment and supply management, the testing and interviewing of patients, the organization and coding of data, and the interpretation and writing. She was responsible for establishing relationships with other doctors, nurses, hospital administrators, and the hospital staff that were essential for the proper execution of the project. Her careful handling of data, her personal ability to deal warmly with people, and her persistence—even after work hours and on weekends—was invaluable to the quality of the project.

Dr. John J. Curry, co-investigator of the project and director of the coronary care unit, initiated the research idea and sought assistance at NIH to bring the project into being. He participated in working out the final methods of procedure, assumed responsibility for all research and medical care activities in the coronary unit, and contributed to the literature search. Problems of medical responsibility were referred to him. Problems of data collection and professional cooperation were referred to him when they could not be handled at lower levels.

Susan Tracie Haggerty, research technician, was Frances Brayfield's major assistant throughout the course of the project. Her role required administering the various psychological tests, helping to solve the day-to-day problems of equipment and supplies, performing secretarial duties, sharing the interpersonal demands of the project, and assisting with the psychopolygraphic recording and the administration of the nursing care procedures. She assumed the role of field director of the project during Ms. Brayfield's vacation periods.

John F. Bradshaw, medical technologist and research assistant, administered the stress task, drew blood samples, prepared and froze plasma, and transported it by air to Nashville. There he initiated and carried out the procedures for analyzing plasma 17-hydroxycorticosteroids (17-OH-CS) and nonesterized (free) fatty acids (NEFA) under supervision. He participated in the design and pilot work to develop the stress task. He also assisted in other activities of the project, such as data scoring and reduction.

Nat Heidorn, medical technologist and research assistant, also performed the drawing of blood and the administration of the stress task. She assisted in other activities, such as data scoring and transporting plasma to Nashville. She also volunteered time beyond the call of duty during times when the project greatly needed her services.

Barbara E. Siebelt, head nurse in the coronary unit and nursing consultant in our project, was the major liaison to help interface the procedures of research with the activities in the coronary care unit. Her efforts did much to maintain the high morale among the research staff, nurses, patients, and, I am sure, the director of the coronary care unit.

Dr. Mary Headrick Haynes, my postdoctoral fellow in psychopharmacology, was in charge of the psychopolygraphic aspects of the project. (This aspect of the project began late. Permission was requested from NIMH during the second year to purchase equipment to perform this part of the project.) Dr. Headrick participated in the research design of the stress task procedure and was solely responsible for designing the analysis of psychopolygraphic measures, putting the equipment into operation, training the field staff to operate it, supervising the data reduction, and completing the data analyses.

Carol Raff Tarica, project research associate for computer analysis, worked with Ms. Brayfield to set up the data analysis. She was responsible for getting it punched, verified, and subjected to the several multivariate analyses outlined by Dr. Butterfield and me. Finally, she worked with me on the interpretation of print-out sheets and the additional analyses that followed the initial interpretation.

Mary Lou Norvich assisted in the analysis of plasma 17-OH-CS.

Lee Wilhite assisted in the analysis of NEFA.

Dr. James V. Dingell, associate professor of pharmacology, supervised the plasma 17-OH-CS analysis in his laboratory. He also assisted in getting the NEFA analysis procedure set up and in preparing the report of findings.

Dr. Murray Heimberg, supervised the analysis of NEFA in his laboratory later in the project.

Dr. Grant Liddle and his staff and Dr. John Mason offered helpful advice concerning the research on plasma 17-OH-CS. Dr. H. C. Meng advised on the plasma storage and analysis for NEFA. Dr. John Lacey consulted on some of the psychophysiological aspects of the study. Drs. Ray Rosenman and David Jenkins consulted on the aspects of personality investigation. Drs. Richard Gorsuch and James Hogge consulted on the statistical procedures. Ellen Durham Davis consulted on the nursing aspects of the study. Dr. Albert B. Craig gave helpful advice on exercise physiology.

Reba Moore was the fiscal and administrative secretary. Nita Peak participated in the typing of initial manuscripts.

Opal Barylski, Sue Willis, and Ruth Franck typed the final manuscript. Patricia Dwyer assisted editorially and in proofreading.

Finally, the nurses, house staff, maintenance staff, private practitioners, data scorers, patients, and spouses of patients who gave willingly of their time and effort are extremely numerous and greatly deserving of our appreciation.

Rue L. Cromwell

PART ONE

A STUDY OF STRESS, PERSONALITY, NURSING FACTORS, AND RECOVERY

Chapter 1

UNANSWERED QUESTIONS IN CORONARY CARE AND RECOVERY

The first part of this book reports the results of a prospective investigation of the role of nursing care and personality in patients' recovery from acute myocardial infarction. (Hereafter, we will usually refer to this disorder as MI.) For the patients who participated, our study began when a decision was made, usually in the emergency room, to admit them to a coronary care unit with suspected acute MI. The major part of the study occurred while the patient was on the coronary unit and terminated when his progress had been tracked through the remaining days of hospitalization and a final follow-up had been made at home 12 weeks after his attack.

A number of critical questions were studied during this period. Most important of all, what are the factors that influence recovery? Are any conditions and events linked to death, positively or negatively, during the 12 weeks following an acute MI? How can one predict who will have a subsequent MI during these 12 weeks?

Less important, but economically relevant, what events and conditions are linked to length of coronary unit and hospital stay? To return to work?

On the level of psychological well-being, what influences a patient's feeling of comfort (or lack of it) during this stressful period? What factors influence his cooperation with nurses and doctors? Do these factors affect the patient's health and physical recovery?

QUESTIONS CONCERNING STRESS

We used the concept of stress to guide our formulation of questions concerning recovery, comfort, cooperation, and length of care. We did not view stress as a condition defined in terms of environmental events alone. Instead, we thought of it as an intervening concept that links environmental conditions to biological and behavioral responses of the subject. Used in this way, stress is an organizing principle, not a cause or effect. It encompasses both environmental input and human response.

On the input side, it is safe to assume that having a heart attack and being removed from one's customary living situation arouse stress. Pain and extreme temperature also elicit stress, as does failure when one is expecting success.

On the output side, stress is accompanied by certain biological changes. These include increased plasma level of 17-hydroxycorticosteroid (17-OH-CS) and nonesterized fatty acids (NEFA). Changes occur in psychophysiologic reactions such as galvanic skin response (GSR), breathing, heart rate, and blood flow in the extremities. Psychological changes of mood also occur. To determine if recovery from acute MI is influenced by stress, this project examined certain stress-related output variables and also those routinely collected clinical measures thought relevant to cardiac recovery.

One of the most important but often implicit assumptions in coronary treatment is that proper nursing and psychological approaches to the patient reduce stress. The possibility that stress may play a role in recovery from acute MI is well reflected in three questions that are often asked by physicians and nurses: How much should the patient be told about the nature and severity of his condition? How much diversional stimulation should he be allowed? Should the patient participate in his own treatment activities, whenever possible, or should he be kept low in activity and participation? To answer these questions, patients in this research were randomly assigned to treatment groups that reflected different combinations of nursing care practices. When patients are systematically studied in this controlled fashion, the effect of information, diversion, and participation can better be understood. Moreover, it can be determined whether certain patients, as individual personalities, benefit from one combination of nursing care procedures while other patients with different personalities benefit from a different combination.

QUESTIONS CONCERNING PERSONALITY

The role of certain personality factors in physical illness and recovery were also examined. Physicians and nurses, and even psychologists, have differed in their assumptions about how personality relates to coronary and other illnesses. As human beings, we can all point to attitudes and actions that we feel are psychologically good for a sick person. We can do this without knowing the personality of the individual, the nature of his illness, or the life stresses that accompany the illness. Some physicians and nurses assume this "psychological care" should be given because it is the human thing to do. Others assume, in addition, this care has a direct effect on physical well-being and recovery.

Some physicians and nurses assume that a more technical knowledge of the patient's emotional state and personality, as assessed psychologically, is useful in prescribing care for him. They believe that different people should be handled differently, depending on specific and measurable personality factors. Others assume that the same basic rules of "good care" apply to everyone and that these psychological discriminations are not important. They see no need for psychological data beyond what they themselves, as nurses and physicians, can assess intuitively.

Some physicians and nurses who adopt the approach that patients differ go one step further. They assume that good psychological care can be determined only when one understands personality differences, life environment differences, and interactions among them. That is, what is stressful to one personality may be satisfying and challenging for another. What is good nursing care for one personality may be the opposite for another. Other physicians and nurses may assume that such distinctions do not exist, are not strong enough to be of practical importance, or that as practitioners they are just not sufficiently sophisticated to make good use of such distinctions.

Going back to the physicians and nurses who make the assumption that these personality and nursing care factors do have a direct bearing on physical illness, still another distinction can be made. Some assume that the personality–illness (i.e., psychosomatic) relationship is disease specific. For example, some assume that personality factors contribute directly to some diseases but not others. This assumption is reflected in the concept of the "coronary-prone personality." Other practitioners assume that personality factors are important in determining a susceptibility to illness, but that organic (nonpsychological) factors determine what illness will be manifested.

In the same vein the environmental factors of life stress and, on the other hand, desirable nursing care are assumed by some to be illness specific. To others these influences from the outside world are assumed to be inherently beneficial or detrimental in themselves, regardless of the type of illness or personality.

Understanding the role of personality and illness, taking a position on the foregoing issues, or even studying them are not simple matters. We recognize this, and our intent is not to pontificate or to sell a point of view. Different positions have too often been taken without adequate supporting data. From the viewpoint of the nurse and the physician, taking a strict position is often not necessary. The issues reduce themselves to a simple set of questions: Are there psychological factors operating in the illness? If so, what should I be doing (or doing differently or not doing) to help the patient? No single research project is capable of providing inclusive and final answers, but well-conceived research can provide important guides to clinical practice. This project was designed to study how certain personality, nursing care, stress response, and biological factors affect the recovery of acute MI patients. Comparisons are made among MI patients and two groups of control patients—one coronary unit group of patients suspected for acute MI but later disconfirmed and one group of hospitalized patients who were comparably ill but did not have cardiovascular involvement.

Too often, the role of personality and other psychological factors are studied separately from the physiological and physical treatment factors. This shortcoming allows camps of inflexible opinion to develop regarding the relative importance of one or the other. Whenever possible in this study, the relative potency of psychological and biological factors was compared. For example, biological and psychological factors were studied together with respect to their value in predicting a recurrence of acute MI. It seems important for physicians and nurses to know the relative importance of biological and psychological contributions to an illness.

MODE OF APPROACH

We exercised several explicit strategies when designing this study. The foremost of these was the choice of a controlled research design rather than a clinical naturalistic study. We are committed to the notion that systematically controlled studies are possible with seriously ill human subjects and that the results of controlled studies are more definitive and generalizable. No clinical case histories or naturalistic observations will be presented here—not because they are unimportant. Indeed, they are vitally important in revealing patterns and principles necessary to understanding the individual patient and his treatment. They are even important for the generation of hypotheses for research. The purpose of this project, however, is to identify patterns and principles that can be confirmed and generalized across the total population of people with myocardial infarction.

Prospective studies are preferable to retrospective studies. A prospective study attempts to identify factors that will predict an outcome before it occurs. A retrospective study is one where the relevant factors are sought after the outcome has occurred. This project is a prospective study of recovery. If it were focused upon who gets an initial MI, it would be retrospective. This study has only limited indirect and no direct relevance to initial onset of MI but relates instead to factors in recovery. Retrospective data are nevertheless of some value in identifying patterns and principles that need further investigation in a controlled prospective setting. Accordingly, some retrospective data are reported, because they suggest new ideas about the role of stress in the etiology of MI.

A theoretical point of view is often considered necessary to set the direction of a research project. On the other hand, when much is yet to be known, a theory-*bound* project will have the risk of proceeding little further than the variables and organizing principles already in its focus. Much value is therefore to be gained from an empirical approach, since it opens the way to identifying relationships not previously expected among the variables studied. Accordingly, this project has both theoretical and empirical aspects. Some previous theoretical notions of the coronary-prone personality help set the direction of the study, but other unforeseen relationships are identified and then cross-validated.

In a project theoretically focused on certain questions but designed to examine other empirical interrelationships among variables, a number of by-products emerges. For example, in this study it was possible to examine the concept of severity of myocardial infarction. What represents a severe heart attack as compared to a mild one? Do the indices of severity agree with each other from case to case? Does severity of acute MI indicate a poor prognosis (as might reasonably be expected), or is severity independent of prognosis?

Another topic resulting from our "by-products strategy" concerns *how* to collect historical and psychological data, as well as what to collect. Can personal history be more reliably collected from a spouse or close relative who answers questions as he or she thinks the patient would answer? If so, this would relieve the ill patient from part of the diagnostic workup. Or, on the other hand, is the relative a less reliable and dependable reporter during this "helpless spectator" period? These and other by-products, sometimes of scientific significance beyond the study of myocardial infarction, were gleaned from this study.

Chapter **2**

ANSWERING THE QUESTIONS
methods and procedures

SUBJECT SELECTION

The subjects of the study were 309 patients of Holy Cross Hospital in Silver Spring, Maryland. This group includes 229 patients who were admitted to the coronary care unit for suspected myocardial infarction and 80 off-ward non-MI control patients who were comparably ill but without cardiovascular involvement.

The 229 coronary care unit patients were selected in the following way. During the period of the project, all patients under the age of 60 and with suspected myocardial infarction were considered as potential candidates for study. Patients over 60 were rejected for study because of the possibility of other factors complicating their illness. The total number of admissions of these potential candidates was 377 coronary patients. Of this group, 30 were found to be readmitted patients who had already participated in the study. This left a total of 347. Thus, the 229 indicated above who were actually studied represented 66% of the eligible admissions. The remaining 34% (118 patients) who failed to be in the project, even under partial study, were mostly excluded because their coronary stay was too short. In other cases the patients or personal physicians or both declined informed consent. Also, some patients were considered by us to be too severely ill to participate in the study. In one instance the patient was a psychologist whose sophistication with our testing procedures made him an inappropriate candidate.

Next, a distinction is made between those patients who participated in the nursing care part of the study and those who did not. Typically, a patient who remained in the unit long enough to have valid data on the effects of the nursing care variables had complete or almost complete data on all variables of the study. For those who were not in the nursing care study, much valid data were nevertheless collected and are reported here as part of the total patient sample. A patient was considered to have valid data in the nursing care study if he had spent at least three full days on the coronary unit. (The modal time for patients on the unit was five days.) Thus, again, an

Table 2-1. Factors in the subject selection for total study
(including nursing care study)

		N		%	
Patients in nursing care study		183		53	
Patients excluded from study		164		47	
Stay too short on coronary unit	65		19		
Physician/patient declined consent	32		9		
Unmonitored bed in coronary unit	27		8		
Condition judged too severe	23		7		
Staff vacations, meetings, etc.	5		1		
Staff developing skill in procedures	4		1		
Patient was psychologist	1		0		
Unrecorded	7		2		
Total potential candidates		347		100	

attrition occurred. Of the 229 coronary unit patients in the project, only 183 stayed long enough to give sufficient data to be included in the nursing care aspect of the study. This number represents 80% of the coronary patients who participated in some way in the study and 53% of the 347 potential candidates admitted to the coronary unit during the project.

The remaining 47% (164 patients) of the 347 potential candidates were studied partially or not at all. The selective factors that occured to prevent these patients' complete participation are summarized in Table 2-1.

The importance of the selective factors just described may be seen in the mortality rate during the period of time the study was taking place. During this period the mortality rate on the coronary unit was 18%; the mortality rate for coronary patients included in our study was zero. The mortality figure of 18% is comparable to the mortality rates reported in other electronically monitored coronary care units during the same period. The mortality rate with myocardial infarction has been estimated to be 40%. For those victims who remain alive long enough to be admitted to a regular hospital ward, the mortality rate is 30%. The mortality on coronary care units represents a substantial reduction and thus has increased the application of the coronary unit concept. While selective factors regarding the kind of patient entering a coronary unit may affect this improved rate (negatively or positively), the increased quality and speed of care are usually considered the significant factors. Twenty-four hours per day monitoring of heart rhythms, the ability to detect a patient in distress within seconds without his beckoning, and a staff specifically trained for coronary care and resuscitation techniques seem to be among the relevant factors leading to improvement. Once admitted to the coronary unit, the mortality rate during the first 24 hours is by far higher than the rate during later periods. After this marked decrease, the rate continues to decrease more gradually during the subsequent days. The first five days following a heart attack are typically considered to be the critical ones. During this period, the physician makes a judgment as to when the patient will be transferred to a regular hospital ward to begin a longer period of convalescence. When the patient is discharged to go home, there is typically another period recommended by the physician before he returns to work.

While the mortality rate for our subject sample was zero on the coronary care unit, four patients died after being transferred from our coronary unit study to the regular hospital wards. Four died within 12 weeks but after returning home. Thus, the statistical analysis of death data was computed on the basis of these deaths after transfer from the coronary unit. The 18% coronary unit mortality during this period was attributable to those patients too old to be in our study and to the 7% judged by us upon admission to be too severely ill to participate.

After our study of a patient was completed and after he was transferred from the coronary unit to a regular hospital ward, a final diagnosis was made retrospectively. The 377 potential candidates of the study were divided at this time into 186 confirmed acute myocardial infarction patients and 191 patients who were disconfirmed for acute myocardial infarction. Thus, 49% of the patients were confirmed and 51% were disconfirmed. Most coronary units have about one-third to one-half of their admissions confirmed for acute myocardial infarction. Thus, the ratio of confirmations to disconfirmations of acute MIs in this unit suggests that the diagnostic criteria for myocardial infarction were fairly strict but within the usual range. This final diagnosis was made by a cardiologically oriented United States Public Health Service physician who examined the accumulated clinical data with a uniform set of criteria. The cardiologically oriented USPHS physician was a full-time resident on the coronary unit as a function of a USPHS project concerning the utilization of cardiac monitors in coronary units. The private physician of each patient also gave a final diagnosis, but these diagnoses were not used in the present project because they were not based upon a uniform set of criteria. The group that was retrospectively confirmed is referred to herein as the MI group. The group that was suspected but disconfirmed is referred to as the on-ward non-MI control group.

Table 2-2 presents the summary of MI and on-ward non-MI control patients in the total eligible group, the participating sample, and the full (nursing care) participant sample. As will be observed, the ratio of MIs to non-MIs increases as one successively compares the eligible candidates, the participating sample (either fully or in part), and the full participants. In fact, this ratio proceeds from 0.9 to 1.3 to 1.7 respectively. This finding, as might be expected, results from the fact that non-MI patients tended to be transferred early and did not remain long enough for extensive participation in the study.

The fact that acute myocardial infarction cannot be firmly diagnosed upon admission provided the on-ward non-MIs as a valuable control group for many of the hypotheses studied. While these patients were being studied, the nurses and staff, the physicians, and the investigators were all assuming that these patients had had a heart attack. Only after data collection and confirmed diagnosis was the acute MI group separated from the on-ward non-MI control group.

After being admitted with suspected acute myocardial infarction, the on-ward

Table 2-2. MI and on-ward non-MI admissions to coronary unit who were eligible candidates, partial participants, and full (including nursing care) participants in the study

	MI		Non-MI		Total	
	N	%	*N*	%	*N*	%
All coronary unit admissions under 60	186	49	191	51	377	100
All coronary-unit-eligible patients under 60 (i.e., excluding readmitted patients)	161	46	186	54	347	100
Patients with at least partial participation	131	38	98	28	229	66
Patients in full study including nursing care study	115	33	68	20	183	53

control group patients were later given diagnoses such as cardiac exhaustion, pancreatitis, or duodenal ulcer. In most cases cardiovascular involvement occurred in the current illness; in some cases it did not. In no case was there evidence of an acute MI with the current illness.

Since the practical demands of the clinical treatment situation did not allow every subject to be assessed on every variable, a small amount of data is sporadically missing on various patients even in the case of those referred to as "full participants." Therefore, the actual number of patients (N) varies from analysis to analysis. In addition, the psychopolygraphic equipment was acquired late in the study. Therefore, the total number in this portion of the study is small.

The off-ward non-MI control group subjects were 80 patients on the hospital's intensive care unit or elsewhere in the hospital. They were without cardiovascular involvement, but their illnesses were comparable in severity. They were not assessed on certain measures either because the hypotheses of the study did not require it or because the appropriate equipment was not available on the ward where the off-ward control patient was located. Therefore, the number of patients involved will be reported separately for each analysis of results.

THE CORONARY CARE UNIT

The coronary care unit of Holy Cross Hospital of Silver Spring, Maryland, was a six-bed unit.* It was designed specifically for patients with myocardial infarction, suspected MI, or serious arrhythmias. Each patient was under the care of his own private physician. All medical procedures, however, were supervised by the coronary unit medical staff. This staff consisted of several nurses, a medical director, who was also chief of the electrocardiographic department of the hospital, and a board-qualified or board-certified internist with cardiology training. The latter person functioned as the in-unit assistant to the director. This position was held by two part-time physicians during the major portion of this study. Both physicians and the

---

*Description of the coronary care unit of Holy Cross Hospital is based upon the initial construction, which occurred in 1965.

nurses played vital roles in disseminating information systematically to patients in the study.

The nurses were selected for training and duty with the approval of the unit medical director, and approximately 45 to 60 hours of special didactic training were required. At least two registered nurses were on duty at all times, as were the necessary auxiliary personnel. In the event of emergencies, additional nursing staff were temporarily available from nursing service or a back-up team came from an adjacent medical wing.

For five of the six beds, there was a cardiac monitor to which the patient was attached by means of chest electrodes as soon as he was admitted. He remained connected to the monitor throughout his stay, which was typically five to seven days. The coronary nurse in Fig. 2-1 is in the process of adjusting a cardiac monitor above one of the beds. The relationship of the cardiac monitor to the patient's bed can be seen.

There was a continuous oscilloscopic display of the patient's electrocardiogram on the bedside monitor and on an oscilloscope at the nurses' station. A blinking light on both oscilloscopes, as well as a beeping tone on the oscilloscope at the nurses' desk, reflected the heartbeat of each patient. For clear perception by the nurses, the beeping tone volume was usually lowered for all but the most severely ill patient. The remaining heartbeats were monitored from the blinking lights. The range of desired heart rate could be set on the bedside monitor. Should the patient's rate fall below or rise above that desired range, an audiovisual alarm was sounded at the nurses' station, and an automatic 30-second ECG printout was recorded at the bed-

Fig. 2-1. Coronary nurse adjusts cardiac monitor at patient's bed.

side. By means of a memory device, the ECG of the 15 seconds prior as well as the 15 seconds subsequent to activation was printed. This made it possible to examine ECG during the period that immediately preceded the alarm. The alarm could be discontinued only at the bedside monitor, which assured a nurses' going into the patient's room at the time of the alarm.

The ECG also could be scheduled to print a 30-second strip at intervals of from 1 to 60 minutes. Typically, the monitor was set for printout once every hour. In addition, should any abnormal ECG pattern appear on a patient's oscilloscope at any time, the printout could be activated either from the nurses' desk or at the bedside monitor by pressing a button.

A variety of equipment, such as a defibrillator, intubation set, pacemakers, and so on were readily available for emergencies.

During the day the coronary unit was always kept well lighted. A carpeted floor and acoustical ceiling controlled the level of sound. At the time this study was conducted the coronary unit concept was new, and professional visitors were frequent. With the nurses, nurses' aides, physicians, and research staff, the number of hospital staff typically exceeded the number of patients during most of the day. Therefore, the average level of stimulation and attention given each patient, regardless of the research group to which he was assigned, was probably somewhat above that of the average hospital ward setting.

NURSING CARE STUDY

As patients in the project came to the hospital with suspected myocardial infarction, a decision was made by the personal physician or by the house staff in the emergency service to assign them to the coronary care unit. Once admitted to the coronary unit, a patient was immediately assigned to an empty bed in an individual roomette that was furnished with equipment for carrying out a predesignated set of nursing care procedures. Each patient was then assigned by the research staff to one of the nursing care treatment combinations. The assignment of patients to beds and to nursing care treatment procedures was on a restricted random basis. The availability of beds at the time of admission was the factor restricting assignment. (Each bed was equipped for certain nursing care conditions and not others.) Near the end of the project, to equalize the number of patients in each of the different groups, certain groups were considered filled to quota, and the assignment of patients would go only to groups with unfilled quotas. Otherwise, the assignment was random. In this way, group and bed assignments were made independently of severity, personality, or other factors.

Once the bed and nursing care group assignment was made, the inclusion of the patient in the project was still tentative. Part of the work of the first day was to determine the patient's eligibility for the project. His admitting diagnosis was checked to make sure he had a suspected myocardial infarction. His age was recorded. His condition was observed closely. Patients were excluded from the project if they were found ineligible on any one of the following criteria:

1. Age over 60 years
2. Illness judged to be too severe to take part in the study
3. Admitting diagnosis other than myocardial infarction
4. Mental incompetence to the extent of being unable to comply with instructions and personality assessment
5. Refusal of informed consent by patient or his physician

All patients were checked for anemia during their first day. While positive evidence of anemia was to have been a basis for exclusion from the study, no patient who otherwise fit the criteria for the study was excluded on this basis.

If a patient did not stay on the coronary care unit at least three days, his data were considered too minimal to be in the nursing care study. However, the data collected in this short period were used in other aspects of the study.

For purposes of administering experimental procedures, the day the patient arrived was considered day 1 of the study if he arrived before 3:30 PM. If he arrived after 3:30 PM, the following day was considered day 1 of his period of study. If the patient arrived either heavily sedated or too weak and severe in symptoms to participate immediately in the project, day 1 was moved forward to the time he could participate in the experiment. Research procedures on each patient were carried out according to the designated day of the patient's stay on the coronary care unit, but recorded length of coronary unit stay was measured from actual time of admission.

Patients were assigned to one of eight nursing care conditions, which are illustrated in Fig. 2-2. In a 2 × 2 × 2 design, each patient was given either high or low amounts of information about the nature of his heart condition, diversional stimulation, and participation in his own treatment. For example, as may be seen in Fig. 2-2,

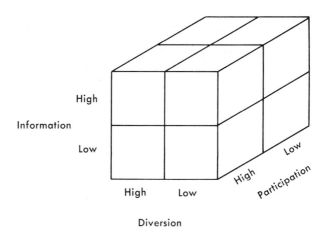

Fig. 2-2. Diagram of research design to study eight patient groups with respect to high versus low information, high versus low diversion, and high versus low participation in self-treatment.

a patient might receive high information, high diversion, and low participation. Another patient would receive a different combination of levels of information, diversion, and participation. All possible combinations of information, diversion, and participation were represented in the eight nursing care treatment groups.

The research staff, house physicians, nurses, and private physicians were instructed personally, through notes in the patients' charts and by letter codes attached to the foot of each patient's bed, about the nursing procedures to be followed with each patient. Also, detailed instructions were kept in the nurses' station for ready access to visiting physicians.

The procedures that differentiated the "high" and "low" levels of the nursing care dimensions are as follows.

High information. Patients in the four groups who received high information listened to two tape recordings. The longer one, called the high information tape, explained the nature of a heart attack, its causes, and its treatment (see Appendix A). When the high information patients asked to hear this tape again or when their relatives asked to hear it, they were allowed to do so. The shorter tape, called the low information tape, gave limited information but described the environment of the coronary unit and gave support and reassurance (see Appendix B). Literature from the American Heart Association and other sources was read by the high information patients. This literature included explanations of heart attacks, the cardiovascular system, the functions and operation of the coronary care unit. The coronary unit house physician assigned to each patient explained extensively the same information.

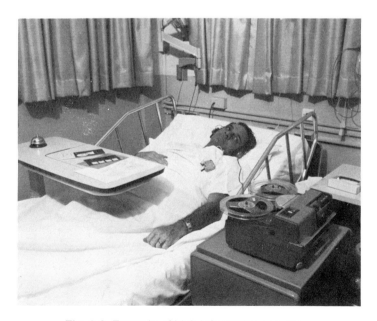

Fig. 2-3. Example of high information condition.

The nurses were encouraged to give full explanations to the patients' questions about heart disease and about the coronary unit. The private physicians who agreed to be a part of the study were told personally and through the patients' charts to be as informative as possible to the patient about his condition.

One of the two coronary unit house physicians was naturally inclined to give full explanations to the patients about their conditions and the other was not. Therefore, the house physicians were selectively assigned to patients so that the one who elaborated more fully had the "high information" patients and the one less inclined to elaborate had the "low information" patients. Fig. 2-3 is an example of the high information condition.

Low information. The patients in the four groups who received low information were given only the shorter of the two tape recordings (i.e., the low information tape). This tape was oriented toward support and reassurance with limited information. No literature on heart disease was made available to these patients. The house physician assigned to each patient limited his comments to support, reassurance, and generalities. The personal physicians also limited their comments to support and reassurance with a minimum of factual explanation. The nurses declined to answer questions and referred the patient to the physician in a traditional manner.

Each patient was given a test on cardiac information at the end of his coronary unit stay. On this test the high information patients scored better than the low information patients. This finding verified that the high and low information groups were in fact being given differential treatment to a measurable extent.

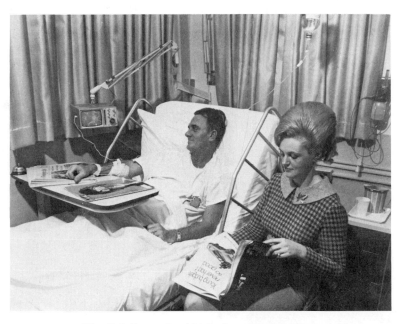

Fig. 2-4. Example of high diversion condition.

High diversion. The patients in the four groups who received high diversion were assigned to a bed that had a television set and a large window beside the bed. A mobile art object was suspended outside the window. Beds for the high diversion condition were located near the entrance to the coronary unit, so that the traffic represented additional stimulation. Patients in this condition had full access to magazines, books, and newspapers. They had expanded visiting privileges. So long as the patient desired company, their visiting privileges were unlimited. However, if the patient gave some indication of being tired or averse to visitation, it was limited according to his needs. The nurses and coronary unit staff were encouraged to engage in friendly conversation with the patients in this group. The clergy were allowed to visit as long as they wished (Fig. 2-4).

Low diversion. Patients in the four treatment groups who received low diversion were assigned to beds that had no television and that had limited visual stimulation. No books, magazines, and newspapers were allowed. The only reading materials were the occasional personality inventories brought by the research staff. Visits were limited to the immediate family and for a restricted time. The clergy were encouraged to limit the time of their visits. Nurses and coronary unit staff visited the rooms of these patients to carry out their routine duties but not for purposes of casual conversation.

High participation. Patients in the four groups receiving high participation were

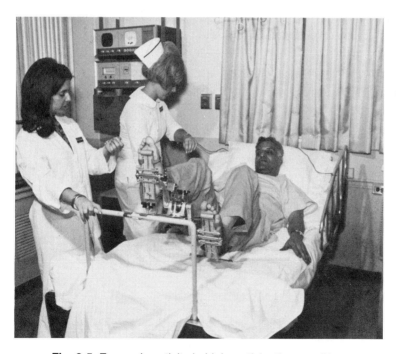

Fig. 2-5. Exercycle activity in high participation condition.

told that they should be doing things to participate in their own treatment and recovery. They were instructed to use the switch to activate their own cardiac monitors to secure ECG tracings whenever they felt some symptom. This ECG tracing was appropriately identified and given to each patient's personal physician at the end of the day. Patients were instructed to perform each day a regime of mild isometric exercises designed to reduce the probability of embolism. Upon medical determination, they were given a foot pedaling exercise with an exercycle attached to the foot of each bed. Blood pressure, ECG, and heart rate were monitored during the exercise. Each period of exercise was for six minutes at a speed that elevated the patient's heart rate 20 beats per minute above his own resting rate (Fig. 2-5). The psychological atmosphere of high participation was deliberately confounded with the amount of physical activity level, and only high participation patients exercised.

Low participation. Patients in the four low participation groups were given the previously standard medical procedure of complete bed rest, except for self-feeding. They were told to lie quietly and that all their needs would be taken care of by the nursing staff. Emphasis was placed upon reduced physical movement.

The patient in Fig. 2-6 is in the group receiving low information, low diversion, and low participation. This group was not stimulus deprived. Instead, their experience was closely comparable to that of a regular hospital patient who could not afford a television set. In this research-oriented coronary care unit, the staff typically outnumbered the patients. The "low-low-low" patient could look out of his room and see at least part of the nursing station. He also had some observation into the room of the patient opposite him. He received all the attention necessary for high quality physical care. He had personality inventories to read and complete. In short, the low-low-

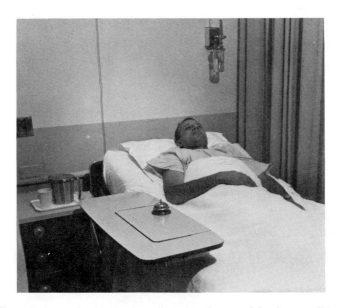

Fig. 2-6. Low information, low diversion, low participation condition.

low procedures were like those of a typical coronary care unit, and the high experimental nursing care procedures were additional to routine procedures.

Comment on the nursing care dimensions

The on-ward control group received the same nursing care assignments as the myocardial infarction group. The off-ward non-MI control group received none of the nursing care treatment procedures under investigation. The research staff did not know during the study of a patient whether he was a confirmed or disconfirmed myocardial infarction case. Throughout the project the medical, nursing, and research staffs were unable to predict the impact of the nursing care procedures on such variables as recovery. Observations from day to day led most of the staff to feel that the high versus low diversion condition would have the greatest impact. Many patients who received low diversional stimulation complained that they were bored and unhappy. (One important goal of the study, as will be shown later, was to examine whether such a bored low-stimulus state is deleterious or advantageous for the patient.) On the other hand, the high versus low participation condition seemed to make no overt impression on the patients—in fact, most observers, including the research staff, felt that this was the one part of the project that would show no results. Therefore, the actual results with respect to these two variables were surprising and had not been anticipated during the project.

At the time this project was conducted, research on the role of exercise in myocardial infarction had not been widely communicated among physicians. Therefore, while some participating physicians were receptive to the use of the exercycle during the acute phase of illness, others were averse to it. The exercycle procedure was included because of the opinion by some cardiologists that mild exercise is valuable to the healing process of the vascular system around the area of the infarct in the myocardium. In addition to the informed consent procedures for the study as a whole, we required a separate informed consent from physician and patient for this procedure. Consequently, only 17 of the 58 patients assigned to the high participation condition actually received the exercycle condition. Failure to participate in the exercycle procedure resulted primarily from the decisions of personal physicians rather than of patients. Each physician typically made his decision for his patients as a group rather than individually. Thus, this situation fortuitously provided a built-in control group with minimal selective bias in order to compare the exercyclers with the nonexercyclers within the "high participation" group of patients. Meanwhile, no negative effects that could be associated with the exercycle procedure, such as arrhythmias, fibrillation, or cardiac arrests, occurred on the coronary unit. As noted previously, the research staff doubted that the participation variable had any potency until the data were analyzed.

Personality variables in the nursing care study

Parallel to the three nursing care procedures, three personality variables were studied to see if they would affect comfort, cooperation, and recovery. These were repression-sensitization, scanning, and locus of control. After patients were assigned to nursing care conditions and their eligibility for the project was established, each of the three personality traits was measured.

On day 2 each patient was given the Ullmann (1962) repression-sensitization measure. This scale, sampled in Appendix C, attempts to measure whether individuals cope with stress by repressing or by becoming increasingly sensitized to it. This scale, usually referred to as a scale of facilitating versus inhibiting anxiety, has item validity for the repression-sensitization dimension and was chosen because of its superior reliability. Usually the patients filled out this objective personality inventory themselves, but if appropriate, the patient was read the items of the test. After all the data of the project were collected, the patients' test scores were separated at the median into repressor and sensitizer categories.

The scanning test was a perceptual task rather than a paper and pencil personality inventory. This test was typically administered on day 3. However, if the patient was in exceptionally good condition or if he was scheduled to leave the coronary care unit shortly or both, the test was given on day 2. The scanning measure was a test of visual size estimation.

Visual size estimation has been demonstrated to be related to scanning (Silverman, 1964). Size overestimation is indicative of minimal scanning. Size underestimation is indicative of extensive scanning. The examiner stood at a standard distance at the foot of the bed of the patient and presented in order a series of 11-by-14-inch cards containing a pen and ink picture. The subject was given a brief description of the picture. After ten seconds, the card was removed and replaced with a card of identical size which had a 2×3 array of six versions of the same picture, each varying in size. The subject was asked which of these six pictures was the same size as the one he had just seen. This procedure was repeated for all six pictures: a square, a tree and bush, and four mother-son scenes of acceptance, rejection, dominance, and overprotection (Harris, 1957; Cromwell, 1968). The patient's score was the average extent of his over- or underestimation of the pictures' sizes. The patients were divided at their median size estimation score, that is, into low and high scanners.

On day 2 the locus of control measure was also administered. This is an objective paper and pencil inventory that measures the degree to which people see the outcome of life events as under their own control rather than under the control of chance or outside forces. This scale, together with filler items that are not scored, is sampled in Appendix D. Again, after data were collected, the distribution of patients' scores was divided at the median to separate patients into internal and external locus of control groups.

In addition to the arbitrary dichotomizing of patients into two groups along these personality dimensions, the continuum of scores on these variables were used directly in several analyses of the results.

Dependent measures of recovery, comfort, and cooperation

The results of the nursing care study were analyzed in terms of 21 dependent variables related to recovery, comfort, and cooperation. The 16 variables related to recovery were the following:

1. Number of days spent in the coronary unit.
2. Number of days spent in hospital after leaving coronary unit.
3. Number of low rate monitor alarms.
4. Number of high rate monitor alarms.
5. Highest sedimentation rate while in coronary unit.
6. Highest uric acid level while in coronary unit.
7. Highest cholesterol level while in coronary unit.
8. Highest SGOT (serum glutamic oxaloacetic transaminase) while in coronary unit.
9. Highest LDH (lactate dehydrogenase) while in coronary unit.
10. Highest WBC (white blood cell count) while in coronary unit.
11. Highest temperature while in coronary unit.
12. Number of days after leaving hospital before return to work.
13. Rehospitalization again within 12 weeks of admission with another acute myocardial infarction. (Occurred = 1. Did not occur = 0.)
14. Death within 12 weeks of admission from another acute myocardial infarction. (Occurred = 1. Did not occur = 0.)
15. Change in severity rating of symptoms while on coronary unit. See Appendix E.
16. Change in temperature (based on first and last 4:00 PM measures) while on coronary unit.

The three variables related to comfort were the following:

1. Comfort interview (structured questions leading to a score on degree of comfort). See Appendix F.
2. Change in Minnesota Multiphasic Personality Inventory (MMPI) Depression score while on CCU. (Hathaway and McKinley, 1943.)
3. Mood change while on coronary unit (algebraic difference between last and first day scores on Nowlis Mood Adjective Checklist). (Nowlis, 1965.) See Appendix G.

The two variables considered to be related to cooperation are as follows:

1. Cooperation interview rating (structured questions to assess stated intent of patient to cooperate with medical instructions after going home). See Appendix H.
2. Nurses' cooperation rating (a combined nurses rating to assess the patient's cooperation with staff and procedures while on coronary unit). Five-point scale.

Interviews and questionnaires were administered at bedside, as shown in Fig. 2-7.

Most of the measures of recovery were recorded from the patient's chart. These were recorded by an assistant without knowledge of the research grouping and hypotheses of the research study. These included days of treatment, monitor alarms, laboratory blood analyses, temperature, and severity ratings. This information was recorded for all patients in the coronary unit. The only exceptions were the information on number of days before return to work, evidence of recurrent MI, and evi-

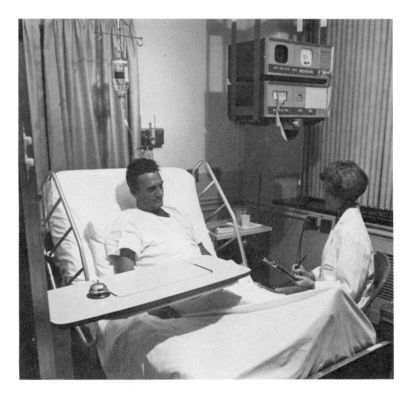

Fig. 2-7. Administering interviews and questionnaires.

dence of death after the patient left the hospital. To gather this information a telephone call or letter survey with return postcard was conducted 12 weeks from the time of admission to the coronary care unit.

The severity rating was based on a 3-point scale developed for use in the USPHS project associated with this study. (See Appendix E.)

The dependent variables designed to measure comfort involved pre- and posttests, that is, measures at the very beginning and at the very end of the coronary unit stay. Shortly after each patient had been admitted to the unit and the necessary medical care procedures had been conducted, the patient was visited by a member of the research staff. The staff member introduced herself, spent a few moments establishing rapport, and observed carefully the manifest energy and response level of the patient. She then explained the purpose of the research in order to provide a basis for informed consent. If the patient consented to the study, the Nowlis Mood Adjective Checklist and the Depression Scale of the MMPI were administered. These measures were referred to as MACL I and Depression I respectively. Administration was repeated on the last day of the patient's stay in the coronary unit. They were recorded at that time as the MACL II and Depression II scores. In this way, premeasures, postmeasures, and difference scores could all by analyzed. The final measure of comfort, the comfort interview, was given only at the end of the coronary unit stay, on day 5 or later. On the day of the patient's discharge, the nurses prepared their rating of his cooperation with them.

The results of the nursing care study are reported in Chapter 3.

PREDICTION STUDY

The purpose of the prediction study was to identify and clarify relationships among all the recorded variables for purposes of prediction of recovery, comfort, and cooperation. The experimental variables of the nursing care and MI versus non-MI comparison study (yet to be described), the demographic variables, and the clinical variables of diagnosis, treatment, and follow-up were all combined into a single multivariate analysis. A total of 207 measures were taken. The psychopolygraphic variables from the stress experiment, to be described later in this chapter, were omitted from the prediction study because the number of subjects was too small for adequate correlational statistics. Sporadic data omissions, resulting from equipment unavailability, shortness of stay of the patient on the coronary unit, and the priority of treatment over research caused the sample size to vary among the different correlations.

The results of the prediction study are reported in Chapter 5.

MI VERSUS NON-MI COMPARISONS

The purpose of the MI–non-MI comparisons was to determine how acute MI patients differed from non-MI patients in various measures under investigation. In this respect the comparison study was an extension of the investigation of MI–non-MI comparisons with respect to stress. Several other personality and clinical indices were also compared, as described in Chapter 6.

Two different sets of comparisons were made. A comparison of MIs and on-ward non-MIs were made on all of the dependent variables. A comparison of the MIs and the off-ward non-MIs could be made with those variables that were studied in the latter group.

THE STRESS EXPERIMENT

To establish whether the acute MI patient reacts differently to psychological stress than a non-MI patient, a standardized procedure was developed and pretested. A psychologically stressful task was introduced, and various indicators of stress reaction were observed as a consequence. A task was needed that would be sufficiently stressful to elicit a valid and observable stress response but not so stressful as to be of harm to the health or survival of the patient. A binary prediction task was the first procedure tried, and it appeared to meet these criteria. For ethical reasons no further attempts were made to refine it, to test its boundary conditions, or to develop alternative procedures. The task was modeled after studies of probability learning in which a typical paradigm is to present one of two stimuli and ask the subject to predict which stimulus will occur next. With a random series in which each stimulus is presented 50% of the time, the subject is unable to anticipate the next stimulus more than half the time. To produce ego involvement, the subject is told that the procedure is a test of his intellectual competence and that he must try to master the task to a level of perfect performance as soon as possible. The random series of stimuli gives the appearance of a regular but complex pattern that somehow remains just outside the range of the subject's complete solution. Chance runs of two, three, four, and sometimes five consecutive correct guesses serve to reinforce this notion. Moreover, once perceiving the task as a genuine one, the motivated subject becomes increasingly frustrated and is left with a feeling of failure after the task.

For this study, binary prediction tasks were developed in which the subject was presented a series of cards with Xs and Os and was asked to guess which stimulus would occur next. In a pilot study, these cards were presented in random order to each of six heart patients. Plasma 17-hydroxycorticosteroids were measured before and after administration. Plasma measures were also taken on six comparison patients who had no intervening activity. The increase in steroid level with the binary prediction task was greater than without it, so the decision was made to adopt this task for the study. While yielding an observable stress response, this procedure creates less stress than would be expected from an exciting bridge game or television program.

The binary prediction task was incorporated into the procedure of the project in the following way. First, a solvable version of the task was administered. Patients were presented a repeated sequence of X-O-X-X-O-O-O. All subjects solved this task in less than six minutes. The solvable task was referred to as the "control task." The unsolvable (random series) task was referred to as the "stress task." It is important to note that the "control task" also had stressful elements, such as ego-involving instructions, needle punctures for blood, application of electrodes, and the use of other psychopolygraphic transducers. As will be seen in Chapter 4, certain stress reactions are apparent under these circumstances. However, the failure experience, as defined by lack of solution, was present only in the "stress task."

The control task was presented on a day previous to the stress task. This procedure intentionally confounded (i.e., covaried) the sequence with the stress-control comparison; the control task was necessarily first to get baseline measures prior to the stress task experience.

Plasma 17-hydroxycorticosteroids

A number of dependent variables were studied in relation to these two binary prediction tasks. Plasma 17-hydroxycorticosteroid level was the object of greatest interest. The changes in levels of 17-hydroxycorticosteroids were examined according to the schedule in Fig. 2-8. As may be seen, the control task (A) and the stress task (B) were presented between 10:45 AM and 11:00 AM. This standard time of presentation was necessary because the level of 17-hydroxycorticosteroid changes in accordance with a circadian rhythm. Unless some clinical procedure, condition of the patient, or availability of staff caused a postponement, the control task was typically on day 3 and the stress task on day 4. By this time the patients had become accus-

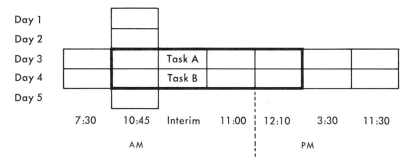

Fig. 2-8. Schedule of blood sampling with respect to the administration of solvable control task (A) and unsolvable "stress task" (B).

tomed to the coronary care unit, yet the acute MI patients were not likely to have been transferred. The plasma levels of major interest are indicated within the block with heavy lines in Fig. 2-8. These were at 10:45 AM, just prior to the task; 11:00 AM, just after the task; and 12:10 PM, a time 70 minutes later. The second posttest, 70 minutes later, was chosen because of evidence that 17-hydroxycorticosteroids have approximately a 70-minute half-life in the bloodstream. The blood samplings and the tasks were administered while the patient was propped in bed at a 45° angle.

In addition to these times of focal interest, we also investigated the circadian rhythm of 17-hydroxycorticosteroids throughout the days of the control and stress tasks. To get information on the circadian rhythm with a limited number of blood samples and without cannulation, blood samples were taken at 7:30 AM, 3:30 PM, and 11:30 PM on the control and stress task days.

Finally, since past evidence indicates that the plasma 17-hydroxycorticosteroid levels of patients—especially acute MI patients—are elevated when hospitalized, a daily scan of steroid level of all project patients in the coronary unit was conducted at 10:45 AM.

The emphasis upon plasma 17-hydroxycorticosteroid (17-OH-CS) as an index of stress came from research evidence (Lazarus, Speisman, and Mordkoff, 1963) that stressful movies elevate it. Wehmer (1966) demonstrated that only six minutes were necessary for an elevation after the stressful point in a movie. Also, he established that a significant correlation existed between plasma 17-OH-CS level and two moods (anxiety and fatigue) as measured on a mood adjective checklist given at intervals during a half-hour stressful movie. Since stress has been hypothesized to play a role in the etiology of heart attacks and since this project focuses on the effect of stress during the treatment situation on recovery, the measure has special interest.

Free (nonesterized) fatty acids

Another lipid that elevates in response to stress is nonesterized fatty acid (NEFA). At a moment of stress this substance is dumped into the bloodstream from the adipose stores in the body. It is metabolized quickly and has a half-life in the bloodstream of only approximately three minutes. Because of its rapid metabolism, it is difficult to design an experiment so that blood is sampled at just the right moment. Also, the NEFA level is affected by food intake from a typical diet. In the present study the analysis of plasma NEFA was conducted for blood samples just before (10:45 AM) and just after (11:00 AM) the stress and control tasks. The follow-up analysis at 12:10 PM should be viewed with caution because of (1) the rapid metabolism of NEFA following stress and (2) the serving of lunch to patients between 11:00 AM and 12:10 PM. We do not know whether these particular times of measurement were optimal. The data were collected because of the potential role of lipids and stress in myocardial infarction.

Blood pressure

At the time blood samples were taken at 10:45 AM, 11:00 AM, and 12:10 PM on the control and stress task days, systolic blood pressure was also taken. The standard cuff method was used, and no attempt was made to monitor blood pressure continuously.

Psychopolygraphic measures—heart rate, breathing, blood volume, pulse amplitude, and galvanic skin response

At 10:00 AM on the control and stress task days electrodes and other transducers were attached to the coronary unit patient for the purpose of psychopolygraphic recording. These procedures are described in greater detail in Chapter 4, which presents the psychopolygraphic findings. At approximately 10:37 AM on these respective days, a six-minute resting sample of psychopolygraphic activity was recorded. At the end of this period came the blood sampling and blood pressure measures. Then, during the binary prediction task, another six-minute sample of psychopolygraphic activity was recorded. Following the task and the posttask measures of blood sampling and blood pressure, approximately at 11:00 AM, a third six-minute sample of psychopolygraphic activity was taken. These measures allowed an assessment of approximate baseline activity, activity during the task, and activity after the respective success or failure experience with the task.

Polygraphic recordings were not taken on all patients. The equipment was acquired and put into operation late in the project. Artifacts in recording led to discarding some protocols and all of the GSR data.

Chapter 3

PATIENT RESPONSES TO NURSING CARE

A major part of the project was a controlled study of three nursing care factors. How much should an acute MI patient be told about the severity of his condition? How much diversional stimulation should he have? To what extent should he participate in his own treatment? Should these questions be answered differently for patients of different personalities?

Three personality factors were chosen as relevant to these nursing care questions. Repression-sensitization refers to repressing rather than becoming more anxious when coping with a threatening situation. Which patients would repress or become anxious when given information about their heart conditions? Scanning level refers to the customary rate of an individual in seeking and processing new information. Some individuals would be expected to seek a level of diversional and other stimulus input that others would consider an overload. Locus of control refers to the tendency for some to see themselves in control of the outcome of events through their own efforts and for others to see the same events as a result of external forces or chance. Individuals differing in locus of control belief might respond differently to participating in their own treatment.

These nursing care and personality factors were studied in relation to their effect upon the patient's recovery, comfort, and cooperation. Specifically, the three nursing and three personality factors were studied with respect to the 21 variables of recovery, comfort, and cooperation listed in the previous chapter. To analyze these data for MI patients separately, for non-MI patients separately, and for these two groups combined, a total of 315 factorial and mixed analyses of variance were computed. In addition, numerous subanalyses were performed when initial analyses indicated this was required. To prevent this book from being a compendium of statistical results, only the salient and useful findings are reported and discussed in the text. Tables describing all analyses are included in the appendix. A guide to statistical symbols and interpretation is presented in Appendix I for those who are unaccustomed to interpreting statistical results.

THE IMPORTANCE OF INFORMATION COUPLING

The first set of analyses examined the effects of the three nursing care manipulations upon the 21 dependent variables (see Appendix J, Table J-1). The major

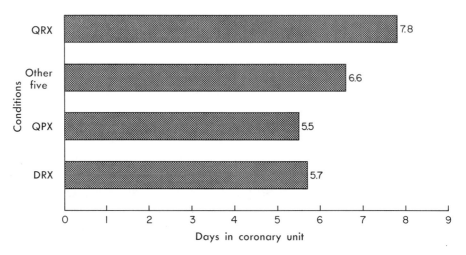

Fig. 3-1. Days in coronary unit as function of different nursing treatment conditions. *QRX* = high information, low diversion, low participation. *QPX* = high information, low diversion, high participation. *DRX* = high information, high diversion, low participation.

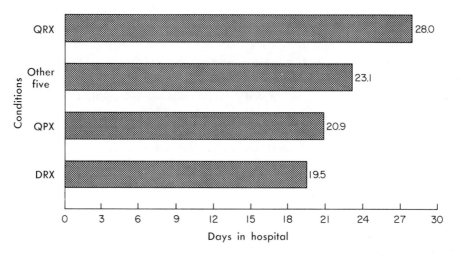

Fig. 3-2. Days in hospital as function of different nursing treatment conditions. *QRX* = high information, low diversion, low participation. *QPX* = high information, low diversion, high participation. *DRX* = high information, high diversion, low participation.

findings, as shown in Figs. 3-1 and 3-2, concern length of stay in the coronary unit and in the hospital. These major findings are closely interrelated and are clearly interpretable. They are reliable, as demonstrated by split-half analyses. Split-half analyses refer to the dividing of the subject population randomly into two groups and determining whether the same findings occur in both groups. When they do, the findings are said to be reliable.

The three nursing factors—information, diversion, and participation—produced a significant triple interaction ($p = .01$) with respect to length of stay in the coronary unit. This finding indicates that our original questions (how much information, and so on) cannot be answered simply. The role of any one nursing care factor depends upon the other two. Additional analyses indicate that information may lead to quick or slow discharge from the coronary unit depending on what it is coupled with. If information is coupled with low levels of diversion and participation, the stay tends to be long. As may be seen in Fig. 3-1, high information coupled with low diversion and low participation leads to an average of 7.8 days in the coronary unit. If information is coupled with one high level condition, diversion, or participation, the stay tends to be short. Again, as may be seen in Fig. 3-1, the coupling of high information with high participation lends to an average of only 5.5 days in the coronary unit. If coupled with high diversion rather than high participation, the high information led to 5.7 days on the average in the coronary unit. The other five conditions in Figs. 3-1, collapsed together for a mean of 6.6 days coronary stay, may be examined separately in Appendix J, Table J-2.

These results brought an humbling message home to us: an everyday common-sense interpretation of the findings seems to surpass any more sophisticated interpretation. If you are going to tell an acutely ill MI patient about the severity of his condition, you should also give him something to do about it or at least something to divert his mind from it.

This major message of the findings was repeated independently with the analysis of length of stay in the hospital after transfer from the coronary unit. Again, a triple interaction ($p = .02$) was found, and the results were interpretable in the same way. As may be seen in Fig. 3-2, high information with no other high condition coupled with it led to a long hospital stay (mean, 28.0 days); high information coupled with either high diversion (mean, 19.5 days); or participation (mean, 20.9 days) led to a short hospital stay. The other five groups, combining for an average of 23.1 days average stay in the hospital, may be examined separately in Appendix J, Table J-2.

These results were striking because the nursing care conditions were administered only on the coronary unit. Their impact carried over after their termination.

Other analyses revealed trends ($p > .10$) that add further support to these two major findings and the information-coupling interpretation. If information and participation are both high (or both low), then the number of cardiac monitor alarms for critically high or low heart rate are relatively few. However, if one condition is high and the other low, the number of alarms is greater. This finding occurred separately for both high heart rate monitor alarms ($p = .06$) and low heart rate monitor alarms

($p = .05$). Thus, the information-coupling interpretation is further bolstered. High information produces heart rate alarms unless it is coupled with opportunities to act on it by way of self-treatment. Moreover, neither the information nor self-treatment activities should be given alone. Giving information without a way to act on it and giving self-treatment activities without an informational context increased heart rate alarms.

In addition to the converging findings above, another separate trend ($p = .08$) toward a triple interaction indicates that the specific combination of low information, low diversion, and high participation also leads to a deviantly large number of high heart rate alarms. While similar, this trend emerged as separate from the preceding one, and no other analysis corroborated it. If valid, this finding indicates that action taken toward participation in self-treatment without a rational information base or without diversion is undesirable.

When the patient comfort factor was analyzed, the MI patients had a nonsignificant trend ($p = .07$) to be influenced by the interaction of information and participation. Again, the results were consistent with the information-coupling interpretation. If information was appropriately coupled with participation (high with high or low with low), reported comfort was higher than when information was inappropriately coupled with participation (high with low or low with high).

To what extent can confidence be placed in the findings concerning information coupling? This cluster of findings, although imminently reasonable, was not predicted prior to the collection of data. Also, even though the sample size is large for the total study, the group size for each nursing care combination is inevitably small (usually 16). On the other hand, small sample statistics are designed to correct for sample size, and positive results are no easier to obtain than with large groups. Some of the findings are trends that fall short of statistical significance, but the total cluster of findings presents a consistent conceptual picture. Ideally, these investigations would be replicated in another setting. Regarding the length of coronary unit and hospital stay the private physician who transferred a patient from the coronary unit is the same one who discharged him from the hospital; thus, physician differences in "keeping patients on" may have been operating. On the other hand, over 30 different private physicians were cooperating in the study; therefore, it is highly unlikely that a random assignment of their patients into the various nursing care conditions could allow the results to occur as a function of bias in physicians' practices. Moreover, the judgmental habits of the individual physicians could not have accounted for the supporting findings concerning high heart rate and low heart rate monitor alarms and the comfort interview. Consequently, appreciable confidence may be placed in the information-coupling results.

At the same time it must be recalled that the nursing care conditions had no effect, positively or negatively, on death of the patient or recurrence of an MI within 12 weeks. The information-coupling findings did not occur among the non-MI patients. This is not surprising, since they tended to be discharged earlier and were no doubt told as soon as possible by their physicians that they had no actual heart attack.

Therefore, the nursing care findings have importance only for the MI and not all coronary patients.

Three interpretations of the findings suggest themselves. The first concerns stress, and it is consistent with the viewpoint we adopted prior to data collection.

We assumed that certain nursing care conditions were more stressful than others, that the stress would serve to retard the recovery of the patient, and that the physician would take note of such instances of slow recovery and keep the patient under treatment longer. Giving a patient extensive information and then limiting his other activity (diversion, participation) should facilitate his learning of the information. Early studies on human learning, retroactive inhibition, and proactive inhibition (e.g., Ebbinghaus, 1913) amply support this proposition. Once the information is well learned, however, the patient would have nothing to do but brood, become anxious, or feel helpless about his fate. On the other hand, the patient who receives extensive information about his condition *and* is given something to do about it, for example, participation in self-treatment, should experience less stress, optimal recovery, and quicker discharge.

Now that the findings are at hand, two other interpretations present themselves. One concerns the reporting of relevant symptoms. As mentioned above, the patients in the high information condition who received low diversion and low participation had the optimal basis for efficient learning and retention. And, indeed, they were given a miniature education about coronary illness. Consequently, they may have been "reporting the right symptoms" to their physicians. If so, this in turn may have created alarm in the physicians and caused them to exercise greater caution in discharging the patient "too soon." While this interpretation does not account for the advantages of coupling with high participation (or diversion) or the monitor alarm results, it does provide a possible explanation for the group with the longest coronary unit and hospital stay.

The third interpretation concerns selective protest by the patient. Almost all patients want to go home; they express this desire to their physicians and sometimes, with help from relatives, pressure their physicians for discharge. Physicians inevitably respond to these influences as well as to the health status of the patient. Therefore, it may be that the patient who is highly informed about the seriousness of his illness and otherwise is left fairly alone to think about it may conclude that the hospital is where he should be. Consequently, he remains quiet at a time when other patients would question or complain about being in the hospital. On the other hand, the patient who is given extensive information, a boring existence with limited visitors, no television, no recreational reading, and instructions to participate in his own treatment may conclude he is well enough to go home. And he may say so. Thus, physicians may respond differentially to these two situations.

THE IMPORTANCE OF INTERMEDIATE LEVELS OF ACTIVITY

In addition to information coupling a second finding is present. Diversion and participation, the two conditions that require the most activity of the patient, interact (see Appendix J, Table J-1). This interaction indicates that either high or low amounts of activity are associated with long coronary unit and hospital stay. Intermediate amounts are associated with short coronary unit and hospital stay. This trend falls short of significance ($p = .09$) for the coronary unit stay; however, it is statistically significant ($p = .02$) for total hospital stay. The trend may be detected in two ways. First, as far as high activity is concerned, it will be noted (from Appendix J, Table J-1) that the "high-high-high" group has the second longest coronary care unit stay. Within the context of the information-coupling finding, it is clearly beneficial to couple information with either diversion or participation but not both. One cannot utilize information and divert oneself from it at the same time. The longest coronary stay was for the "high-low-low" group. This result apparently derives from both the activity level and the information-coupling effects. Second, at the other extreme of short coronary stay, the two extreme groups have one condition high and the other low for diversion and participation. Similar but stronger findings occurred for total hospital stay as for coronary unit stay.

The implication from these results is that an intermediate amount of physical activity is optimal for a short coronary unit and short hospital stay. As far as watching television, receiving visitors, conversing with the staff, taking exercises, operating the cardiac monitor, reading, and so on are concerned, the guideline is moderation. Demanding that the patient exert great control over his activity and forego all diversional pleasures leads to long treatment, perhaps because of the stress of these demands or perhaps because the patient becomes convinced he needs to stay. At the other extreme, unloading a wide range of activities on him without ample opportunity for some private, quiet, undemanding time is also unfavorable to an early discharge.

Further support for the desirability of moderate activity comes from the total amounts of external information to process as opposed to the amount of physical activity. Whereas diversion and participation are conditions that are high on activity, information and diversion are conditions high on external informational input. The near-significant interactions between information and diversion were in a direction to indicate that an intermediate amount of input leads to fewer high ($p = .05$) and low ($p = .07$) heart rate alarms than does low or high input. A tape recording concerning coronary disease, heart attack literature, watching television, reading, and dealing with visitors all demand the processing of informational input, and the trend of these results suggests that an intermediate amount yields fewer cardiac alarms.

Other findings suggested that high participation, in and of itself, had some unfavorable aspects. Patients with high participation in self-treatment had less tendency to express cooperative attitudes regarding medical instructions than patients with low participation ($p = .01$). This finding is compatible with the previously stated interpretation that low participation patients became more impressed with the seriousness of their condition than high participation patients. A second finding indicated low participation patients to become less depressed, as compared to high participation patients, while on the coronary unit ($p = .04$).

Nursing care and the non-MI patients

The pattern of results for the MI patients did not occur for the non-MI patients. Thus the two groups should be considered different from each other (see Appendix J, Table J-3). The non-MI patients typically have the tentative diagnosis of an acute MI disconfirmed. They are not suffering the physical effects that accompany an acute MI. They tend to be transferred from the coronary unit earlier. Non-MI patients on high diversion tend to spend significantly more time in the coronary unit (p = .05) and hospital (p = .04) than non-MI patients on low diversion. This is undoubtedly because the low diversion patients are more bored and feel well enough to complain to be released. Consistent with this is the finding that low diversion non-MI patients have lower ratings for cooperation while on the coronary unit (p = .05).

The exercycle

The exercycle procedure in the high participation condition was conducted after we acquired a separate informed consent. The physician was almost always the one to dissent and, if dissenting, usually did so for all his patients. As may be seen from Table 3-1, the majority of physicians chose not to have this procedure administered to their patients. The fact that other physicians did consent allowed a comparison of the two groups. Of the 21 dependent variables analyzed, four reached statistical significance. In the favorable direction, the users of the exercycle had a significantly greater drop in temperature during their stay on the coronary care unit. They also had a significantly lower uric acid level. On the unfavorable side, cholesterol level and the probability of returning to the hospital with another MI was significantly greater among the exercyclers than the nonexercyclers.

Unfortunately, one cannot conclude from these data whether the exercycle is favorable or unfavorable. The finding on subsequent MIs arouses the greatest alarm. Concerning this finding, the following reminders should be made. First, since no patient in the study had a subsequent MI (or death) while on the coronary care unit, this finding results from a delayed or residual effect rather than an immediate one. One possible explanation, offered previously, is that the exercyclers, through being asked to participate in this unusual procedure during the acute phase of their illness, may have concluded that they were not seriously ill and may not have followed

Table 3-1. Analysis of recovery as a function of the use of the exercycle among the MI patients

Dependent variable	Exercyclers		Nonexercyclers		
	Mean	**N**	**Mean**	**N**	**p**
Temperature change	−0.4°	17	+0.4°	41	.05
Uric acid	4.9	15	6.2	33	.05
Cholesterol	289.8	14	250.0	35	.05
Subsequent MIs	1.1	16	1.0	40	.05

adequate medical precautions after leaving the coronary unit. Such a conclusion by the patient should be preventable with proper instructions to him.

PATIENT PERSONALITY AND NURSING CARE

One of our major questions was whether the nursing care dimensions interacted with personality to influence comfort, cooperation, and survival. Instead of a simple proneness concept in personality or a hypothesis that the benefit of a given nursing care environment is the same for everyone, we preferred an interactional hypothesis. That is, we were guided by the possibility that what is stressful (or beneficial) for one personality may not be for another. For example, information about one's condition may be calming to a sensitizer but disquieting when forced upon a repressor. Diversional input may be distressing to a minimal scanner, but an extensive scanner may be distressed without it. Participation in self-treatment may be a threatening demand to an external-locus-of-control personality, but it may be the prime source of solace to the internal-locus-of-control person.

While some interactional findings occurred, their extent and importance were not as great as we had expected. The effect of nursing care factors independent of personality, as described in the previous section, has been greater than expected. Even stronger effects, as will be shown in the next chapter, exist between personality and recovery, independent of environment. With these cautions in mind, here are the few interactional results that were found.

Information and repression-sensitization

The amount of information provided and the personality factor of repression-sensitization interacted ($p = .05$) to influence number of high heart rate alarms. Sensitizers who receive low information and the repressors who receive high information tend to have a greater number of high-rate monitor alarms. The sensitizers who receive high information and the repressors who receive low information tend to have fewer high-rate alarms. This finding is in line with our initial hypothesis that high information is stressful to the repressor but unstressful to the sensitizer, but the finding is not supported by data from other indices of recovery, so it should be viewed with caution.

As predicted, cooperation with nurses was a function of the interaction between information and repression-sensitization. Repressors with limited information about their cardiac illness and sensitizers with extensive information tended to cooperate more with the nurses. Sensitizers with limited information and repressors with extensive information were rated as less cooperative. The least cooperative group were the sensitizers with low information. The most cooperative group were the repressors with low information. This finding suggests that giving the sensitizers (the more anxious patients) ample information and giving the repressors (the less anxious patients) less information would tend to increase cooperation with the nursing staff.

Other findings on MI patients may be found in Appendix J, Table J-4.

Among the non-MI patients the number of days spent in the coronary care unit was found to be strongly related to the degree of congruence between nursing care and personality. The repressors who received limited information and the sensitizers who received extensive information were transferred out of the coronary care unit sooner (mean, 2.7 and 3.3 days respectively). By contrast, the sensitizers who received low information and the repressors who received extensive information remained in the coronary care unit longer (mean, 4.2 and 4.3 days respectively). The direction of this finding supports the initial hypothesis but only among non-MI patients (51% of those admitted to our coronary care unit).

The non-MI repressors markedly dropped in level of depression from the beginning to the end of their stay in the coronary care unit. The non-MI sensitizers showed a slight increase.

Other findings on non-MIs are shown in Appendix J, Table J-5.

Diversion and scanning

A summary of the analysis of variance of recovery, comfort, and cooperation factors as a function of diversion and scanning in MI patients indicates the number of significant findings does not greatly exceed what would be expected by chance. Therefore, the findings reported here should be viewed with great caution.

The strongest finding in the analysis was an interaction ($p = .002$) between amount of diversion and scanning behavior as related to the number of monitor alarms indicating high heart rate. Contrary to prediction, the high number of alarms came from the *congruent* nursing-personality combination. The minimal scanners with low diversion had an average of 3.5 alarms, and the extensive scanners with high diversion had an average of 2.4 alarms. In the incongruent combinations, the extensive scanners with low diversion had an average of 1.6 alarms, and the minimal scanners with high diversion had an average of 1.9 alarms. Other than chance, no explanation suggests itself for these unexpected findings. Minimal scanners who were given the quiet condition reported less personal comfort in the interview than the other three groups. The other three groups were fairly equal in reported comfort. Again, no explanation for this unpredicted finding occurs to us.

Other analyses of MI patients are reported in Appendix J, Table J-6.

The peak white blood cell count on the coronary unit among the non-MI patients was found to be a function of the interaction of diversion and scanning. Patients with the congruent combinations were relatively low in white blood cell (WBC) count during the peak period. Patients with incongruent combinations were relatively high in peak WBC. In other words, minimal scanners given the quiet condition and extensive scanners given the diversion condition were lower than the incongruent groups (extensive scanners given the quiet condition and minimal scanners given the diverse condition). Although this finding is in line with prediction, no explanation is available for how the relationship between the nursing-personality interaction and the biological dependent variable is mediated. Therefore, the interpretability of this result is guarded until replication and further study is conducted. Even then, the finding would probably reflect a mechanism at normal levels of WBC and would be obscured if a bodily lesion produced high WBC levels.

Other findings on non-MI patients are reported in Appendix J, Table J-7.

Participation and locus of control

Two trends just short of significance seem worthy of note, since they involve subsequent MI and death. Regarding participation in self-treatment and locus of control, no one in the congruent combinations (internal locus of control—ILC—with high participation and external locus of control—ELC—with low participation) returned to the hospital within 12 weeks ($p = .06$) or died within 12 weeks ($p = .06$). All those who had recurring MIs or who died had the incongruent combinations (ILC with low participation and ELC with high participation). These findings are in the predicted direction. As may be noted, the lack of statistical significance results solely from the low total number of deaths, since all findings are in the same direction. This finding is a candidate for future study, and it might merit clinical consideration now.

Since no patient in the study had another heart attack or died while on the coronary unit, the question may be raised as to how the nursing care conditions on the unit could have such a long-term effect on the patients after they had been transferred onto the regular hospital ward or had been discharged to go home. The only interpretation offered here concerns the motivation to delay once initial symptoms of recurrence occur. The patient whose nursing care treatment was incongruent with his personality may have resisted the decision to return to the hospital when these crucial symptoms of another MI appeared. Therefore, a subsequent fully developed MI or subsequent death would be more likely to occur. This interpretation would not explain a different frequency in recurrent MIs to begin with.

Other analyses are in Appendix J, Table J-8.

No interactions occurred between participation and locus of control among the non-MI patients (Appendix J, Table J-9).

PRACTICAL IMPLICATIONS

Drawing clinical implications from research findings often discomforts both the scientist and the clinician. Deciding which research findings merit strong conclusions and which result from complex interplay of chance factors is always partly arbitrary. Scientific conservatism dictates great interpretive caution. But in an area of such vital importance as heart disease, urgent answers are sought and drawing practical conclusions is necessary. Even best guesses from controlled research data may have value over the suggestions of uncontrolled clinical observations. To present any finding places it under public scientific scrutiny so that it may be more clearly confirmed or disconfirmed in later years. With all these considerations in mind, we have included a digest of our findings and their possible implications at the end of this and the following chapters.

Findings on which the discussion is based are either presented earlier in the chapter or are in the appendixes. Neither nonpredicted interactions nor the main effects that accompany nonpredicted interactions are discussed. Some analyses of personality factors are referred to in this section because of relevance, but they are reported more fully in the next chapter. For the personality variables, correlational statistics reported in the next chapter are more sensitive and appropriate than the analyses of variance reported in this chapter.

Death

Our ultimate dependent variable was death. It was importantly related to factors of subject selection and to our experimentally measured variables. In a coronary unit where the mortality rate was 18%, the rate for patients in this study before transfer from the coronary unit was 0%. The elimination of patients over 60 and of patients too ill to participate in psychological testing undoubtedly accounts for the high survival rate of our studied patients. Within 12 weeks after admission 5 (3.8%) of the 131 MI patients and 1 (1.0%) of the 98 non-MI patients had died from a subsequent MI, giving a total of 6 (2.6% mortality) for the 229 coronary unit patients.

With this small mortality rate, not much can be said for sure about variables related to death. However, by virtue of small-sample statistical techniques, the following findings have been described precisely. Patients who later died came mostly from the high diversion groups. This finding would suggest that extensive diversion (TV, reading materials, telephone, visitors, and so on) should be viewed with concern or caution.

All patients who died were "incongruent" in personality with respect to locus of control and anxiety, that is, either internal control with high anxiety or external control with low anxiety. Very little by way of intervention can be suggested from this finding, since these personalities were years in development. Nevertheless, death may be expected more frequently in those who view themselves as responsible but probably unsuccessful in gaining positive outcomes in life. Death should also be expected more frequently among those who feel out of control of life's circumstances, never self-motivating, and never highly anxious. All patients who died had personalities incongruent with the ward treatment variables, more specifically internal locus of control with low participation or external locus of control with high participation. No ILC patient under high participation or ELC patient under low participation died within 12 weeks. These findings suggest that MI patients who see themselves as controlling outcomes of events should be given assignments of self-care and treatment on the coronary unit in order to improve their chances of surviving. Conversely, people who are resigned to fate and control by others should not be given self-care and treatment responsibilities.

Subsequent myocardial infarctions

Our second vitally important measure is the occurrence of a subsequent myocardial infarction. Within 12 weeks of admission to the coronary unit, 12 patients suffered a recurrence of acute myocardial infarction. These patients were prone to be extensive scanners and highly anxious. No intervention seems likely to be effective in changing these long-term personality characteristics; however, situations arousing anxiety or demanding excessive attention and concentration should be avoided. As we shall see in the next chapter, the results clearly indicate that personality factors, rather than enzyme levels or cardiographic data, are the most useful and powerful in predicting recurrence of acute myocardial infarctions.

Coronary unit and hospital stay

In terms of health economics the strongest findings of practical importance concern the length of stay in the coronary unit and in the hospital. These findings have strong monetary implications for the patient, insurance companies, and the state. The findings have implications for physicians and nurses in maintaining an efficient flow of patients through limited specialized facilities.

Both nursing care procedures and patient personality are important determinants of an MI patient's length of stay. Of greatest importance are the findings relevant to information coupling. MI patients who were given extensive explanation about the nature of their condition but were neither encouraged to participate in their own treatment nor given diversional stimulation had unusually long stays, both in the coronary unit and in the hospital after leaving the coronary unit. By contrast, MI patients who were given extensive information and were also encouraged to participate in their own treatment had the shortest stays. As a second best undertaking, the coupling of information with diversion is favorable to a short stay, but the use of both participation and diversion should be avoided. Even though these nursing care approaches were conducted only on the coronary unit, their effects carried over to affect later length of hospital stay in an identical way.

How much should the MI patient be told? It all depends upon what he is able to do with the information after he gets it. The practical message suggested by these findings is that if an MI patient is given extensive information about the nature of his condition, he should also be given "things to do" by way of self-treatment or, otherwise, something to occupy his mind. Coupling either self-treatment or diversion, but certainly not both, to the health information is favorable to a shorter stay. By contrast, to give a patient such information about the seriousness of his condition and then leave him deprived of either diversion or opportunities to "do something for himself" leads to an unusually long hospital stay.

A mnemonic that can help you remember these information-coupling findings is to associate the acute MI victim and the astronaut going into outer space. A new experience is confronting each. It is stressful. Pain or physical discomfort may be expected. The threat of death is apparent. In each case, however, the stress in the situation is greatly reduced by (1) adequate information about what is going on, (2) clearly prescribed duties to perform, for example, obtaining information relevant to survival, and (3) very little diversional stimulation from sources irrelevant to the problems at hand.

These findings in coronary unit and hospital stay may result from (1) stress leading to greater illness, (2) selective reporting of relevant symptoms to the physician, (3) reduced protest by the patient or his family toward getting released, or all of these. Whatever the reasons, the patients in the favorable nursing care combination tended to be released from the coronary unit two to three days before patients from the least favorable nursing care condition. For total hospital stay, a seven-to-eight-day difference existed between the favorable and unfavorable groups. No evidence existed whatsoever to indicate that the early-discharged patients had any more or less favorable outcome than those who were discharged later. Therefore, the information-coupling procedure is economically sound and seems in no way damaging to health.

A secondary factor affecting length of coronary and hospital stay concerns the overall amount of activity during the acute phase of illness. The results indicated that moderate activity is optimal. If the patient was deprived of diversion (TV, reading materials, extensive visitation, and so on) and participation in self-treatment, a longer stay resulted. If he was given both, a longer stay resulted. With one or the other, a shorter stay resulted. This interpretation toward moderation is also supported by the fact that coronary patients with an intermediate combination of information and diversion have fewer monitor alarms for high and low heart rate. Especially the high participation condition combined with low information and diversion yields frequent low-rate cardiac monitor alarms.

This intermediacy finding, taken together with the information-coupling finding, suggests that coronary units deemphasize diversional materials and increase self-participation opportunities. In this way, both factors could be controlled to the advantage of the patient.

Besides the nursing care factors, certain personality variables among the MI patients are correlated with length of stay. Patients with attitudes of internal locus of control get transferred from the coronary unit before those with external attitudes. In particular, MI patients with internal locus of control, low level of anxiety, and the tendency toward extensive scanning have a short initial hospital stay. The practical implications of this finding are not great, except the finding suggests the kind of patients who will and will not appear ready for early discharge.

For suspected but disconfirmed (non-MI) patients, the average number of days of coronary unit stay was much shorter, and the variables affecting stay were somewhat different. Patients given limited diversion had shorter stays than those with more diversion, possibly because the low-diversion patients without acute MIs were more bored and wanted to leave. Again, from a health economic standpoint, this finding would argue for limiting diversional opportunities on the coronary unit. Another finding among non-MI patients concerned the giving of information about heart disease to anxious and nonanxious patients. The findings suggest that the anxious patient wants such information and the nonanxious (repressor) patient does not want it. In both cases where the amount of information apparently fit the needs of the patient, an early release from the coronary unit occurred. As for hospital stay, the patient with internal locus of control attitudes, high anxiety, and extensive scanning tendencies appeared to remain longer.

Cardiac symptoms and related indices

The typical symptoms of myocardial infarction were only minimally influenced by the nursing care variables studied here; however, they were markedly related to the patient personality patterns. Coronary unit patients had fewer cardiac monitor alarms for high heart rate if the amount of information given was congruent with their personalities. That is, giving extensive information to highly anxious and limited information to nonanxious patients led to fewer high rate alarms than the incongruent combinations. These findings suggest that the physician and coronary nurse should use the anxiety level of the patient as a positive indicator to judge how much information he should receive (and then should follow through with assignments of self-treatment). The anxious person becomes distressed if he is deprived of such information, contrary to the intuitions of many physicians and nurses.

Personality of the patient has several other relationships to cardiac symptoms. The symptoms of nonanxious MI patients tend to decrease more after the first 24 hours on the coronary unit, as compared to anxious patients. The anxious patients also tend to have a higher peak sedimentation rate. The same is true for the extensively, as opposed to minimally, scanning patient. The highly anxious and extensively scanning MI patient tends to have a higher peak temperature while on the coronary unit. Finally, LDH is higher in MI patients with high anxiety, external control attitudes, and minimal scanning.

The locus of control personality variable stands out in its relationship to biological variables related to myocardial infarction. Except in two cases where internal locus of control is coupled with high anxiety, the external locus of control attitude was always associated with undesirable outcomes. Patients who tend to see the outcome of life circumstances as under control of others or of chance rather than of themselves tend to have high sedimentation rates, higher SGOT levels, higher LDH levels, higher peak temperatures, less drop in temperatures during CCU stay, longer stays on the coronary care unit, and longer stays in the hospital. These findings tend to hold with MI and non-MI patients alike on the coronary care unit. For MI patients in particular, those with internal locus of control and high anxiety tend to have higher sedimentation rates. Those MI patients with internal locus of control and high anxiety have the highest cholesterol—especially if they are minimal scanners.

Even though locus of control is related to these biological factors, it is not directly related to recurrence of MI or death. However, the consistency of the findings is impressive. One interpretation is that patients with these elevated biological indices are sicker, and a temporary shift to external locus of control is elicited. If this is true, it is contrary to previous studies that have failed to produce abrupt shifts in locus of control. Assuming on the other hand that the locus of control measure is stable, the findings strongly suggest more future research be directed toward linking lifelong habit patterns to biologic states.

Further support for the suggestion to study personality-biochemical relationships comes from data on the non-MI patients. These patients had enzyme and other biochemical levels well below that of the MI patients. The statistically significant findings that occurred for them were often different from those for the MI patients. For example, both SGOT and LDH were higher among the high diversion non-MI patients than among the low diversion non-MI patients. Minimal scanners had higher cholesterol than extensive scanners. Extensive scanners under high diversion and minimal scanners under low diversion had low white blood cell counts, but the counts were elevated for the incongruent combinations. Taken together, these findings suggest that the energy demands of diversional stimulation and of a hyperscanning personality produce an observable but mild stress in the non-MI patient. With an active lesion such as myocardial infarction and the subsequently elevated enzyme levels, this pattern of change resulting from diversional stimulation and scanning is apparently obscured.

Cooperation

Cooperation of patients depended slightly more upon the personality of the patient than upon the nursing care factors studied here. One exception was that an attitude of cooperation with medical instructions after release was more positive with those given the low participation condition than with those given the high. While high participation, combined with other factors, had many positive aspects, the high participation patients apparently did not take their heart conditions as seriously as those who were told to rest and be waited on by the coronary staff. Thus, the pattern of results is complex. Participation in self-treatment is important, especially when extensive information is given. Of great importance, however, is the fact that special steps should be taken by the cardiologist to impress the high participation patient about the seriousness of his condition and the need to cooperate after he leaves the hospital.

As for personality, the results are straightforward. As expected, coronary patients who feel they have control over what happens to them are more cooperative. Likewise, the seemingly withdrawn patient who is less attentive to his surroundings is more cooperative than one who is responding excessively to what is going on.

Cooperation with nurses while on the coronary unit was complex in its relations with personality and nursing care variables. Better cooperation is revealed by the congruent combinations of information and anxiety; that is, the anxious MI patients who are given extensive information and the nonanxious who are given limited information have higher cooperation ratings. The incongruent combinations are lower in cooperation. For coronary patients in general, the congruent combinations of scanning and participation yield greater cooperation. That is, extensive scanners with high participation and minimal scanners with low participation have higher cooperation ratings. The incongruent combinations cooperate less. Among MI patients the highest cooperation level was found among patients with internal locus of control, low anxiety, and minimal scanning. Paradoxically, among non-MIs the highest cooperation was found among patients with internal locus of control, high anxiety, and minimal scanning. These findings point to a crucial demand on nurses and on nursing education. It is not enough simply to learn a "correct role" of nursing care that can be performed regardless of the type of the personality of the patient. More understanding is needed of personality, how one patient needs one nursing approach and another patient needs a different one. Finally, the greatest challenge is for the coronary nurse who experiences the frustration and annoyance of an uncooperative or otherwise offensive patient. The reality must be faced that this is a manifestation of the patient's stress and is as much in need of treatment as the physical symptoms that occur. Ordinarily, the natural human response to an obnoxiously anxious patient is to feel angry or rejecting and to avoid him—or even to punish him for his behavior. The findings here call for the opposite. They suggest approaching and giving extensive information to anxious patients—in spite of the complaining ways in which anxiety is expressed. This finding illustrates the importance for nurses to acquire adequate technical knowledge of personality treatment. Otherwise, response of personal emotion and avoidance on the nurse's part would represent a failure in nursing care.

Keeping in mind the importance of differential nursing care, another challenge is offered to nursing education. Traditionally, nurses in deference to the physician have been instructed in the past to divulge no information to the patient. Even the simple facts, such as temperature and blood pressure, have been withheld under the false presumption that this will *cause* anxiety. Our data indicate that this withholding of information is indeed more stressful to some patients than receiving it. The nurse, with her more extensive personal contact with the patient, is often the more appropriate person to play this informative role.

Comfort

Patient comfort measures on the coronary unit, as with cooperation and recovery, were more dependent upon personality than upon the nursing care variables under study. First, all patients showed an increase in positive mood from beginning to the end of their coronary unit stay. This could be expected because of the apprehension at admission and the positive mood on the day of their release. In addition, if the patients who are hyperalert in scanning are given self-treatment chores, they will be more comfortable. Again, the implications for differential nursing care are evident.

Patients with attitudes of internal locus of control become less depressed during their coronary unit stay. Among the MI patients with internal locus of control, those with low anxiety become even less depressed than those with high anxiety. The non-MI patients with internal locus of control had the most positive change in mood during coronary unit stay. Non-MI patients with high anxiety become less depressed than those who are nonanxious.

Return to work

Time before returning to work was influenced by personality and nursing care variables but was not related in any way to the indices of severity of the myocardial infarction. Patients with an MI and those given high information were slow in returning to work. Patients returned to work more quickly who were low in anxiety and high in scanning. Non-MI patients who had internal locus of control and who were given minimal information about the nature of heart disease returned to work quickly. Patients also returned to work quickly who were congruent in scanning and information. Extensive scanners receiving information and minimal scanners given limited information returned to work much more quickly than those with the incongruent combinations. Again, these results suggest giving more information to the anxious and the hyperalert scanners than to the low anxious and the minimal scanners. The findings also suggest that the physician's advice about returning to work should be based upon patient's personality to a greater extent than from the severity of the infarct.

Chapter **4**

PATIENT RESPONSE TO STRESS*

As noted in Chapter 2, one part of the project was an examination of stress responses among myocardial infarction and nonmyocardial infarction patients. Nurses and physicians will find few treatment implications in this part of the study, but the findings will help them and researchers to conceptualize how the acute MI patient responds to stress. Differences between acute MI patients and the other groups were indeed found. Physicians and nurses have asked us whether these differences occur only during the time of the acute lesion (giving them diagnostic significance) or at some time before the lesion (making them relevant to coronary proneness). This study does not answer that important question. It identifies differences in stress response among the groups at the time they were compared, but it cannot say whether the differences would have been found before the MI.

The stressing event was a binary prediction task. The patients tried to guess which of two alternatives (X or O) would be presented next. The task occurred between 10:45 and 11:00 AM on days 3 and 4 of the coronary unit stay. It was described as a brief measure of intelligence, the purpose of which was to observe how patients responded physically to such tests. On day 3 the task was solvable; on day 4 it was not. The task was chosen because it produced a mild but measurable stress response (see Chapter 2 for details).

The dependent variables chosen to assess the stress response were (1) plasma 17-hydroxycorticosteroids, (2) plasma nonesterized (free) fatty acids, (3) heart rate, (4) blood volume, (5) pulse amplitude, and (6) blood pressure. Breathing and GSR measures were also collected but not analyzed as dependent variables. Blood was drawn according to the schedule in Fig. 2-8 in order to assess change in steroid level across days, throughout the circadian rhythm of the two days of task administration, and

---

*This chapter was written in collaboration with Mary Headrick Haynes, Ph.D., and James V. Dingell, Ph.D. Actively contributing to this part of the project were John Bradshaw and Murray Heimberg, M.D., Ph.D. Their specific roles are described in the Introduction.

44

immediately before and after the task and 70 minutes after the task on each day. The NEFA analysis of blood plasma was conducted only on the samples drawn immediately before and after the tasks. Chest electrodes and a finger plethysmograph were used to collect data during six-minute periods before, during, and after the task administrations. Cuff blood pressure measurements were conducted immediately before, immediately after, and 70 minutes after the task.

At 3:00 PM on day 4 the examiner met with each subject and explained in full detail the nature of the procedures, their importance in understanding the patient's response to mild stress, and the reasons for withholding the specific details of unsolvability on the second day.

The following research questions were asked of the data: (1) Do acute MI patients differ from non-MI patients in their plasma responses across days in the coronary unit? (2) Do acute MI patients differ from non-MI patients in the circadian rhythm of plasma 17-OH-CS? (3) Do acute MI patients differ from non-MIs in the change of plasma level resulting from a standardized stressful task situation? (4) Do acute MI patients differ from non-MI patients in plasma 17-OH-CS at a period 70 minutes following the stressful task? (5) Do significant correlations occur between plasma levels and other variables in the project? (6) Do the autonomic nervous system indices of stress (heart rate, blood volume, pulse amplitude) show differences among pretask, during-task, and posttask measures? (7) Are these autonomic changes shown in high rate levels, low rate levels, high-low differences, or variability in each case, respectively?

SUBJECTS

The subjects of the 17-OH-CS study were 36 acute MI patients, 28 on-ward non-MI patients, and 20 off-ward non-MI control patients. Patients were fewer in number than in the total study because (1) this aspect of the project was initiated later than the nursing care study, (2) occasionally staff was not available to draw blood samples and test the patients, and (3) occasionally a plasma sample would be broken or ruined in transport from Silver Spring, Maryland, to Nashville, Tennessee, where it was analyzed.

The subjects of the NEFA study were 17 acute MI patients, 21 on-ward non-MI patients, and 12 off-ward non-MI patients from among the total group described in Chapter 2. These represented the final subjects studied in the total project, since the NEFA analysis was set up last of all. A few subjects were missed when weekends and unavailability of staff precluded their testing.

Psychopolygraphic data was collected on 35 coronary unit patients. Data were fully analyzed only if both the heart rate and finger plethysmograph data (blood volume, pulse amplitude) were complete and scoreable on both the control and stress task days. A total of seven MI and seven non-MI records were included in the final analysis. Ten records were discarded because only the control task data were obtained. Eleven additional records were discarded because of movement artifact, equipment failure, or experimenter error on either or both of the two testing days.

PLASMA 17-HYDROXYCORTICOSTEROIDS ASSAY

The assay of the plasma samples was based on a procedure described by Silber and Porter (1957). Ten milliliters of heparinized whole blood was centrifuged at 2500 rpm for 10 minutes. Five-milliliter specimens of plasma were transferred to acid-washed centrifuge tubes and frozen. A few dozen frozen samples at a time were transported to the laboratory site for assay. There the specimens were thawed. To each 4 ml of plasma, 16 ml of petroleum ether was added at room temperature. The mixture was vigorously shaken for 30 seconds in a test tube with a Teflon-lined plastic cap. After centrifugation the solvent layer (top) was removed by aspiration and discarded. Two milliliters of this washed sample was extracted by shaking 30 seconds with 15 ml of chloroform that had been redistilled until it was virtually fluorogen free. The mixture was centrifuged, and the aqueous layer was carefully removed by aspiration and discarded. One milliliter of $0.1N$ NaOH was added, and the tube was shaken for 15 seconds and centrifuged. This preparation was centrifuged at 1400 rpm for four minutes. Pipetting beneath the NaOH, 10 ml of the chloroform extract was removed and placed in a test tube containing 2 ml of $30N$ H_2SO_4. The tube was capped and shaken vigorously for 30 seconds. The cap was then removed carefully, and the tube was centrifuged. After removal of the chloroform by aspiration the acid phase was transferred to a cuvette. The fluorescence was determined within 20 minutes using an Aminco-Bowman Fluorimeter with a 1P-21 photomultiplier. Measurements were made at wavelength for excitation and emission that gave maximum fluorescence with the fluorophore. Blanks and standards consisting of distilled water and aqueous solutions of hydrocortisone in place of plasma were carried through the entire procedure.

NEFA ASSAY

The assay of free fatty acids was performed on plasma taken from the same storage tubes from which plasma 17-OH-CS was assayed. This assay was conducted through the use of an extraction procedure (by columns method), which has subsequently been described by Kohout, Kohoutova, and Heimberg (1971).* Following this, the assay was determined by the colorimetric procedure described by Duncombe (1963).

PSYCHOPOLYGRAPHIC APPARATUS

The electrocardiographic (ECG) tracing, the cardiotachometric transformation of R-R intervals into beats per minute (BPM), blood volume (BV), pulse amplitude (PA), breathing rate and amplitude, and skin resistance (GSR) were recorded on a six-channel Grass Model 7 Polygraph.

Heart rate was obtained by coupling the output of the General Electric cardiac monitor with a Grass 7P4 preamplifier. The R wave of the QRS complex was used to

---

*The NEFA assay procedure was conducted in the laboratory and under the supervision of Murray Heimberg, M.D., Ph.D.

trigger the tachometer side of the 7P4. The latter was calibrated with a Grass TRC1 calibrator so that each millimeter of pen displacement represented a two-BPM change in instantaneous rate. The ECG tracing was also recorded so that R-R intervals could be determined manually and transformed to BPM when cardiotachometer tracings were interrupted by artifacts.

Blood volume and pulse amplitude measures were obtained using a single Grass PTTI-7 photoplethysmograph that was capacitance coupled with a Grass 7P9 matching panel. The photocell transducer was placed on the fifth digit of the dominant hand at the base of the nail. The light source was on the opposite side of the finger from the transducer so that deep rather than surface opacity was obtained. The patient's hand was placed in an opaque black felt "mitten," which effectively reduced ambient light. The time constant of the 7P9 was ten seconds. The plethysmograph channel was centered prior to testing, and the amplitude of the pulses was set initially at 1.5 cm. This setting was not changed during the 18 minutes of testing.

Respiration measures were obtained using a 6-inch Hg strain gauge and plethysmograph (Parks Electronics). The strain gauge was attached 2 inches below the sternum under tension induced by stretching at 20% of its unstretched length.

Skin resistance was obtained using Fels zinc-zinc-chloride palmar electrodes with an impressed current of 50 microamperes provided by a Grass 7P1 PGR preamplifier.

Paper speed was 10mm/sec except when artifactual or electrical interference affected cardiotachometer function, in which case the paper speed was 25 mm/sec.

Psychopolygraphic data quantification

Fig. 4-1 helps explain how we reduced the data. The upper left corner of the figure shows our 2 × 3 experimental design. Besides two groups (MI, non-MI) under three phases (pretask, task, posttask), a third dimension, not noted in the figure, is days (control task day, stress task day). Each six-minute period of recording within this design was divided into 36 ten-second segments.

In the middle of the figure is an actual specimen record of three such segments. For heart rate, blood volume, and pulse amplitude, each ten-second segment provided a number of measures, as may be seen on the right-hand side of the figure. The cardiotachometer tracing of BPM equivalents was observed for each ten-second segment. From it, the highest recorded beats per minute, the lowest recorded beats per minute, and the high-low difference were determined.

From the finger plethysmograph ten-second segments, blood volume was measured through observing the pen deflection from a constant arbitrary baseline during the interpulse interval (diastole). That is, during the successive points at which the pen had reached the valley in between the upward deflections resulting from pulses of blood, the distance of these points from an arbitrary constant baseline below the tracing was recorded. Again, the highest level (relative dilation), the least level (relative constriction), and the high-low difference was recorded for each ten-second segment.

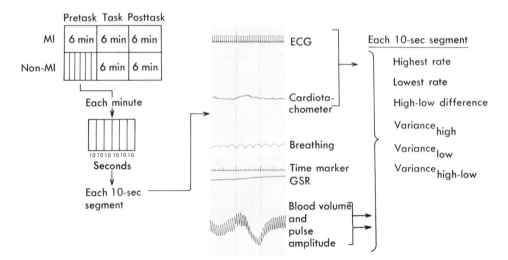

Fig. 4-1. Reduction and extraction of six dependent variables from psychophysiological measures.

For pulse amplitude, once the highest and lowest blood volume measures were identified within each ten-second segment, the amplitudes of the pulses (from valley to peak) immediately thereafter were recorded in millimeters. These were referred to as the high and low pulse amplitudes respectively. Absolute high and low pulse amplitudes within each ten-second segment were not recorded. Again, the high-low difference was also calculated.

At this point, 36 scores (one for each segment) were recorded for each of the three indices (high rate, low rate, high-low difference) for each of the three measures (heart rate, blood volume, pulse amplitude). Means and standard deviations of these 36 scores were computed, so that each subject had one score for each six-minute period (heart high rate, pulse amplitude high rate, and so on).

All data were transformed into scaled scores representing percentage of change from the pretask period:

$$\frac{\text{Task (or posttask) score} - \text{Pretask score}}{\text{Pretask score}} \times 100$$

Visual observation of the data indicated that no important results would emerge from the high-low difference or from the three variance scores. Therefore, further analysis of these variables was dropped at this point. High rate and low rate indices yielded essentially identical results, so the description of results does not deal separately with these two indices.

RESULTS
Plasma 17-hydroxycorticosteroids

The daily scan of plasma 17-OH-CS at 10:45 AM for MI patients as compared to the combined non-MI control group is illustrated in Fig. 4-2. As may be seen, the

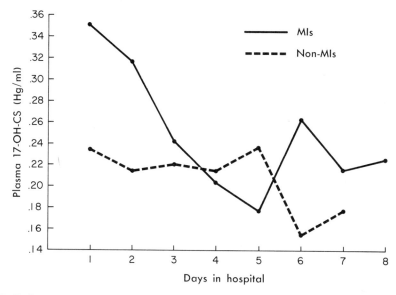

Fig. 4-2. Daily levels of 10:45 AM plasma 17-hydroxycorticosteroids in acute MI and the combined non-MI control patients following hospital admission.

mean levels of the MI patients are higher than those of the non-MI patients on every day except days 4 and 5. The higher levels among MIs reach statistical significance on days 1, 2, and 6. The sample sizes for days 1 through 8 for the MIs are 21, 27, 24, 23, 20, 27, 22, and 12 respectively. For the non-MIs they are 23, 45, 52, 39, 27, 11, 10, and 4 respectively. Thus, fluctuation in levels may be attributed to selective discharge as well as changes over time within the same patients. Lack of staff information of new admissions on weekends in order to collect first-day blood samples is probably an unimportant selective factor but should not be overlooked.

The plasma 17-OH-CS levels for the on-ward and off-ward non-MI patients are presented in Fig. 4-3. As may be seen, the levels of the on-ward non-MI group (suspected but disconfirmed for MI) are consistently higher than those for the off-ward non-MI group. However, the difference is significant only on day 5. The sample size for the on-ward non-MI group for days 1 through 8 are 16, 31, 34, 26, 16, 7, 5, and 2 respectively. For the off-ward non-MI group, it is 7, 14, 18, 13, 11, 4, 5, and 2 respectively. Again, changes in level may be due to selective discharge, changes in level within the same patient, or less likely, selective entry into the plasma study.

The circadian drop in plasma 17-OH-CS throughout the day is depicted in Fig. 4-4. As may be seen, the levels drop throughout the day. However, the disruption in the circadian change as a function of the mildly stressful tasks is notable. Disregarding the stress task data at 10:45 AM, 11:00 AM, and 12:10 PM, no significant difference occurs in the circadian rhythm between MI and non-MI patients. Also, no significant difference occurs between stress and control task days. Even when including the

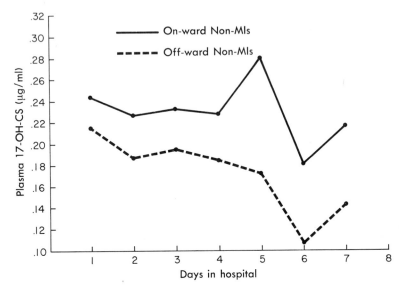

Fig. 4-3. Daily levels of 10:45 AM plasma 17-hydroxycorticosteroids in on-ward and off-ward non-MI control patients following hospital admission.

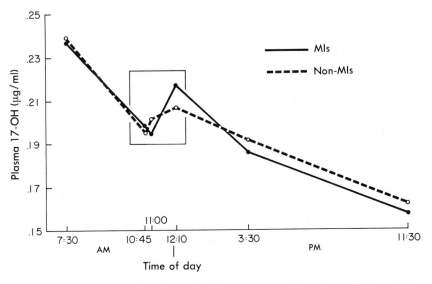

Fig. 4-4. Plasma 17-hydroxycorticosteroid levels of acute MI and non-MI hospital control patients at time points throughout day for stress and control task days combined.

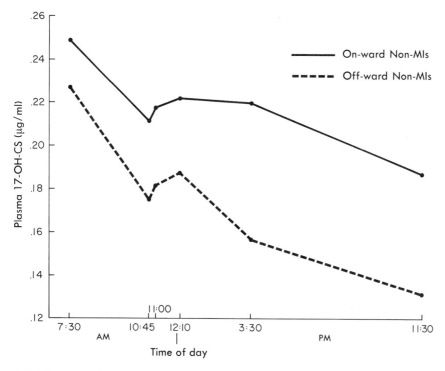

Fig. 4-5. Plasma 17-hydroxycorticosteroid levels of on-ward and off-ward non-MI control patients at time points throughout day for stress and control task days combined.

stress task data, differences between patients are greater in both groups at 7:30 AM than at any other time.

The circadian rhythm data for the on-ward and off-ward non-MI groups separately are shown in Fig. 4-5. As may be seen, the on-ward non-MI subjects were again consistently higher in steroid level than the off-ward non-MI subjects. This is true for both the control and stress task days.

From the data within the rectangle in Fig. 4-4, the reaction to stress may be examined. These data were subjected to a mixed analysis of variance with groups (MI, non-MI) as a "between" dimension and time (10:45 AM, 11:00 AM, 12:10 PM) and days (control task day, stress task day) as "within" dimensions. A significant interaction occurred between time and groups ($p < .05$). As may be seen in Fig. 4-6, the MI and non-MI groups reacted differently at the three time periods. The non-MI control group displayed an immediate but slight response to stress and 70 minutes later tapered off in accordance with its circadian rhythm. The MI group showed no immediate response to stress but 70 minutes later showed a highly elevated plasma 17-OH-CS level. The latter difference was statistically significant ($p < .005$).

The stress reactions of the on-ward and off-ward non-MI groups were compared in a similar analysis of variance design. No significant differences were found.

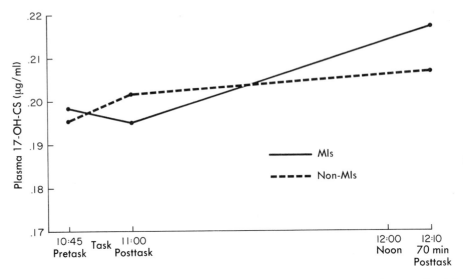

Fig. 4-6. Plasma 17-hydroxycorticosteroid levels before, after, and 70 minutes after intellectual task performance under solvable and unsolvable conditions.

The influence of drugs (barbiturates, anticoagulants, analgesics, and pheno-thiazines) and of sleep (on day shifts) on the control and stress task days respectively was examined for effect upon the steroid response. No findings were significant.

Discussion. The major finding is the delayed plasma 17-OH-CS response to stress among the MI patients. The non-MI response is mild and immediate; the MI response is delayed and exaggerated. These findings contradict speculations that MI patients have adrenal exhaustion, and they suggest that data indicating adrenal exhaustion may have been collected soon after the stressful situation. The findings suggest that non-MI patients respond to stress immediately but briefly. By contrast, the MI patients' data suggest that they deal with the stress situation while it is occurring; then, when it is over, they obsess or ruminate about the event, which elevates their steroid levels. The findings for MIs are like those for depressed patients, who also accumulate, rather than dissipate, steroids following a stressful situation (Wehmer, 1966).

Notably, the steroid response was not associated specifically with failure. It occurred on control and stress days. It is important to remember that both days are stressful in that blood is sampled, special electrodes are attached, instructions and administration of an intellectual task are given. The only difference is the added stress of personal failure on the second day. This latter type of stress does not apparently affect steroid level, or if it does, it is masked out by the day-to-day, circadian rhythm or other factors affecting steroid level. This lack of apparent differential response in steroids to control and stress tasks is different from the psychopolygraphic data, which does show such differences.

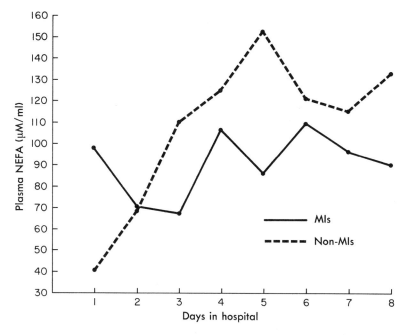

Fig. 4-7. Daily levels of 10:45 AM plasma nonesterized (free) fatty acid levels in acute MI and combined non-MI control patients following hospital admission.

The findings of this study support prior findings concerning the higher steroid level in acute MI than in other patient groups. Moreover, the data also indicate a trend for the on-ward non-MI control group to have higher steroid levels than the off-ward group. This finding may be related to the cardiovascular symptoms leading to a suspected MI among the on-ward control group, subclinical manifestations of MI that were not included within the strict diagnostic criteria, or different lengths of time since admission.

No difference between MIs and non-MIs can be attributed to the pattern of circadian rhythm. Both groups were high in the morning, showed fluctuations during the stressful task period, and were low in the evening.

Nonesterized (free) fatty acids (NEFA)

The levels of NEFA at 10:45 AM on different days in the hospital are shown in Fig. 4-7. The non-MI patients showed a tendency to increase in NEFA level across days. The sample sizes for the MI patients from day 1 to day 8 were 12, 17, 13, 17, 15, 19, 15, and 7 respectively. The sample sizes for the non-MIs from day 1 to day 8 were 10, 26, 33, 22, 14, 6, 6, and 2 respectively.

In Fig. 4-8, the non-MI data are separated for on-ward and off-ward groups. Both groups increase during the first five days. The off-ward levels are higher than the on-ward levels until day 7. The sample sizes for the on-ward non-MIs from day 1 to day 8 were 8, 17, 21, 15, 7, 4, 2, and 0. The sample sizes for the off-ward non-MI

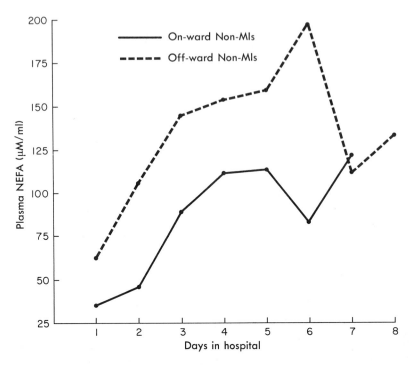

Fig. 4-8. Daily levels of 10:45 AM plasma nonesterized (free) fatty acid levels in on-ward and off-ward non-MI control patients following hospital admission.

patients from day 1 to day 8 were 2, 9, 12, 7, 7, 2, 4, and 2. These sample sizes are not sufficient to test statistical significance.

The levels of NEFA during the control and stress task days are shown in Fig. 4-9. As may be seen, no circadian rhythm was shown for NEFA as for plasma 17-OH-CS. Elevations occurred around the stress task period (10:45 AM, 11:00 AM, and 12:10 PM). Elevations even occurred at 10:45 AM, as compared to 7:30 AM, suggesting that at least for the on-ward patients the attachment of electrodes and preparation for blood sample and blood pressure in advance of the binary prediction task may have been stressful. The non-MI patients showed a greater elevation than the MI patients during the stress task. Then, at 3:30 PM, the levels of NEFA were uniformly low in both groups on both days. At 11:30 PM, the non-MI patients displayed an elevated NEFA, but the MI patients did not. When the non-MI patients were broken down into on-ward and off-ward groups, the data were similar until 11:30 PM, when the on-ward MI patients showed much higher elevations in NEFA than the off-ward non-MI patients (see Fig. 4-10). The latter elevation was probably due to a late evening snack for patients on the coronary unit. In order to examine the NEFA response to the stress tasks, a mixed analysis of variance was performed with groups (MI, non-MI) as a "between" dimension and days (control task day, stress task day) and times (10:45 AM, 11:00 AM) as "within" dimensions. The 70-minute follow-up

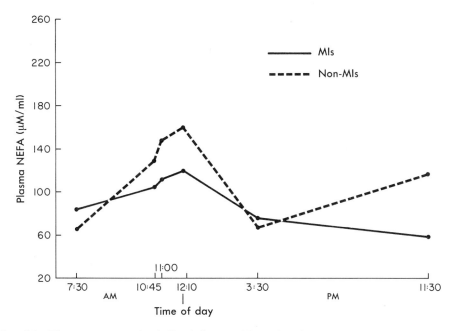

Fig. 4-9. Plasma nonesterized (free) fatty acid levels of acute MI and non-MI control patients (on and off coronary unit) at time points throughout control and stress task days.

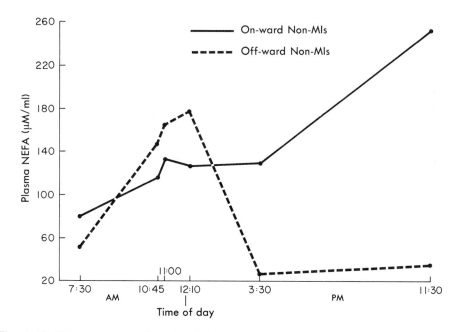

Fig. 4-10. Plasma nonesterized (free) fatty acid levels of on-ward and off-ward non-MI patients at time points throughout control and stress task days.

data at 12:10 PM was omitted because of the assumption that the noon meal between 11:00 AM and 12:10 PM would contaminate the results. (Actually, in retrospect, the correlational data of the next chapter indicate that the 12:10 PM NEFA data were not altogether valueless in their reflection of stress response.) The results of these data, shown in Fig. 4-11, indicated a significant increase ($p < .05$) in NEFA from before (10:45 AM) to after (11:00 AM) the stress task. This substantiated that an elevation occurred in NEFA in association with the stress and control task situations. A nonsignificant trend occurred for groups as a result of the overall level of NEFA being higher among the non-MI patients on all occasions. Of greatest importance, the curves from 10:45 AM to 11:00 AM were parallel. There was absolutely no evidence that the MI and non-MI patients have differential NEFA responses to the task on either the control or stress task days.

The NEFA data in response to the control and stress tasks were also analyzed with caloric intake being covaried out on the days of the control and stress tasks. This analysis made the statistical results stronger but the same as reported in the preceding paragraph.

The NEFA responses of the on-ward and off-ward non-MI patients were compared in a similar Groups × Days × Time mixed analysis of variance. Again, only time (10:45 AM versus 11:00 AM) was significant ($p < .025$). Thus, while the posttask NEFA exceeded the pretask NEFA, no difference occurred between the two control groups on either day.

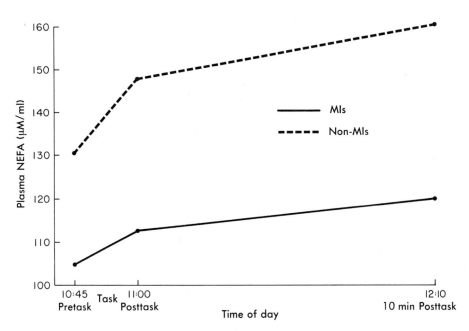

Fig. 4-11. Plasma nonesterized (free) fatty acid levels of acute MI and non-MI control patients before, after, and 70 minutes after intellectual task performance under solvable and unsolvable conditions.

Discussion. MI and non-MI patients respond with similarly increased NEFA levels to a standardized stress task and to caloric intake. However, the correlational findings on death, which are reported in Chapter 5, show that elevated NEFA levels among MI patients, particularly after the stress task, are significantly associated with death from another MI within 12 weeks. Thus, the hypothesis of association between NEFA and myocardial infarction received a measure of support despite the foregoing results.

The following trends in the data merit future investigation: (1) Non-MI patients increased in 10:45 AM NEFA from day to day; MI patients did not. (2) On-ward non-MI patients were unusually high in NEFA at 11:30 PM, in contrast to MI patients. (3) On-ward non-MI patients tended to have lower NEFA levels from day to day than off-ward non-MI patients. Whether these findings result from differences in coronary unit and regular hospital diet could not be determined in this study.

Psychopolygraphic measures

Heart rate. Heart rate levels are shown in Fig. 4-12. The fact that each heart rate level during the task is well above the arbitrary zero pretask baseline shows that both the tasks (control and stress) raised heart rate (control day, $\overline{X} = 8.7\%$, $F = 10.43$, $df = 1/12$, $p = .003$; stress day $\overline{X} = 6.5\%$, $F = 6.05$, $df = 1/12$, $p = .015$). The elevation of heart rate in MI patients was less than in non-MI patients, but the difference fell short of significance ($F = 2.97$, $df = 1/12$, $p = .11$).

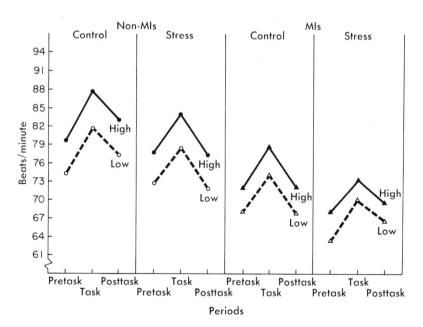

Fig. 4-12. Heart rate levels of acute MI and on-ward non-MI control patients during 6-minute periods before, during, and after stress and control tasks.

There was a nonsignificant tendency for all subjects to be less responsive on the second (stress task) day. This effect could not be fully examined, since day sequence had been deliberately confounded with the control versus stress task in the design.

The only reliable difference between groups occurred during the posttask period on the control day. The non-MI subjects failed to restore heart rate back to baseline level during that period ($\bar{X} = 4.02\%$, $F = 7.98$, $df = 1/12$, $p = .015$). With this exception, the heart rate was usually restored to pretask level during the posttask period. However, variability in scores prevented the Groups × Periods × Days interaction from reaching significance.

Blood volume. The blood volume levels are shown in Fig. 4-13. There was very little difference between the (arbitrarily zero) pretask levels and those during the task. However, remarkable differences occurred between the task and posttask levels on the stress day. This resulted in a significant interaction among groups, periods, and days ($F = 10.84$, $df = 1/12$, $p = .006$). Fig. 4-13 indicates that the blood volumes of non-MI patients sharply decreased and those of MI patients increased following the failure experience. Although the magnitude of change in the non-MIs was greater, an analysis of individual response patterns indicated greater stability among the MI responses. The sharp decrease of the non-MIs was accounted for greatly by one deviant subject. The increase of lesser magnitude among the MI patients was more uniform; six of seven MI patients showed this trend.

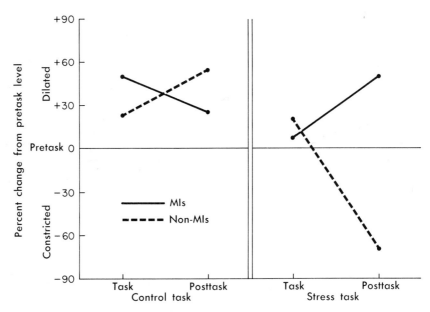

Fig. 4-13. Digital blood volume (between pulses) in acute MI and on-ward non-MI control patients during and after the stress and control tasks, expressed as deviations from "arbitrary zero" pretask levels, at the most dilated blood volume point within each ten-second segment.

Pulse amplitude. The pulse amplitude response levels are presented in Fig. 4-14. The non-MI patient group decreased its pulse amplitude on both days from the pretask level (arbitrarily zero) to the level during the task. Likewise, the MI group decreased from before to during on the control task; on the second (stress) day, there was an increase. These trends do not reach statistical significance on the control day, but they are statistically reliable on the stress day.

From during to after the task, Fig. 4-14 clearly indicates little change in subject groups on the control day. However, following failure on the stress day, there was a sharp increase among non-MI patients and a sharp decrease among MI patients. Statistical analyses indicate a significant interaction of groups and periods on the stress day (F = 10.82, df = 1/12, p = .007). When these group trends were examined separately, however, only the increase of the non-MI patients was significant (F = 5.90, df = 1/12, p = .03). While the mean decrease in MI patients was not significant, six of the seven patients showed a decrease.

The overall pattern of changes in pulse amplitude assessed by a multivariate contrast were found to be significant by exact likelihood ratios (F = 4.61, df = 4/9, p = .03) and by chi square (X^2 = 24.59, df = 4, p = .0002).

Discussion. The polygraphic findings indicate that acute MI patients respond differently from non-MI patients. The heart rate findings were few but consistent. The MI patient was less responsive than the non-MI patient. Overall heart rate was

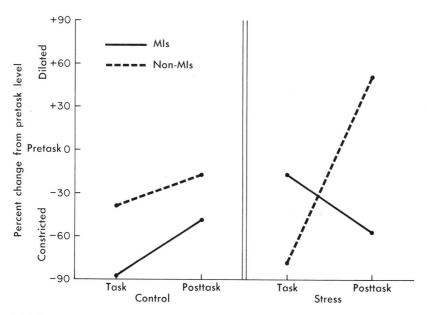

Fig. 4-14. Digital pulse amplitude in acute MI and on-ward non-MI control patients during and after the stress and control tasks, expressed as deviations from "arbitrary zero" pretask levels, at the most dilated blood volume point within each ten-second segment.

slightly lower among the MI patients. The increase in heart rate during the binary prediction tasks was less among the MI patients. During the posttask period, the MI patients were more consistently restored to their pretask baseline rate.

Slight habituation in heart rate was observed in both groups on the second day; the deliberate confounding of control versus stress task and day sequence in the design probably did not allow a full expression of the habituation effect.

The finger plethysmographic data of blood volume and pulse amplitude taken together support the notion that MI patients are different from non-MI patients in their responses to failure. From a psychological point of view, failure in an ego-involving goal-directed situation should have different characteristics than either physical stress or the psychological stress resulting from the demands of a success-fully completed but difficult task. However, heart rate, plasma 17-hydroxy-corticosteroid elevation, and NEFA elevation showed no distinction between the patients' reactions to failure and success. With blood volume and pulse amplitude, however, there were differences, and the characteristic reactions of MI patients were opposite to those of non-MI patients. Following failure, the blood volume of MI patients increased, and pulse amplitude decreased. Blood volume of non-MI patients decreased following failure, and pulse amplitude increased. Whether the pattern observed here in MI patients is also present in coronary-prone and in postcardiac individuals or whether the difference occurs only in association with an acute lesion in heart tissue, cannot be determined by this study. The strength of the result warrants further investigation.

A note of clarification is needed regarding the reference to increased and de-creased blood volume as dilation and constriction respectively. Past evidence has indicated that while some peripheral nerves effect a dilation (e.g., on the face, neck, and chest in blushing), others effect only constriction (e.g., in the hands and feet) (Brown, 1967). From this evidence alone one would conclude that the term dilation should not be used to describe finger response but, instead, only the presence or absence of constriction. However, while this innervation for constriction occurs in the vascular plexus near the skin surface, it is not clear whether the finding applies also to the deeper muscles in the finger. Surface measures with finger plethysmo-graph are likely to be sensitive to only or primarily the vasculature near the surface, and in such cases blood volume and pulse amplitude tend to be positively corre-lated. Our transducer measured blood volume through the diameter of the digit, therefore measuring the deep as well as surface vasculature. It is evident from our data that this technique allows pulse amplitude and blood volume to vary in opposite directions. Whether this is because the deeper muscle vasculature is capa-ble of active dilation is a question that future research must answer.

SUMMARY

The stress experiment yielded many results. These results are summarized here as observations before, during, immediately following, and 70 minutes following the stress task. Summarizing them this way allows concurrent changes among the various measures of blood volume, pulse amplitude, heart rate, plasma 17-OH-CS, and plasma NEFA to be compared. Readers who wish to follow the course of specific measures across time should refer to the separate discussions in the chapter.

Prior to the administration of the task, the acute MIs showed a higher steroid level than non-MI patients. This steroid level decreased with increased hospitalization. By contrast, an increase in NEFA level in non-MI patients was observed from day to day. Among the non-MI patients, those with suspected but disconfirmed MIs and still on the coronary unit had higher steroid levels than the non-MI patients elsewhere in the hospital. No difference occurred between MI and non-MI patients in the pattern of 17-OH-CS or NEFA circadian rhythm. This similarity in plasma levels persisted later in the day following the solvable and unsolvable tasks. No significant differences were observed in heart rate between MI and non-MI patients prior to the task administration.

During the task administrations the non-MI patients had an immediate but mild elevation in steroid level that the MI patients failed to show. By contrast, both MI and non-MI subjects had elevated NEFA during the task, and there was no evidence that the two groups differed in NEFA response characteristics. Heart rates increased in all patients, but the elevation was slightly less among MI patients. No change occurred in blood volume from the pretask to the task administration period. Pulse amplitude in MI and non-MI patients decreased on the first test day when given the solvable task. On the second day with the unsolvable task, however, it increased in only the MI patients.

During the period immediately following the task administration the patients have knowledge that they have either failed or succeeded in the task. No immediate effect is shown in steroid level. However, those MI patients showing a high NEFA response to the tasks (regardless of success or failure) have a higher probability of death within 12 weeks (see Chapter 5). Heart rate is lower in acute MI than in non-MI patients. In fact, the non-MI group failed to recover its pretest baseline level on the first day of testing. Of interest, however, is the fact that the MI and non-MI patients react differently to the failure experience. Their opposite responses occurred for both blood volume and pulse amplitude. The MI patients had increased blood volume and decreased pulse amplitude following failure. The non-MI patients had decreased blood volume and increased pulse amplitude following failure. No particular pattern of plethysmographic response was noted following the successful completion of the binary prediction task.

Finally, a striking finding occurred in the plasma 17-OH-CS as measured 70 minutes following the tasks, a time after which a steroid secretion is expected to be at its half-life in the bloodstream. MI patients were markedly elevated; non-MI patients showed a drop in accordance with their circadian rhythm.

Acute MI patients respond differently to stress than other patients, but the nature of their response is highly dependent upon the parameter being measured. Moreover, some parameters are associated particularly with failure, whereas other parameters are associated with the general demands of the situation.

As for practical implications, the clinician who is interested in the response of an MI patient to stress is not likely to find it in the patient's immediate reaction. Like the depressed patient, the MI patient may react very little immediately. But after a while, perhaps as a result of rumination, the stress reaction becomes elevated and clear. Though delayed, the response may be important, since its magnitude (at least as reflected by NEFA) may signal a fatal recurrence of the myocardial infarction.

Chapter 5

ANTICIPATING SUBSEQUENT INFARCTIONS AND OTHER CLINICAL MANIFESTATIONS*

The question this chapter seeks to answer is the prospective one: which variables help predict a recurrence of acute myocardial infarction? The chief interpretive problem with data that might answer the question is separating correlations that have prognostic value from those that are statistically significant but meaningless. Even though the chapter focuses only on correlations relevant to recovery variables, the number of correlations is very large. Since 1 in 20 correlations will be significant at the .05 level by chance alone, the number of these expected spuriously significant correlations will also be large. Therefore, as a first strategic principle, we divided subject groups randomly into halves, computed the correlation coefficients for each split-half, and interpreted results as significant only if they reached the .05 probability level in each group. This cautious procedure provided increased assurance that significant correlations, as reported, described valid relationships in the data rather than invalid chance events. Having met this split-half criterion, the groups were recombined. These more stable correlations for the total group are reported in Table 5-1. The split-half correlations are reported in Table K-1 (MIs), K-2 (on-ward non-MIs), and Table K-3 (off-ward non-MIs) of Appendix K.

The split-half approach is an extremely useful one, but it does not fit every situation. In the present study, for example, very few people had recurring MIs and died. Splitting the sample in half when trying to evaluate the correlates of death would so severely reduce the number of patients in either half that we would likely overlook valid relationships. In cases of death and recurrence of MI, we necessarily relied on correlations from the whole sample. To minimize the possibility of inter-

Text continued on p. 69.

---

*This chapter was completed in collaboration with Carol Raff Tarica.

Table 5-1. Significant predictors of various recovery variables

	r	N	p
Death from recurrent MI			
MI patients			
Mood II: social affection	.32	99	.005
NEFA unsolved task, 12:10 PM*	.63	37	.0005
NEFA, day 1, 10:45 AM*	.59	12	.025
NEFA, solved task, 12:10 PM*	.54	23	.005
NEFA, unsolved task, 11:00 AM*	.45	37	.005
NEFA, day 6, 10:45 AM*	.41	18	.025
NEFA, unsolved task, 10:45 AM*	.38	37	.01
Non-MI, both groups			
None			
Rehospitalization with another MI			
MI patients			
Scanning (size underestimation)	.39	103	.0005
Sedimentation rate	.30	101	.005
17-OH-CS, unsolved task, 3:30 PM*	.40	46	.005
Number cards guessed, solved task*	.36	53	.005
Sensitization-repression (anxiety)*	.31	113	.005
MMPI Depression I*	.30	97	.005
Death from MI*	.30	114	.005
Highest recorded systolic BP*	−.30	51	.025
Non-MI, both groups			
None			
Death or rehospitalization, MI			
MI patients			
Size estimation*	−.26	104	
Repression-sensitization*	−.24	115	
Mood I: anxiety*	.25	114	
Mood I: sadness*	.21	114	
Mood I: skepticism*	.21	114	
Mood II: anxiety*	.18	99	
Proneness scale, scanning*	.17	115	
Proneness scale, perfectionism*	.23	115	
Sedimentation rate*	.19	104	
Cardiac episodes*	.26	80	
Lactate dehydrogenase*	.16	113	
Severity total*	.18	116	
Severity II*	.19	116	
Depression I*	.27	100	
Non-MI, both groups			
Depression II*	.24	92	
Return to work*	.21	111	
Severity I (first 24 hours)			
MI patients			
Severity II (after first 24 hours)	.59	122	.0005
Severity change (drop)	.44	122	.0005
Days in coronary unit	.43	122	.0005
Highest temperature	.42	122	.0005

*These correlations were not submitted to the split-half criterion to be reported as significant. The alpha level was set at .025.

Table 5-1. Significant predictors of various recovery variables—cont'd

	r	N	p
Number days temperature over 99° F	.36	81	.005
Days before testing	.35	122	.0005
SGOT	.32	120	.0005
Severity total	.89	122	.0005
Non-MI on ward			
Severity II (after first 24 hours)	.95	26	.0005
Severity, total	.99	26	.0005
Severity II (after first 24 hours)			
MI patients			
Severity I (first 24 hours)	.59	122	.0005
Number arrhythmias	.47	80	.0005
Severity change (drop)	−.47	122	.0005
Days in coronary unit	.30	122	.005
Days before testing	.30	122	.005
SGOT	.22	120	.025
Number cardiac episodes	.60	81	.0005
Severity total	.89	122	.0005
Non-MI on ward			
Severity I	.95	26	.0005
Days before testing	.55	26	.005
Days on coronary unit	.52	26	.005
Severity, total	.99	26	.0005
Severity, total			
MI patients			
Number cardiac episodes	.52	81	.0005
Number arrythmias	.44	80	.0005
Days in coronary unit	.41	122	.0005
Number days temperature over 99° F	.38	81	.0005
Days before testing	.37	122	.0005
Highest temperature	.35	122	.0005
SGOT	.30	120	.005
Mood change (positive)	.26	98	.005
Severity I (first 24 hours)	.89	122	.0005
Severity II (after first 24 hours)	.89	122	.0005
Non-MI on ward			
Days before testing	.52	26	.005
Severity I	.99	26	.0005
Severity II	.99	26	.0005
Severity change (improvement)			
MI patients			
Number cardiac episodes	−.35	81	.005
Severity I	.44	122	.0005
Severity II	−.47	122	.0005
Non-MI patients			
None			
Days in coronary unit			
MI patients			
Days before testing	.43	129	.0005
Severity I	.43	122	.0005
SGOT	.41	128	.0005

Continued.

Table 5-1. Significant predictors of various recovery variables—cont'd

	r	N	p
Severity total	.41	22	.0005
Number days temperature over 99° F	.38	81	.0005
Days in hospital	.36	131	.0005
LDH	.36	125	.0005
High rate alarms	.33	90	.005
Highest temperature	.32	131	.0005
Severity II	.30	122	.005
Non-MI on ward			
Severity II (after first 24 hours)	.52	26	.005
LDH	.46	95	.0005
Days in hospital	.44	98	.0005
Days before testing	.25	98	.01
Number of cardiac episodes			
MI patients			
Severity II (after first 24 hours)	.60	81	.0005
Severity total	.52	81	.0005
Number arrythmias	.39	40	.05
Severity change (drop)	−.35	81	.005
Denial: complacency	−.28	79	.01
Non-MI on ward			
None			
Number of days before testing			
MI patients			
Days in coronary unit	.43	129	.0005
SGOT	.41	126	.0005
Severity total	.37	122	.0005
Severity I (first 24 hours)	.35	122	.0005
Severity II (after first 24 hours)	.30	122	.005
Highest temperature	.29	129	.0005
Non-MI on ward			
Days in coronary unit	.25	98	.01
Non-MI off ward			
Days in hospital	.52	80	.0005
Number of arrhythmias			
MI patients			
Severity II (after first 24 hours)	.47	80	.0005
Severity total	.44	80	.0005
Number episodes	.39	80	.0005
Non-MI on ward			
None			
Low heart rate monitor alarms			
MI patients			
Denial: self-interest	−.32	85	.005
Denial: hostility	−.22	85	.025
Non-MI patients			
None			
High heart rate monitor alarms			
MI patients			
Days in CCU	.33	90	.005
Non-MI on ward			
Relatives' view: coronary proneness, control of self	−.92	9	.0005

Table 5-1. Significant predictors of various recovery variables—cont'd

	r	N	p
Number of days temperature over 99° F			
MI patients			
Highest temperature	.72	81	.0005
17-OH-CS scan 5	.63	16	.005
LDH	.43	79	.0005
Days in coronary unit	.38	81	.0005
Severity total	.38	81	.0005
Severity I (first 24 hours)	.36	81	.005
White blood cell count	.35	79	.005
Days in hospital	.31	81	.005
Last 4:00 PM temperature	.31	81	.005
Mood I: vigor	−.25	79	.025
Non-MI patients			
None			
Highest temperature			
MI patients			
Severity I (first 24 hours)	.42	122	.0005
Total severity	.35	122	.0005
LDH	.33	125	.0005
Days on coronary unit	.32	131	.0005
Days in hospital	.31	131	.0005
Days before testing	.29	129	.0005
WBC	.25	129	.005
Non-MI on ward			
First 4:00 PM temperature	.58	98	.0005
Last 4:00 PM temperature	.55	98	.0005
WBC	.48	98	.0005
Sedimentation rate	.43	85	.0005
Lactate dehydrogenase (LDH)			
MI patients			
NEFA, day 2	.74	15	.005
SGOT	.71	125	.0005
Number days temperature over 99° F	.43	79	.0005
Days in coronary unit	.36	125	.0005
WBC	.33	125	.0005
Highest temperature	.33	125	.0005
Non-MI on ward			
Days in coronary unit	.46	95	.0005
SGOT	.37	95	.0005
Serum glutamic oxaloacetic transaminase (SGOT)			
MI patients			
LDH	.71	125	.0005
Relatives' view: repression-sensitization (anxiety)	.49	31	.005
Days before testing	.41	126	.0005
Days in coronary unit	.41	126	.0005
Severity I (first 24 hours)	.32	120	.0005
Severity total	.30	120	.005
Severity II (after first 24 hours)	.22	120	.025

Continued.

Table 5-1. Significant predictors of various recovery variables—cont'd

	r	N	p
Non-MI on ward			
Blood pressure	.52	33	.005
LDH	.37	95	.0005
Diversion	.29	71	.01
White blood cell count (WBC)			
MI patients			
Number days temperature over 99° F	.35	79	.005
LDH	.33	125	.0005
Highest temperature	.25	129	.005
Mood II: egotism	.21	99	.025
Non-MI on ward			
Relatives' view: repression-sensitization (anxiety)	.68	13	.005
Highest temperature	.48	98	.0005
Sedimentation (sed) rate			
MI patients			
Relatives' view: coronary proneness (repression-sensitization)	−.40	30	.025
Subsequent hospitalization, acute MI	.30	101	.005
First 4:00 PM temperature	.28	113	.005
Scanning (size underestimation)	.28	94	.005
Non-MI on ward			
Highest temperature	.43	85	.0005
Last 4:00 PM temperature	.37	85	.0005
Mood I: vigor	−.30	47	.025
Scanning (size underestimation)			
MI patients			
Subsequent hospital acute MI	.39	103	.0005
Depression I	.37	97	.0005
Sedimentation rate	.28	94	.005
Non-MI on ward			
None			
Non-MI off ward			
Days in intensive unit	−.66	19	.005
Mood II: Social affection			
MI patients			
NEFA, day 1	−.76	12	.005
NEFA, day 7	−.76	12	.005
Mood I: social affection	.48	99	.0005
Mood II: surgency	.45	101	.0005
Mood II: elation	.38	101	.0005
Death, MI, within 12 weeks	−.32	99	.005
Participation	.27	100	.005
Mood II: concentration	.26	101	.005
Non-MI on ward			
Mood I: social affection	.58	48	.0005
Mood II: elation	.53	50	.0005
Mood I: concentration	.45	48	.005
Coronary proneness scale: control of self	.42	49	.005
Mood II: surgency	.42	50	.005
Education	−.41	45	.005
Repression-sensitization (low anxiety)	−.38	49	.005

Table 5-1. Significant predictors of various recovery variables—cont'd

	r	N	p
Familial history of heart disease			
MI patients			
None			
Non-MI on ward			
None			
Previous MIs or heart history			
MI patients			
None			
Non-MI on ward			
None			
Uric acid			
MI patients			
Sex (male)	.38	108	.0005
Cardiac information test	.32	89	.005
Analgesics	−.28	106	.005
Mood II: fatigue	.24	87	.025
Non-MI on ward			
Analgesics	−.35	80	.005
Cholesterol			
MI patients			
17-OH-CS, day 3	.68	22	.0005
17-OH-CS, unsolved task, 11:30 PM	.66	33	.0005
17-OH-CS, unsolved task, 7:30 AM	.55	41	.0005
17-OH-CS, solved task, 7:30 AM	.53	37	.0005
17-OH-CS, solved task, 11:30 PM	.51	36	.0005
17-OH-CS, unsolved task, 10:45 AM	.51	42	.0005
17-OH-CS, unsolved task, 3:30 PM	.51	42	.0005
17-OH-CS, unsolved task, 10:45 AM	.49	36	.005
Non-MI on ward			
None			
Number days before return to work			
MI patients			
None			
Non MI on ward			
None			
Blood pressure (systolic)			
MI patients			
None			
Non-MI on ward			
SGOT	.52	33	.005

preting spurious correlations we examined and interpreted patterns of predictive relationships. When related variables agreed in predicting a particular outcome, we had greater confidence in each related finding. We did this both judgmentally and with the help of factor analysis. The results of the factor analysis also were used to decide how to order the results presented in this chapter as well as to bolster our judgments about which correlations could be interpreted most confidently.

As a second strategic principle, we examined correlations separately for the MI and non-MI groups. If a significant correlation occurs in the acute MI group but in neither of the non-MI groups, it may be interpreted as specifically relevant to acute myocardial infarction. If a correlation emerges significantly in non-MI as well as MI groups, then it may relate to general recovery or to the fact that cautious diagnostic criteria left a number of subclinical or marginally clinical acute MIs assigned to the on-ward non-MI group. The opposite pattern of findings could also emerge; some factors may predict only non-MI recovery.

DEATH

MI patients. As noted in Table 5-1, the only psychological variable correlated with death that reached split-half significance was stated mood for social affection at the end of the coronary unit stay. The lower the stated mood for social affection, the greater the likelihood of subsequent death within 12 weeks. While decreased social affection may be a part of the "giving up" syndrome (Schmale, 1964), this was not one of the variables we expected to predict death. In the total MI sample the highest seven correlations all involved nonesterized (free) fatty acids (NEFA). The higher the NEFA levels, the greater likelihood of death within 12 weeks. The highest correlation was with NEFA level at 12:10 PM following the stressful (unsolvable) task. As was seen in Chapter 4, this is the same time at which the plasma 17-hydroxycorticosteroids (17-OH-CS) were elevated in MI patients. Death was also significantly correlated with NEFA measured at 10:45 AM on day 1, 12:10 PM on the control (solvable) task day, 11:00 AM immediately after the stress task, 10:45 AM on day 6, 10:45 AM at the beginning of the stress task, and at 10:45 AM on day 7. It is notable that almost all these positive correlations occur around times associated with the psychological stress.

Non-MI patients. No variables were significantly correlated with death for the on-ward and off-ward non-MI patients.

REHOSPITALIZATION WITH SUBSEQUENT ACUTE MYOCARDIAL INFARCTION

MI patients. Two variables were strong correlates and predictors of subsequent hospitalization with an acute MI. The strongest is the level of perceptual scanning. The higher the scanning level, the more likely the readmission within 12 weeks. The second variable was peak sedimentation rate while on the coronary care unit. The higher the sedimentation rate, the more likely the readmission.

Scanning is the most powerful predictor of recurrent MIs. The high scanner, oriented to a high rate of processing information, is prone to recurrence. One interpretation is that the higher scanner more readily detects his own symptoms and gets back to the hospital. If this interpretation is valid, then lower scanners may have infarcts that go unidentified. Another interpretation comes from the psychophysiological evidence on orienting from Lacey (1958) and Broekema's research groups (Warner, 1973; McCormick, 1974). According to these studies, high scanning or orienting activity, shown here to be highly frequent among recurring MIs, is associated with momentary decreases in heart rate. It is possible that the slowing of heart rate, even within normal limits during intensive scanning, may lower the threshold for fibrillation or other heart activity associated with a rehospitalization.

The second stable correlate, sedimentation rate, is regularly monitored in coronary patients. These results suggest that relations should be examined more closely between sedimentation rate and psychological and biological variables related to stress, scanning, and infarction.

In the analysis of the total MI sample, the nine highest correlations with acute MI readmission were plasma 17-OH-CS level at 3:30 PM on the day of stress testing, scanning, number of cards guessed on the solvable control task, NEFA level on day 2, repression-sensitization, MMPI Depression score on admission, peak sedimentation rate, death from MI, and low measures for the highest recorded systolic blood pressure during coronary unit stay. Since these correlations were not significant in both split-half analyses, they should be viewed primarily as leads for future research. As shown in the previous chapter, MI patients have elevated plasma 17-OH-CS at 12:10 PM following the binary task. The present correlations suggest a high probability of recurrent MI for those patients whose plasma levels have not returned to the baseline level of the circadian rhythm by 4½ hours after the stress task. Also, greater effort on the control task, as shown by the number of cards guessed, indicates goal orientation and extensive scanning for the recurrent MI patients. This is consistent with the coronary-prone characteristics described by Freedman and Rosenman (1974).

The higher the anxiety level, the more likely the recurrent MI, as indicated by the total group correlations.

The greater the depression upon admission, the more likely the recurrent MI. Interestingly, the depression measure at the end of the coronary unit stay is not significant, perhaps because of mild euphoria among patients who have just learned that they have recovered enough to be transferred off of the coronary unit.

The lower the peak blood pressure, the more likely the recurrence of MI. Unfortunately, only the highest blood pressure during coronary unit stay was recorded in the research records. The lowest blood pressure during coronary unit stay was not recorded. It is therefore unknown whether the lowest reading would have been more predictive than the peak reading.

Non-MI patients. No correlations were significant that involved subsequent MIs.

Death or rehospitalization from subsequent MI

We kept data on death separate from data on rehospitalization without death. When they were combined, additional findings emerged beyond those already described. No split-half analysis was performed on this combined group.

Psychological factors continued to play a dominant role. Patients who either die or become rehospitalized with another MI within 12 weeks enter the coronary unit with high moods of anxiety, sadness, and skepticism. They also leave with high anxiety. In response to the coronary proneness scale devised for this project, the recurring MI patients score high in self-reported scanning and perfectionism. On the biological side, besides sedimentation rate, these MI-recurrent patients had a greater number of cardiac episodes that required nursing assistance on the coronary unit, a higher lactate dehydrogenase (LDH), and a higher total severity rating during their coronary unit stay.

SEVERITY

MI patients. Ratings of the severity of symptoms during the first 24 hours after admission (Severity I) and during the coronary unit period thereafter (Severity II) have a number of common elements. Both measures are positively related to the number of days spent in the coronary unit. Both are related to the number of days' delay before psychological testing began. SGOT is related to both. The two severity measures are related to each other and to other severity measures. Nevertheless, certain differences arose.

Severity of symptoms during the first 24 hours is more associated with temperature, and severity during the following period is associated more directly with cardiac dysfunction. The highest peak temperature and the number of days with temperature over 99° F are significantly related to Severity I. Severity II reflects the number of cardiac episodes and the number of recorded arrhythmias.

Severity total, the combination of these two measures, is significantly correlated with all the aforementioned variables plus one other. The greater the overall severity of symptoms on the coronary unit, the more positive the mood change. Apparently, those patients with a sustained severity of symptoms who, by the way, spend a longer time on the unit, have a greater mood improvement during coronary unit stay. That is, they have a lower initial mood or a greater elevation in mood when they learn they are going to be transferred.

Most patients have fewer severe symptoms after the first 24 hours. Thus the variable of change in severity of symptoms was analyzed. The number of times the patient needed assistance because of cardiac symptoms was the only variable correlated with severity change. As expected, the more episodes, the less the usual decrease (or the more the increase) in severity.

The severity measures are notable not only for what they are related to but also for what they are not related to. For example, severity has no relationship to long-term prognosis. The factor analysis, reported later, further clarifies this finding.

On-ward non-MI patients. As might be expected, the ratings of severity for those with suspected but disconfirmed MIs had limited correlation with other variables. Severity I and Severity II were indeed correlated. Severity I had no other correlate. Severity II was positively correlated with the number of days before project testing began and the number of days of coronary unit stay. Combining the severity measures led to no new results. Also, severity change was not significantly related to other variables.

Off-ward non-MI patients. Severity measures, which pertained specifically to cardiac illness, were not administered to control patients off the coronary care unit. In view of the results for the on-ward non-MI patients we believe that few significant results would have been obtained for this off-ward control group. Below, we have mentioned these patients only in connection with the variables that were collected from them.

LENGTH OF STAY IN CORONARY UNIT AND HOSPITAL

MI patients. The number of days spent on the coronary care unit was significantly correlated with ten other variables in both split-half samples. The number of days our research staff delayed testing was a predictor of length of stay. Apparently the same visible signs of illness that led to the delay in testing also led to a prolonged stay in the unit. This finding indicates that the decision to delay testing was a valid one. It also indicates that informal judgments of severity can be made reliably. The formal severity ratings were also correlated with the length of coronary unit stay. Severity of symptoms during the first 24 hours, severity of symptoms thereafter, and the combination of these two scores were all associated with a longer stay.

Five specific indicators of illness were related to the length of coronary unit stay. These included SGOT level, LDH level, the number of days in which the body temperature exceeded 99° F, the highest temperature recorded for each patient on the coronary care unit, and the number of monitor alarms indicating high heart rate. The number of low rate alarms was not a significant predictor of stay on the coronary unit.

Finally, the number of days on the coronary care unit itself was a significant predictor of the number of days spent in the hospital. Days spent in the hospital was not shown in the factor analysis to be relevant to the major clinical predictors. Consequently, the data are omitted from Table 5-1 but are discussed here.

Considered separately, these findings are susceptible to several interpretations. Physicians may have used the information reflected by these specific variables to decide when their patients were to be transferred. Or the physicians may have responded to the general physical condition of the patients as assessed by the severity ratings, and the specific variables are merely correlated with severity. At the time decisions were made to delay testing in our project, however, none of the various ratings and blood work had been completed. Moreover, the delay in testing was a research staff decision, and transfer from the coronary unit was each personal physician's decision. Therefore, whatever led to these decisions had a valid relationship with transfer, severity, and clinical and serological measures.

For length of stay in the hospital, as for length of stay in the coronary unit, temperature is an important predictor. Both the number of coronary unit days in which temperature exceeded 99° F and the highest temperature recorded on the coronary unit were significant predictors of length of hospital stay, even though only coronary unit temperature was considered in the research record.

The level of plasma 17-OH-CS 70 minutes after the completion of the control (solvable) task was also significantly related to length of hospital stay. As was described more fully in the preceding chapter, MI patients tend to have an unusually elevated steroid reaction 70 minutes following the binary prediction task. The greater this elevation on the (first) control task day, the longer the hospital stay.

One finding was in the opposite direction from expectation. The tendency of the relatives (usually the spouses) to describe the patient as internal locus of control (ILC) was also positively related to length of hospital stay. After the fact, this finding would suggest that ILC personalities may feel that remaining in the hospital represents greater control of their destinies. Alternatively, it may suggest that physicians and hospital staff have a subtle or unconscious preference for ILC behavior. The possibly less preferred or less tolerable ELC patients go home sooner.

On-ward non-MIs. For length of coronary unit stay, only four of the ten variables significant for the MI patients were significant for the on-ward non-MIs. LDH, number of days before testing, and severity after the first 24 hours on the unit all predicted the number of days in the coronary unit. The number of days in the unit, in turn, was related to the number of days in the hospital. These results leave open the possibility that LDH is associated with cardiac exhaustion, coronary insufficiency, or some other non-MI condition that prompts admission to the coronary unit.

For total hospital stay, a different group of correlates was significant. The level of social affection on admission to the coronary unit and the administration of anticoagulants were each positively related to length of hospital stay. High social affection may encourage physicians and hospital staff to keep a patient, whereas, low social affection may discourage it. Anticoagulants, at least at the time of this study in the late 1960s, tended to be given to sicker patients for whom there was possibility of clotting. This probably accounted for the longer recovery period in this treatment group.

Off-ward non-MIs. Off-ward non-MIs were sampled from the intensive care unit, which was physically and functionally separate from the coronary unit. The length of intensive care unit stay for the off-ward non-MIs was related to factors different from those for coronary unit patients. Minimal scanning, as revealed by size overestimation, was correlated with length of stay. Based on other findings in this project, the minimal scanner is probably less prone to anxiety, depression, and complaining. The minimal scanner probably exerts less pressure than the extensive scanner to get out of the hospital.

The length of hospital stay was, as expected, correlated with the length of intensive care unit stay.

The length of hospital stay was also positively associated with internal locus of control as reported by the patient. This finding is in the same direction as the relatives' estimates of patients' locus of control and length of hospital stay among the MI patients. Again, an internal locus of control may lead the patient to lobby for longer hospitalization.

The off-ward non-MI patients with longer hospital stay tended to be tested later. This finding resulted from the greater availability of the longer-staying patients, since no tight scheduling procedure was used for them. Low NEFA level 70 minutes after the stress task was also related to longer hospital stay. No explanation can be offered for the latter result. In our judgment, it is a chance finding.

NUMBER OF CARDIAC EPISODES

MI patients. The number of times each patient needed nursing or medical assistance as a result of cardiac embarrassment was associated, as would be expected, with the number of arrythmias recorded from the cardiac monitor. Also, as mentioned earlier, the number of episodes was associated with severity of symptoms after the first 24 hours of coronary unit stay. Those with more cardiac episodes either showed less improvement or became worse in symptoms late in their coronary unit stay. Finally, those patients having more episodes tended to admit rather than deny attitudes of complacency.

On-ward non-MI patients. No correlations were significant.

NUMBER OF DAYS BEFORE TESTING

MI patients. Although not originally viewed as an index of severity or recovery, the amount of delay before our research staff began testing each patient emerged as a highly relevant variable. Delays were based upon a subjective decision by the project field director (a psychologist) and the head nurse. Patients with greater delays before testing spent more days in the coronary care unit. They had higher ratings of severity of symptoms, both during the first 24 hours and thereafter. They had higher temperatures and markedly higher SGOT levels. All this data became available subsequent to the decision to begin testing. Thus the subjective assessment of when a patient can participate in psychological tests is an index of severity.

On-ward non-MI patients. Of all the preceding variables, only three (days on the coronary care unit, severity level after the first 24 hours, and total severity level) were related to the number of days before testing among the on-ward non-MI patients.

Off-ward non-MI patients. As mentioned earlier, the off-ward non-MI patients with greater number of days of delay before testing tended to spend more days in the hospital. Patients with more days in the hospital were more likely to be chosen as controls.

NUMBER OF ARRHYTHMIAS

MI patients. As might be expected, the number of arrhythmias was significantly related to the combined severity ratings for total coronary unit stay. Comparing the two severity ratings, the number of arrhythmias is more relevant to the severity of symptoms after the first 24 hours on the unit. As may be seen in Table 5-1 and below, temperature is more relevant during the first 24 hours. The number of arrhythmias was also related to the number of cardiac episodes that demanded special attention while on the coronary care unit.

On-ward non-MI patients. No correlations were significant.

MONITOR ALARMS FOR LOW HEART RATE

MI patients. The data suggest that the number of monitor alarms for low heart rate is related to neither recovery nor severity. Only two psychological measures, denial of self-interest and denial of hostility, were related to low rate monitor alarms. Both were related inversely. As will be discussed in Chapter 6, MI patients have a greater denial of hostility than off-ward non-MIs. This tends to make the low alarm rate even less useful in the prognosis of myocardial infarction. Obviously, this does not mean that low heart rate or arrest in connection with an acute MI is clinically unimportant.

On-ward non-MI patients. For the on-ward non-MIs, no variables were related to the number of low rate monitor alarms.

Off-ward non-MI patients. No cardiac monitor data were collected for patients off the coronary care unit.

MONITOR ALARMS FOR HIGH HEART RATE

MI patients. As indicated earlier, the greater the number of monitor alarms indicating high heart rate, the longer the stay on the coronary unit. No other correlation was significant.

On-ward non-MI patients. Relatives report less self-control for patients with more high alarms. This finding was unexpected and is unexplained. While the amount of data collected on relatives was very limited, this finding yielded almost a perfect correlation.

TEMPERATURE

MI patients. As has already been indicated, temperature is an important correlate of an infarct, especially during the first 24 hours on the coronary unit. The severity of symptoms during this early period and also the initial low mood measure for vigor are significant predictors of the number of days with a temperature over 99° F. The number of days with temperature over 99° F, in turn, significantly predicts LDH, WBC, peak temperature level, last 4:00 PM temperature before leaving the unit, the plasma 17-OH-CS level on day 5, the number of days spent on the coronary unit, the overall severity of symptoms on the unit, and the number of days spent in the hospital after leaving the unit.

The highest peak temperature has similar significant correlates. Like the number of days over 99° F, the peak temperature is related to Severity I, LDH, WBC, overall symptom severity, length of coronary unit stay, and length of hospital stay. It is also related to the number of days' delay before testing, the first 4:00 PM temperature, and steroid level immediately after failure on the stress task at 11:00 AM and again at 12:10 PM.

The first 4:00 PM temperature reading is less related to other variables than the two temperature measures described above. As already indicated, the first 4:00 PM temperature is related to the highest temperature recorded while on the coronary unit. It is also positively related to sedimentation rate. As might be expected, the higher this initial temperature reading, the more likely the final day's 4:00 PM reading will be lower.

The final 4:00 PM temperature reading on the coronary unit is related to the number of days on which temperature was over 99° F.

On-ward non-MI patients. As expected, temperature had fewer correlates for the on-ward non-MI patients. The highest peak temperature was correlated positively with the initial and final 4:00 PM temperatures, which in turn were correlated with each other. This indicated some stability in temperature among non-MIs during the total coronary unit stay. Other positive and significant correlates of peak temperature were sedimentation rate and WBC, both of which were associated with temperature measures among MI patients also.

The last 4:00 PM temperature, besides being correlated with peak temperature and the first 4:00 PM temperature, is positively correlated with sedimentation rate and social affection upon leaving the unit. The latter correlation is surprising. No explanation is available as to why high final 4:00 PM temperature should be associated with a high final social affection mood. Also uninterpretable—men have a greater drop in temperature than women.

LACTATE DEHYDROGENASE (LDH)

MI patients. The highest recorded level of lactate dehydrogenase, as well as being related to SGOT, was significantly related to other variables, indicating severity of the myocardial infarction. LDH was correlated with the highest recorded temperature, the number of days with temperature exceeding 99° F, white blood cell count, and the number of days before transfer from the coronary unit. NEFA level on the second day in the coronary unit was also found to be positively related to LDH.

On-ward non-MI patients. LDH in the on-ward non-MI patients also was correlated with SGOT. Patients remaining longer on the coronary unit had a higher LDH. As noted previously, this finding suggests LDH may be associated with diagnoses other than acute infarcts.

SERUM GLUTAMIC OXALOACETIC TRANSAMINASE (SGOT)

MI Patients. SGOT is an important concurrent index of infarct severity. SGOT was significantly related to severity ratings of symptoms, both during the first 24 hours and later in the coronary unit stay. The high correlation of SGOT with lactate dehydrogenase (LDH) indicated that the two variables shared about 50% of their variance with each other in both split-half samples. Those patients whose participation in the project was delayed because of the severity of their symptoms were found to be high in SGOT. The higher the SGOT level, the longer the patients's stay on the coronary unit. On the psychological level, SGOT was unexpectedly found to be higher in patients whose relatives reported them to be low in anxiety and to repress problems rather than be preoccupied with them.

On-ward non-MI patients. Like the MI patients, SGOT level in the on-ward non-MI patients tended to be positively associated with LDH. In addition, patients high in SGOT tended to be high in blood pressure and to be in the high diversion condition of nursing care. This latter finding suggests that non-MI patients (perhaps cardiac exhaustion or insufficiency patients), in contrast to MI patients, may find high diversion detrimental to their condition, as gauged by the SGOT level.

Off-ward non-MI patients. SGOT was not regularly recorded on the off-ward control patients.

WHITE BLOOD CELL COUNT (WBC)

MI patients. The highest white blood cell count recorded during coronary unit stay seemed to be another index of severity. It was significantly related to peak temperature, the number of days with temperature over 99° F, and LDH. WBC was also correlated with the MI patients' subjective report of egotism at the end of their coronary unit stay. No explanation is offered for this unexpected finding.

On-ward non-MI patients. Like the MI patients, WBC in the on-ward non-MI patients was associated with high peak temperature. The relative's estimate on the Ullmann scale that the patient is a repressor (low in anxiety) was also unaccountably related to WBC.

SEDIMENTATION RATE

MI patients. Together with other variables, the highest recorded sedimentation rate while on the coronary unit is a significant predictor of subsequent hospitalization for myocardial infarction within 12 weeks after admission to the coronary unit. Also related to sedimentation rate is extensive scanning (size underestimation), temperature at 4:00 PM on the first day in the coronary unit, and the relatives' report that the patient tends toward sensitization (anxious preoccupation with problems) rather than repression. Thus, sedimentation rate seemed to be more related to prognosis and psychological factors than to severity.

On-ward non-MI patients. Among the on-ward non-MI patients, sedimentation rate was again related to temperature and behavioral measures. Those patients with reports of low level of vigor upon entering the coronary care unit, those recording the highest temperature while on the unit, and those having high final 4:00 PM temperatures all tended toward high sedimentation rates.

SCANNING (SIZE UNDERESTIMATION)

MI patients. As reported previously, the underestimation of size of visual stimuli has been established as a valid index of scanning—the tendency of individuals to process information at a high rate. In this study high scanning rate has been found to be associated with rehospitalization with another MI within 12 weeks. In addition, size underestimation is also associated with depression upon entering and the highest sedimentation rate during the stay in the coronary unit. The two variables, size estimation and highest recorded sedimentation rate, are intercorrelated predictors of recurrent MIs. The multiple correlation, using size estimation, repression-sensitization, initial MMPI depression score, sedimentation rate, and cholesterol is + .41 with recurrent MI.

The reader will recall from an earlier part of this chapter that research since the completion of this project (Warner, 1973; McCormick, 1974) has shown that size underestimation in schizophrenics and alcoholic controls is associated with heart rate deceleration when the subject is watching a target stimulus. This decelerative heart response may in some way mediate later heart attacks.

On-ward non-MI patients. No correlations involving size estimation were significant in either split-half samples.

Off-ward non-MI patients. Size overestimation was associated with a greater number of days on the intensive care unit. Although N is small, the magnitude of the relationship is quite high ($r = .66$) and significant. While this finding was not predicted, it suggests that prolonged serious illness is associated with reduction in the rate of processing of stimulus input.

MOOD II: SOCIAL AFFECTION

MI patients. The mood scales of the Nowlis Mood Adjective Checklist were given at the beginning and at the end of the coronary care unit stay. A complete summary of the correlates of these mood scales may be found in Appendix K, Tables K-1, K-2, and K-3. Of major interest here is the mood for social affection at the end of the coronary unit stay. At this point a low mood level for social affection was associated significantly with the probability of death within 12 weeks. As described earlier, this finding may be related to the "giving up" syndrome (Schmale, 1964). In addition, a low mood for social affection was also associated with high NEFA levels on days 1 and 7 in the coronary unit and with the nursing care conditions of low participation in self-treatment. Certain other mood measures from the same scale, as might be expected, were also correlated with the social affection mood.

On-ward non-MI patients. For the on-ward non-MI patients, besides being related to other mood and personality measures, social affection mood II was negatively associated with level of education. That is, the less educated tended to leave the coronary unit with higher social affection moods.

FAMILIAL HEART DISEASE

MI patients. Evidence of heart disease among blood relatives has been known to be associated with an increased probability of MI. However, this study indicates that once an individual has had a heart attack, our knowledge of his family history is not a significant predictor of another one.

On-ward non-MI patients. As with MI patients, no correlations were significant.

PREVIOUS MYOCARDIAL INFARCTION OR
HISTORY OF HEART AILMENT

MI patients. The two variables, previous MI and positive history of heart ailment, were, of course, spuriously correlated with each other but were not related to any of the other variables of the study. Like history of heart attacks in the family (and possibly cholesterol and other variables), these two variables may be important in the prospective analysis of who would become a subject of this study to begin with; however, they are not useful predictors of mortality, length of treatment, recurrence, and so on.

On-ward non-MI patients. Family history of MI or heart ailment was not significantly correlated with any of the other variables in the study. Furthermore, positive instances were so few that the variables did not reach a significant correlation with each other.

URIC ACID

MI patients. Although uric acid is commonly viewed as an index of severity for myocardial infarction or of its prognosis, it was found not to be so for the recurrence of MI in this study. As would be expected, the average male patient had a higher uric acid level than the average female patient. Also, patients with high uric acid levels retained more information about cardiac illness. This finding was based upon a set of questions given each patient at the end of his coronary unit stay regarding the facts given him earlier about the nature of heart conditions such as his. Another finding indicated that the higher the uric acid level, the greater the tendency to report personal fatigue at the end of the coronary unit stay. Finally, patients who were given higher amounts of analgesic medication were found to have lower levels of uric acid.

The finding concerning greater recall of information among higher uric acid patients is consistent with recent evidence that uric acid is a cerebral stimulant that facilitates information processing and intellectual activity (see Mueller, Kasl, Brooks, and Cobb, 1970).

The finding that patients with lower uric acid levels are on higher amounts of analgesic medication suggests several interpretations. The finding is of special interest since the same correlation was statistically significant among the on-ward non-MI patients. One interpretation is that the finding is mediated by the sex of the patient. That is, women, shown here to be low in uric acid level, are known to be more sensitive to pain or to complain more about it or both. This was borne out here when women complained significantly more about needle punctures for sampling blood during the stress tasks. Thus, females would more likely report pain and receive analgesic medication. If this is a viable explanation, the amount of analgesic medication should be higher among females than males. In the total group, this was found to be true for the on-ward non-MI patients but not for the MI patients. Another interpretation is that uric acid tends to block the sensitivity to (cardiac) pain and therefore call for less analgesic medication. This explanation would be compatible with the previous one in that it may partially explain why, beyond cultural reasons, males report less pain. A third interpretation is that analgesic medication, at least some types, reduces the level of uric acid in the body. This explanation is compatible with the notion that analgesic medication in this study may have cancelled out any relationships that existed between uric acid level and myocardial infarction. The project findings do not indicate which, if any, of these interpretations is correct.

On-ward non-MI patients. As indicated and discussed above, the on-ward non-MI patients high in uric acid level tended not to be given analgesics.

CHOLESTEROL

MI patients. The correlations of cholesterol with other variables directly relevant to myocardial infarction were surprisingly weak. In the split-half analysis, each of the significant correlations of cholesterol was with another lipid, 17-OH-CS. For the MI group (with the total group analyses), cholesterol had 35 significant correlations. Of these 35, only 5 were with something other than a lipid, that is, a measure of 17-OH-CS or NEFA. The nineteenth highest correlation $(r = .40)$ indicated that the higher the cholesterol, the more likely a relative would describe the patient as a low scanner. Among the other correlations, the only nonlipid correlation to reach a magnitude of .20 indicated the patient described himself as a low scanner. At still lower levels, phenothiazine medication, positive mood change, and the information condition were significant. However, without the split-half provisions these latter findings should be treated with caution.

Among the high and stable correlations, the highest cholesterol measure during coronary unit stay is related to plasma 17-OH-CS measures during the undisturbed circadian state, that is, not when stress has been introduced to influence the steroid and NEFA level. When all MI patients were combined, the highest correlation indicated that cholesterol had an extremely high correlation $(r = .99)$ with NEFA on day 8. Since a limited number of patients were left in the unit until the eighth day, this would be predominantly a selected group of the more severe patients without information-coupling activities. The small number of cases did not allow this remarkably high correlation to hold up in the random split-half correlations of MI patients.

These findings repeatedly confirm that cholesterol sets the level of 17-OH-CS independently of the circadian and stress fluctuations of the latter substance. To a much lesser extent such correlations were present between cholesterol and NEFA. As was seen in the previous chapter, plasma 17-OH-CS and NEFA clearly show stress responses that differentiate MI and non-MI patients. However, no evidence is found here that cholesterol is significantly related to the severity of an acute MI or to the imminence of a recurrent one. Nor does it significantly differentiate between MI and non-MI patients. Whether cholesterol is related prospectively to the probability of having the first heart attack, a well-known hypothesis, is not clarified by this study.

On-ward non-MI patients. Cholesterol level in the on-ward non-MI patients had no relationship to other variables in the study.

SYSTOLIC BLOOD PRESSURE

MI patients. The highest systolic blood pressure recorded on the coronary unit was not significantly related to any other variable in the split-sample analysis. Examination of correlations for the total MI sample revealed low blood pressure to be associated with subsequent MIs within 12 weeks.

On-ward non-MI patients. Higher blood pressure was associated with higher SGOT levels.

Off-ward non-MI patients. As with MI patients, blood pressure was correlated with no other variables.

RETURN TO WORK

MI patients. Among the 145 other variables included in the correlation matrix, none were significantly correlated with the number of days at home before the patient returned to work. This absence of correlation is somewhat striking, since one might predict that patients with a more severe myocardial infarction would stay at home longer before returning to work. This was not the case. Future researchers should be discouraged from using this variable as a major index of recovery from a myocardial infarction. It may be controlled more by economic need and by psychosocial factors than by anything else.

On-ward non-MI patients. As with MI patients, no significant correlations with other variables were found.

PRINCIPAL COMPONENTS FACTOR ANALYSIS

Because of primary interest in individual variables, this chapter until now has been limited to individual correlations. The analysis of factor structure becomes useful, however, in understanding the relationships among groups of variables. Of special interest in this study are the group interrelationships that occur among variables related to severity and to prognosis. The purpose of this section is to examine these and other factors more carefully than was possible through the individual correlations.

The data analyzed here is from the 131 patients listed in Table 2-1, who were retrospectively confirmed for acute myocardial infarction and who had at least partial participation in the project. This sample of 131 MI patients is 81% of the 161 confirmed MI patients under 60 years of age who were in the study.

A total of 78 variables was chosen for study. These variables, listed in Table 5-2, were chosen partly because the amount of missing data was minimal. All variables have been described in more detail in Chapter 2.

A missing data product-moment correlation matrix was computed for the 78 variables. The principal components method of factor analysis was utilized with unities in the diagonals. All of the principal components whose latent roots exceeded 1.00 were retained and rotated by the varimax method. Twenty-six such factors exceeded this criterion. The items with rotated factor loadings of .30 or greater were used to interpret the factors.

The analysis indicated that the measures of severity separate themselves into different factors. The first severity factor, which was the third factor to emerge in the analysis, is shown in Table 5-3. It is defined primarily by the physician's ratings of severity. Other assessment variables defining this factor are the number of episodes and number of arrhythmias in ECG on the coronary unit. Apparently in response to these clinical and ECG factors, the testing of patients for this project was delayed and the patient was kept on the unit for a longer time. As may be seen, other variables load on this factor to a lesser degree.

Table 5-2. Major variables in the study

Personality variables	Uric acid
Locus of control	Cholesterol
Repression-sensitization	Sedimentation rate
Perceptual scanning	*Comfort, cooperation, and recovery variables*
Nowlis Mood Adjective checklist variables	Comfort interview
MMPI Depression Scale	Future cooperation interview
MMPI Lie Scale	Nurses' rating of cooperation
Katkovsky Denial Scale variables	Number of days on CCU
Coronary Proneness Scale variables	Number of days in hospital after transfer from
Severity variables	coronary unit
Severity rating I (first 24 hours)	Number of weeks before return to work
Severity rating II (subsequent)	Rehospitalization with MI within 12 weeks
High cardiac rate alarms	Death from MI within 12 weeks
Low cardiac rate alarms	*Other unclassified variables*
Cardiac episodes on coronary unit	Age
Number of arrhythmias	Sex
Days of temperature over 99° F	Education
First 4:00 PM temperature	Salary
Last 4:00 PM temperature	Cardiac information test
Highest recorded temperature	Personal history of heart disease
Routine laboratory measures	Family history of heart disease
WBC (white blood cell count)	Number of previous MIs
LDH (lactate dehydrogenase)	Number of days before testing
SGOT (serum glutamic oxaloacetic transam-inase)	Medication

Table 5-3. Factor 3: Clinical and ECG symptom severity

Loading	Variable
.81	Severity rating I
.80	Severity rating II
.49	Number of days in the CCU
.45	Number of cardiac episodes
.42	Number of days before testing
.41	Number of arrhythmias on the CCU
−.34	Coronary Proneness Scale III (Perfectionism)
.30	Mood II: vigor
.30	Number of days of temperature over 99° F
.30	Highest CCU temperature

The second severity factor is shown in Table 5-4. The highest loaded variables on this factor are the enzyme measures of plasma LDH and SGOT. Also, elevated temperature plays a slightly greater role in this factor. White blood cells count is also related to this type of severity. As on the first severity factor, certain decision-making strategies on the coronary unit are reflected. Patients high in severity are delayed in the number of days before starting testing and are kept for a greater number of days on the coronary unit. It also appears that the more severely ill patients tend to receive phenothiazines.

Table 5-4. Factor 20: Enzyme and temperature severity

Loading	Variable
.83	LDH
.80	SGOT
.48	Number of days before testing
.44	Number of days of temperature over 99° F
.41	Phenothiazines
.38	Number of days in the coronary unit
.37	Highest CCU temperature
.32	WBC

In addition to these two major severity factors, three more factors related to severity emerge. They are specific rather than general. They help clarify the roles of specific indices such as high temperature, cholesterol, and white blood cell count. Factor 17 indicates that patients with a higher temperature spent more days in the hospital. Factor 18 indicates that high cholesterol tends to occur in women, in those who have a greater number of arrhythmias on the coronary unit, and in patients of younger age. It would appear that this factor may be describing a fairly rare type of pathway to heart disturbance since only a few young females were MI patients. Factor 19 indicated that patients with high white blood cell count tended to have a greater number of arrhythmias on the coronary unit and took a longer time before returning to work.

The factor associated with recurrence is shown in Table 5-5. The relevant variables are sedimentation rate and the perceptual scanning measure of size estimation. This information is essentially the same as that reported earlier in this chapter. Thus, patients who have a subsequent hospitalization for myocardial infarction within 12 weeks tend to have a high sedimentation rate and to be extensive scanners, that is, hyperalert or overinclusive of stimulus input. While the factor rotation orients toward sedimentation rate, the correlations indicate that the perceptual scanning variable exceeds sedimentation rate in its prediction of a rehospitalization with MI within 12 weeks. No variables except these two are loaded above .30 on this factor.

The factor associated with death is shown in Table 5-6. As expected, a recurrence of hospitalization with another MI indicates a higher probability of death. This factor reveals no information beyond what was already discussed earlier in this chapter.

Other factors, less relevant to severity and prognosis, are reviewed briefly in the following paragraphs.

Factor 1 indicated that an unhappy mood (i.e., skepticism, aggression, egotism, and sadness), especially upon entering the coronary unit, is associated with having low cooperation with the coronary nurses and being given phenothiazines.

Factor 2 indicated that a positive mood (i.e., surgency, elation, vigor, social affection, and concentration), especially upon entering the coronary unit, is associ-

Table 5-5. Factor 15: Recurrence of acute myocardial infarction

Loading	Variable
.79	Sedimentation rate
− .62	Perceptual scanning
.50	Subsequent hospitalization for MI

Table 5-6. Factor 22: Death

Loading	Variable
.80	Death within 12 weeks
− .49	Mood II: social affection
.41	Subsequent hospitalization for MI

ated with having a low salary. This factor has many alternative interpretations. Low socioeconomic persons may have a response set to report more positive things. High socioeconomic persons may have a response set toward open "complaining" upon becoming ill. Low socioeconomic persons may experience so much environmental stress that the personal care and escape into the coronary unit is received in a more positive way. High socioeconomic persons, especially those who get coronaries, may be more prone to the inhibition of positive mood expression.

Factor 4 indicates that tendencies toward denial (including MMPI lie score) are associated with older age and lower salary.

Factor 5 indicates that depression is related to size underestimation (higher scanning), anxiety, and the relative absence of denial of anxiety.

Factor 6 reflects the spurious overlap of the two measures, history of heart ailment, and previous MIs.

Factor 7 indicates that anticoagulants and analgesics were given to those with higher education and higher scores on the cardiac information test.

Factor 8 indicates the positive interrelationship among control of self, perfectionism, reported scanning, anxiety, entering mood of concentration, and the denial of complacency and dependence.

Factor 9 reflected a close relationship between the comfort and cooperation interview responses, possibly due to response set or rating set factors.

Factor 10 describes the interrelationship between the mood fatigue, bottling up tension, overeating, and the mood of anxiety. Other data (Appendix J, Table J-9) indicate this factor could be related to plasma 17-OH-CS elevation.

Factor 11 indicates that MI patients high in uric acid tend to be male, tend not to receive analgesics, and tend to score highly on the cardiac information test.

Factor 12 reflects the interrelationship among temperature measures.

Factor 13 indicates that high exercise is associated with attitudes of higher cooperation toward medical instructions.

Factor 14 indicates that those given high barbiturate medication tend not to deny dependence.

Factor 16 indicates that those patients who had a high number of low and high rate monitor alarms tend to return to work more quickly. As noted earlier in this chapter, such patients tend to openly acknowledge rather than deny self-interest and hostility.

Factor 21 indicates that patients with a history of heart disease in their families tend to be higher in education, more cooperative with nurses, and have a higher mood of concentration upon entering the coronary unit.

Factor 23 indicates that patients with high temperatures over a prolonged period have certain mood and personality characteristics. They tend to have entered the coronary unit with high moods of concentration and social affection, to be low in anxiety, and not to deny dependence.

Factor 24 indicates that people who enter the coronary unit with high moods of concentration and who did well on the cardiac information test tended to leave the coronary unit with negative moods (anxiety, skepticism, concentration, sadness, and aggression).

Factor 25 indicates that people who were transferred from the coronary unit with temperatures still high tended to be younger and to return to work sooner. Also, as would be expected, they had had elevated temperatures for a greater number of days.

Factor 26 indicates that patients with external locus of control tended to bottle up tension, tended to be lower in education, and tended not to deny complacency.

SUMMARY

What do these correlations tell us about recovery from acute myocardial infarction?

Death from another MI within 12 weeks was revealed to be more frequent among those who departed from the coronary unit with a low mood for social affection. Whether underlying physiological states lead to social disaffection and death cannot be determined in this study. NEFA elevation during a psychological stress period was also associated with subsequent death from MI within 12 weeks. This finding suggests that NEFA should be further investigated as a mediator in the death prediction.

In the prediction of rehospitalization with subsequent acute infarctions within 12 weeks, as with death, psychological factors are surprisingly predominant over the blood, electrocardiographic, and clinical symptomatic measures. The most powerful predictor of early recurrent myocardial infarction is the extensiveness of scanning. Second to this is sedimentation rate. Rehospitalization for subsequent MI within 12 weeks was also predicted by plasma 17-hydroxy-corticosteroid still being elevated 4½ hours after a psychologically stressful task, high anxiety, high depression, and a low level of maximum recorded blood pressure during coronary unit stay. These findings, together with those in the previous chapter, suggest that the coronary-prone and coronary-recurrent individual may ruminate about a psychologically stressful event long after it is over.

Combining patients with subsequent MIs, some of whom died and some of whom did not, we found both groups to have moods of high anxiety, sadness, and skepticism upon first admission. They left the unit with a mood of high anxiety, also. They were high in self-reported scanning and perfectionism. Biologically, in addition to high sedimentation rate, they had more cardiac episodes, higher LDH, and higher total severity rating for complete coronary unit stay. Temperature level is highly associated with severity of clinical symptoms of myocardial infarction during the first 24 hours on the coronary unit. In fact, the severity level at that time is useful in predicting the number of days with elevated temperature thereafter. (Temperature is also the major index that determines the patient's report of comfort.) On the other hand, severity of clinical symptoms after the first 24 hours is associated more with direct manifestation of cardiac disturbance, such as arrhythmias and cardiac episodes where the patient requires assistance.

A number of variables of interest in the project had surprisingly little relevance to myocardial infarction, its severity, and recovery. Among these were uric acid; monitor alarms, especially for low rate; drug treatment on the coronary care unit; and the number of days before returning to work. Cholesterol was related to other lipids (plasma 17-OH-CS and NEFA) primarily during undisturbed parts of the day. Uric acid appeared to play a role in cerebral stimulation and in blocking pain sensitivity. It was higher in males. However, it was not related to recurrence of myocardial infarction. The cardiac monitor's recording of arrhythmias seemed more informative than its recording of extreme heart rate changes. Of the latter, however, high heart rate appeared to be important more frequently than low heart rate. While drugs were not the intensive focus of the study, the medications of barbiturates, anticoagulants, analgesics, and phenothiazines turned out to be related to variables relatively unimportant to MI, such as socioeconomic level and certain moods. Return to work was determined by factors other than severity and recovery from the myocardial infarction.

Plasma 17-OH-CS and NEFA both tended to be correlated to one set of factors during stressful periods of the day and to another set during nonstressful periods. Plasma levels during nonstressful periods were related primarily to general cholesterol level and moods, but plasma levels during stressful periods were often associated with reinfarction and death within 12 weeks.

The reports of relatives about personality reactions of the respective patients tend to be useful in some cases but typically not as useful as the patients' own reports.

In general, the pattern of findings, in personality as well as in cardiac symptomatology, indicate that the MI patients are different from both the on-ward non-MIs (suspected but disconfirmed cases) and the off-ward non-MI patients from elsewhere in the hospital. Except for LDH, which may be an index of severity of cardiac exhaustion, insufficiency, congestive disorder, or some other non-MI heart condition, and the fact that temperature elevations tended to remain throughout the entire period of the coronary unit stay, very few useful findings emerged with the non-MI patients.

The following paragraphs summarize the factor analysis findings.

The severity of a myocardial infarction, as measured here, gives limited information about how likely another will occur within the coming few weeks. A severe MI does not necessarily suggest another one will occur soon. A mild MI does not necessarily suggest that another one will not occur again within a few weeks.

Severity, as applied to MIs, is not a simple, clearly assessed concept. The findings indicated a surprising tendency for severity factors to be independent of each other. One type of severity concerns the malfunction of the heart (cardiac episodes, arrhythmias) and the clinical symptoms related to it (circulatory symptoms, prostration, cardiogenic shock). This type of severity seems to reflect how well the heart is performing its task as a blood pump.

The second type of severity appears to assess the extent of myocardial lesion. Thus, the enzymes, LDH and SGOT, are centrally involved. Depending upon the locus and structure of such lesion, this dimension of lesion severity is relatively independent of the dimension of severity of clinical functioning. In this study only temperature was found to bridge the two severity factors as a common element.

Other findings reveal the roles of specific variables. High temperature results in a longer period of hospital recovery. Cholesterol was found to be higher in patients who were female, young, and more frequently victims of arrythmias. White blood cell count was also associated with more arrhythmias and time before returning to work.

Recurrence of MI within 12 weeks was found to be more frequent in extensive scanners and among those who had a high peak sedimentation rate. Death was more frequent among those patients who left the coronary unit with a low mood state of social affection. Thus, psychological variables are found to play a major role in prognosis among acute MI patients.

Chapter 6

UNIQUE QUALITIES OF THE MYOCARDIAL INFARCTION PATIENT

In Chapters 3 and 5 we presented findings observed from the MI, on-ward non-MI, and off-ward non-MI patients as separate groups. However, the MI and non-MI patients were not tested directly against each other except in Chapter 4, where the central question was how acute MI and non-MI patients differ from each other in stress reactions. The purpose of the present chapter is to report other differences between MI and non-MI patients. These differences should not be interpreted as predictive or "proneness" factors but as leads for future studies of proneness. While our research is prospective to recovery, it is retrospective to the initial attack. Research prospective to the initial MI is needed to establish proneness.

PROCEDURE

All MI patients described in Table 2-1 were compared with the on-ward and off-ward non-MI patients on all measures. A set of t tests for independent means were used for each of 143 variables. An alpha level of 5% was used to interpret significance. For the reader interested in particular variables the nonsignificant findings between .05 and .10 probability are listed. However, for the set of analyses in total the reader must not overlook the inevitable fact that a portion of the comparisons emerge as significant by chance alone. Some of the following differences (approximately 5%) would not be expected to be sustained as significant in a repetition of our experiment.

RESULTS

On 12 dependent variables, the MI patients differed from both the on-ward and off-ward non-MI patients. These findings are presented in Table 6-1. Two variables support previous findings that MI patients are higher than non-MI patients in plasma 17-OH-CS. The findings here suggest that the second day of hospitalization is the

Table 6-1. Variables that distinguish acute MI patients from non-MI patients

Variable	Acute MI	On-ward non-MI	Mean differential p	Off-ward non-MI	Mean differential p
LC (external)	8.096	6.614	.0028	7.030	.0125
Sex (M = 1; F = 2)	1.122	1.214	.0667	1.298	.0003
Age (years)	49.870	48.357	.0995	45.629	.0001
TV time (hours/day)	3.469	5.681	.0047		
Familial heart disease (0-4)	1.711	0.611	.0002		
Previous MIs (number)	.225	.439	.0397		
Days CCU/ICU (days)	6.443	3.531	.0000	3.458	.0000
Days hospital (days)	23.076	10.224	.0000	10.051	.0000
History heart disease (0-1)	.369	.971	.0001		
Severity I (0-3)	1.459	.538	.0000		
Severity II (0-3)	1.484	.577	.0000		
Depression I (items)	23.779	22.389	.0970		
Low alarms (no.)	1.156	.356	.0044		
Mood I: sadness (no. adjectives)	3.102	2.022	.0017		
Mood I: egotism (no. adjectives)	1.299	.822	.0303		
Mood II: surgency (no. adjectives)	3.149	3.900	.0988		
Mood II: sadness (no. adjectives)	1.921	1.160	.0563		
Mood II: skepticism (no. adjectives)	1.792	1.220	.0728		
17-OH-CS scan 1 (μg/ml)	35.095	24.375	.0462	23.522	.0276
17-OH-CS scan 2 (μg/ml)	31.667	22.806	.0100	21.533	.0023
17-OH-CS scan 5 (μg/ml)	17.850	28.00	.0160	23.667	.0949
17-OH-CS scan 8 (μg/ml)	22.500	36.000	.0584	15.545	.0216
Sedimentation rate (time)	26.379	19.706	.0001		
Cholesterol (μg/ml)	264.431	248.852	.0798		
SGOT (μg/ml)	140.367	41.619	.0000		
WBC (no.)	150.605	118.867	.0001		
Highest temperature (°F)	100.496	99.255	.0000		
Last 4:00 PM temperature (°F)	98.742	98.327	.0017		
Return to work (days)	11.694	6.895	.0000		
CP scale I (R-S) (items)	3.784	3.140	.0034	3.259	.0064
CP scale II (perfectionism) (items)	5.464		NS	4.789	.0045
CP scale (control of self) (items)	6.048	5.360	.0072	5.367	.0016
CP scale V (exercise) (items)	1.512	1.744	.0930	1.699	.0983
Total CP (items)	20.144	18.512	.0036	18.265	.0002
Relatives' CP I (R-S) (items)	3.710	2.308	.0165		
Relatives' CP V (exercise) (items)	1.194	1.846	.0445		
Relatives' LC (external) (items)	9.161	6.385	.0088		
Severity total (0-6)	2.943	1.115	.0000		
Temperature change (°F)	−0.266	+0.163	.0015		
Blood pressure	107.231	121.353	.0011	125.983	.0000
Cards turned, solvable task (no.)	130.528	143.469	.0031	142.033	.0092
Cards wrong, solvable task (no.)	12.000	6.182	.0125	5.984	.0038
NEFA scan I (μM/ml)	97.750	35.125	.0007	40.600	.0010
NEFA scan 2 (μM/ml)	70.882	46.471	.0961	NS	
Denial: hostility (items)	8.780		NS	7.771	.0124
17-OH-CS solvable task 12:10 AM (μg/ml)	24.273		NS	19.782	.0727
NEFA solvable 11:00 AM (μM/ml)	107.474		NS	154.953	.0747

best time to assess this difference. Differences on other days, while significant, are not as reliable as the second day.

Two of the variables are retrospective to the hospitalization. MI patients do indeed spend more days in intensive care and in the hospital than do non-MI patients.

Four variables seem to reflect symptoms and the weakened state of the MI patient. The MI patient has a lower peak blood pressure, attempts fewer card guesses, gets fewer guesses right on the control task, and has higher NEFA on the first day.

Four personality variables distinguished the acute MI patients from the other two groups. MI patients had greater external locus of control, greater proneness to bottle up tension, greater reported control of self, and greater total score on our coronary proneness test (see Appendix L).

A total of 22 variables were found to distinguish acute MI patients from on-ward non-MI patients only. The greater number of significant variables here is expected because of the higher number and more standard circumstances of measurement among the MI and the on-ward non-MI patients. Also, certain measures were not administered to the off-ward group.

Of these 22 significant differences, three concerned medical history. MIs more often had a personal and family history of heart disease, including previous MIs.

Eleven differences concerned heart symptoms and functioning on the coronary unit. MI patients had higher severity ratings (during the first 24 hours and thereafter), SGOT, LDH, sedimentation rate, WBC, peak temperature, and last 4:00 PM temperature. MI patients also had less drop in temperature from first to last 4:00 PM reading. More low rate monitor alarms occurred in the MI patient than in the on-ward non-MI group. While this finding is consistent with the scanning finding in MI patients described in Chapter 3, it must be recalled that low heart rate monitor alarms did not have severity or prognostic implications (Chapter 5). Another difference concerned a lower plasma 17-OH-CS in MIs on the fifth day. By contrast, MIs had higher steroid levels on earlier days. The reversal in steroid level after three days, described in Chapter 4, is apparently due to selective discharge of non-MI patients; only the severely ill (e.g., cardiac exhaustion or congestive disorder) non-MIs remain.

Finally, seven behavioral variables distinguished the two groups. The MIs reported more sadness and egotism upon entering the coronary unit. They also spent less time watching television. Their relatives reported them to have greater bottling up of tension, less exercise, and higher external locus of control. The MI patients took longer to return to work.

Five variables showed differences between the MI group and the off-ward non-MI control group only. In contrast to the latter group, the MI patients were older males. A trend in this direction also occurred with the on-ward control group also. Finally, while the on-ward non-MI group had a trend toward higher plasma 17-OH-CS on the eighth day, the off-ward non-MI group was significantly lower in plasma 17-OH-CS on this day. In terms of personality, the MI patients claimed more perfectionism and had a greater denial of hostility.

DISCUSSION AND SUMMARY

From a total of 48 potential prospective variables, 19 distinguished our MI and non-MI patients. These 19 may (or may not) have been present prior to the acute MI. For some of the 19, the report of relatives is congruent with the patient's report, and these are particularly good candidates for prospective study.

In brief, the candidates for prospective identification as coronary-prone individuals are older men with positive histories of heart ailment (and MI) in themselves and in their families. They have a personality orientation toward external locus of control, depression, bottling of tension, denial of hostility, self-claimed perfectionism and control of self, and identifiable moods of sadness and egotism. They tend to exercise little and exhibit a nonsignificant trend toward high cholesterol. In agreement with the patients' reports, relatives reported patients to bottle up tension, to be external in locus of control, and to exercise little.

Twenty-nine other variables that differentiate the acute MI patient from the non-MI patients are the inevitable consequences of a cardiac lesion. These include the severity of coronary-related symptoms, more frequent low rate monitor alarms, lower peak blood pressure, and a number of indices that reflect a somatic lesion or body stress (e.g., distinctive steroid and NEFA pattern, sedimentation rate, SGOT, LDH, WBC, and a prolonged temperature elevation). In addition, manifestations of weakness and prostration are indicated by less TV watching, fewer trials attempted and fewer trials correct on the control task, moods of low surgency and of high sadness and skepticism upon leaving the coronary unit, and a longer period before returning to work.

Chapter 7

SUMMARY AND CONCLUSIONS

the scientific perspective

The purpose of this project was to study the role of stress during recovery from acute myocardial infarction (MI). The study had four major parts. In the first part, called the nursing care study, the interactions of nursing care procedures and personalities of the patients were studied with regard to recovery, comfort, and cooperation during coronary care. In the second part, called the stress experiment, MI and non-MI patients were compared in their steroid, NEFA, and psychophysiological reactions to mild stress. The third part concerned the prediction of recurrence of coronary illness, death, and other relevant factors. The fourth part focused upon ways in which MI and non-MI patients differed from each other. Special attention was given to those factors that might be prospective indicators of illness.

Definite strategies were built into the project. It was primarily a prospective study of recovery from acute attacks of myocardial infarction rather than a retrospective study of proneness. It had both theory testing and empirical aspects.

Stress was viewed as the interaction of personality and environmental factors affecting both psychological and biological reaction. The understanding of stress during the recovery from myocardial infarction was viewed as closely linked to the questions often asked of physicians and nurses: How much should the patient be told about his condition? How much diversion should he have? Is it better to have him cared for or to involve him actively in his own treatment?

The setting for the project was a newly developed coronary care unit in a community hospital. After seven months of preparation, the research procedures were phased into the routine clinical program of the unit, and data collection continued for two years.

METHOD

The subjects were 229 of the 347 patients under 60 years of age admitted to the coronary unit during the two-year period. Of these, 131 were MI patients and 98

93

were non-MI patients. This diagnostic distinction was made on the basis of uniform criteria separate from the researchers and after the research procedures were completed. Thus, the 98 served as the "on-ward non-MI control group." In addition, 80 off-ward non-MI patients, without cardiovascular involvement but comparably ill, were studied. Patients judged too ill to participate in psychological testing were excluded. Other coronary unit patients were not studied because their length of stay was too short or for other reasons described in Chapter 2.

In the nursing care study each patient was randomly assigned to "high" or "low" treatment with regard to each of three nursing care factors: (1) amount of *information* about cardiac condition; (2) amount of *diversional stimulation*, such as TV, visitors, reading materials, and so on; and (3) the amount of *participation* in self-treatment. Parallel to these three nursing care factors were three personality variables: (1) repression versus sensitization (often referred to as anxiety); (2) scanning (as measured by a perceptual test designed to reflect rate of processing of stimulus information from the environment); and (3) locus of control (the degree to which an individual views the outcome of life circumstances as under his own control rather than externally controlled). The interactions of these nursing care conditions and personality factors were studied to see how they affected recovery, cooperation, and patient comfort.

NURSING CARE RESULTS

No patients admitted whom we studied died while on the coronary unit. Only six died after transfer to a regular ward or after discharge within 12 weeks. This low mortality rate contrasts with a rate of 18% on the total coronary unit. It can be attributed to not including the older and most severely ill patients into the study. The available mortality data did reveal significant results. For example, more deaths occurred among patients with internal locus of control and high anxiety, that is, among those who feel responsible for what happens to them but who at the same time are apprehensive about this outcome.

Patients who were extensive scanners or highly anxious or both were more likely to have another MI within 12 weeks.

The lengths of stay in the coronary unit and in the hospital were strongly affected by a factor referred to here as information coupling. Although this factor was revealed in different ways, its common element concerned how an individual was given information about his cardiac condition. If the information was coupled with chores for him to do to foster his recovery, then his stays in the hospital and in the coronary unit were short. If, on the other hand, the patient was given information not coupled with other procedures, that is, without participation in his treatment or without diversion, his stays in the coronary unit and the hospital were much longer.

A second, and less important, factor affecting length of coronary unit and hospital stay was the overall amount of activity (total amount of diversion and participation). Moderate activity led to shorter stays than either high or low amounts.

The typical symptoms and indices of acute MI were influenced markedly by patient personality patterns but only moderately by nursing care factors. Coronary unit patients had fewer cardiac monitor alarms for high heart rate if the amount of information given them was congruent with their personalities. This finding suggests that highly anxious patients should be given extensive information and nonanxious patients should be given limited information. Separate from the information factor, nonanxious patients tend to decrease more in symptoms during the first 24 hours than anxious patients. The anxious patients and also the extensive scanners have higher peak sedimentation rates during coronary unit stay. Among MI patients the highly anxious and the extensive scanners reach a higher peak temperature while on the coronary unit. Lactate dehydrogenase was found to be higher in MI patients with high anxiety, external locus of control attitudes, and scanning.

Locus of control, as a personality variable, stands out in its relation to biological variables related to myocardial infarction. Except when internal locus of control is coupled with high anxiety, the external tendency is unfavorable. Patients with external locus of control have higher sedimentation rates, higher SGOT levels, higher LDH levels, higher peak temperatures, less drop in temperature during coronary unit stay, longer stay in the coronary unit, and longer stay in the hospital. These findings hold for both MI and non-MI heart patients. The direction of cause between locus of control and these biological variables remains an open question.

For MI patients in particular, those with internal locus of control and high anxiety tend to have higher sedimentation rates. They also have the highest cholesterol levels—especially if they are minimal scanners.

Among non-MI patients, who had lower enzyme levels, certain relationships occurred that did not occur with the MI patients. Both SGOT and LDH were higher among the non-MI patients in high diversion than in low diversion nursing care. Minimal scanners had higher cholesterol levels than extensive scanners. Extensive scanners under high diversion and minimal scanners under low diversion had low white blood cell counts, but the counts were elevated for the incongruent combinations. Taken together, these findings suggest that the energy demands of diversional stimulation and of a hyperscanning personality produce mild stress reactions in non-MI coronary unit patients. With an active lesion such as myocardial infarction, however, this pattern of low level changes is obscured.

Cooperation of patients depended slightly more upon the personality of the patient than upon the nursing care factors studied here. An attitude of positive cooperation with medical instructions after release was greater with those given the low participation condition than with those given the high. Participation in self-treatment speeds recovery, especially when extensive information is given; high participation patients apparently do not take their condition as seriously as those told to rest and be waited on by the coronary staff. For this reason, special steps should be taken to impress the high participation patient about the seriousness of his condition and the need to cooperate.

As for personality factors affecting cooperation, internal locus of control patients, as might be expected, had a greater attitude of cooperation. Minimal scanners had a more positive attitude than extensive scanners.

Cooperation with nurses on the coronary unit was greater in the congruent combinations of information and anxiety. That is, the anxious MI patients given extensive information and the nonanxious MI patients given minimal information had higher cooperation ratings than the two incongruent combinations. For coronary patients in general, the congruent combinations of scanning and participation yielded greater cooperation: extensive scanners with high participation and minimal scanners with low participation had higher cooperation ratings. The incongruent combinations cooperated less. Among MI patients, the highest cooperation level was found among those patients with internal locus of control, low anxiety, and minimal scanning. Paradoxically, among non-MIs the highest cooperation was found among patients with internal locus of control, high anxiety, and minimal scanning.

Patient comfort was also more dependent upon personality than nursing care. All patients developed more positive moods while in the coronary unit, undoubtedly due to their apprehension upon admission and a feeling of elation upon learning of their transfer orders. Patients with the congruent combinations of scanning and participation (high participation for extensive scanners and low participation for minimal scanners) reported greater comfort during their stay than did the incongruent combinations.

Patients with attitudes of internal locus of control became less depressed during their coronary unit stay. Among the MI patients with internal locus of control, those with low anxiety became even less depressed than those with high anxiety. The non-MI patients with internal locus of control had the most positive change in overall mood state during their coronary unit stay. Non-MI patients with high anxiety became less depressed than those who were nonanxious.

Time before returning to work was greater for MI than for non-MI patients. Among the MIs, time before returning to work was unrelated to severity of the infarct. Patients who were given high information stayed home longer before returning to work. Patients high in anxiety and scanning also took longer to return to work. Non-MI patients with internal locus of control and who were given minimal information about the nature of heart disease returned to work quickly. Patients with congruent combinations of information and scanning (high information to high scanners and low information to low scanners) returned to work more quickly than patients with the incongruent combinations.

RECOVERY PREDICTION RESULTS

Death from another MI within 12 weeks of admission was more frequent among patients who departed from the coronary unit with a low mood for social affection. Whether this psychological factor is a crucial mediator or whether underlying physiological states lead to the unfavorable mood and to death remains to be seen.

NEFA elevation in response to a psychologically stressful period is associated with subsequent death from MI within 12 weeks.

In the prediction of subsequent hospitalization with another MI within 12 weeks, as with the prediction of death, psychological factors were surprisingly predominant and more powerful than blood, electrocardiographic, and clinical symptomatic measures. As noted earlier, the most powerful predictor of an early recurrent MI is the extensiveness of scanning. Second to this is sedimentation rate.

At a less strict criterion of inference, rehospitalization for subsequent MI within 12 weeks was also predicted by elevated plasma 17-hydroxycorticosteroids 4½ hours after a psychologically stressful task. High anxiety, high depression, and a low level of maximum recorded blood pressure during coronary unit stay were also predictive of rehospitalization for subsequent MI within 12 weeks. These findings, together with those in the comparison and proneness search study, suggest that the coronary-prone and coronary-recurrent individual may ruminate about a psychologically stressful event long after it is over.

Combining those patients who died and those who were rehospitalized with another MI within 12 weeks, additional findings emerged. This combined group entered the coronary unit with moods of high anxiety, sadness, and skepticism. They departed with moods of high anxiety. They had more cardiac episodes while on the coronary unit. Lactate dehydrogenase, as well as sedimentation rate, was higher. The total severity rating was higher. On the coronary proneness scale the "death and/or rehospitalization" group was high on reported scanning and perfectionism.

Temperature level is the key factor associated with clinical symptoms of myocardial infarction during the first 24 hours on the coronary unit. In fact, the severity level at that time is useful in predicting the number of days with elevated temperature thereafter. (Temperature is also the major index that determines the patient's report of comfort.) On the other hand, severity of clinical symptoms after the first 24 hours is associated more with the direct manifestation of cardiac disturbance, such as arrhythmias and cardiac episodes where the patient requires assistance.

A number of variables had unexpectedly little relevance to recurrence of a new myocardial infarction. Among these were cholesterol, uric acid, monitor alarms, especially for low rate, drug treatment on the coronary unit, and the number of days before returning to work. Cholesterol level was related to other lipid levels (plasma 17-OH-CS and NEFA) during undisturbed parts of the day. Uric acid, higher in males, appeared to play a role in cerebral stimulation and in blocking pain sensitivity. The cardiac monitor proved more important in recording arrhythmias than in recording heart rate changes. Among the heart rate changes, however, high heart rate was predictively important more frequently than low heart rate. While drugs were not the intensive focus of the study, the level of medication of barbiturates, anticoagulants, analgesics, and phenothiazines was related to relatively unimportant variables, such as socioeconomic status and certain moods. Length of time to return to work was determined by factors other than severity and recovery from myocardial infarction.

Plasma 17-OH-CS and NEFA were both correlated to one set of factors during stressful periods of the day and another set of factors during the nonstressful periods.

The reports of relatives about personality factors in the respective patients tended to be useful in some cases, but typically they were not as useful as the patient's own reports.

GROUP FACTOR ANALYSIS FINDINGS

The severity of a myocardial infarction is minimally related to recurrence within 12 weeks. Besides this relative independence of severity and prognosis, severity of myocardial infarction is a complex concept. Different indices of severity were independent of each other. One type of severity concerns the malfunction of the heart (cardiac episodes, arrhythmias) and the clinical symptoms related to it (circulatory symptoms, prostration, cardiogenic shock). This type of severity seems to reflect how well the heart is performing as a blood pump. A second type of severity appears to assess the extent of myocardial lesion. Thus, the two enzymes, LDH and SGOT, are centrally involved. Depending upon the locus and structure of such lesions, this dimension of lesion severity is relatively independent of the severity of clinical functioning. Temperature was the only element common to the two severity factors.

Other findings reveal the role of specific variables. High temperature is associated with a longer period of hospital recovery. Cholesterol was found to be higher in patients who were female, young, and the victim of many arrhythmias in the coronary unit. White blood cell count was also associated with number of arrhythmias and longer time before returning to work.

STRESS RESPONSE

A major comparison of acute MI and non-MI patients was made during a mildly stressful psychological task. This task, although not as stressful as an exciting bridge game or television program, was sufficiently stressful to produce a measurable elevation in plasma 17-hydroxycorticosteroids. The acute MI group, after showing no immediate response, gave a delayed (70 minutes) but highly elevated 17-hydroxycorticosteroid response. By contrast, non-MI patients had an immediate and mild response but no delayed response.

The acute MI patients also had a higher steroid level throughout the day than non-MI patients, this level decreasing with increasing days of hospitalization. The on-ward non-MI patients (those with suspected but disconfirmed MIs and still on the coronary unit) had higher steroid levels than the non-MI patients elsewhere in the hospital.

No differences between MI and non-MI patients were found in the pattern of circadian rhythm of plasma 17-OH-CS. Also, no differential plasma 17-OH-CS response resulted from failing versus succeeding on the psychological task; both showed the stress response of plasma elevation.

The acute MI patients had no characteristic pattern of NEFA response to stress that is different from non-MI patients. No difference in NEFA response to success or failure was shown. No circadian rhythm was identified. As expected, the elevation of

NEFA occurred with the stressful task and with caloric intake of hospital diet. Non-MI patients increased in 10:45 AM NEFA from day to day, whereas MI patients did not. Non-MI patients were unusually high, in contrast to MI patients, in the nighttime NEFA measure (11:30 PM). On-ward non-MI patients tended to have lower NEFA levels from day to day than off-ward non-MI patients. Whether these findings resulted from differences in coronary unit as compared to regular hospital diet could not be determined.

Increased heart rate occurred among all patients during the psychological task. The increase among the acute MI patients was slightly less than among the non-MI patients. Immediately following the task the heart rate of MIs dropped back to the previous level more uniformly than did the heart rate of the non-MI patients. In brief, the acute MI patients have a less responsive heart rate than non-MI patients to the task.

Following a failure experience on the task, the finger plethysmographic response of acute MI patients was clearly different from the non-MI group. The MI patients increased their blood volume and decreased their pulse amplitude following failure. The non-MI patients decreased their blood volume and increased their pulse amplitude following failure. No such pattern of response occurred following success-ful completion of the task.

COMPARISON AND PRONENESS SEARCH

In general, the acute MI patients differed from the non-MIs by being older men with a positive history of heart ailment (including previous MIs) for themselves and blood relatives; being more oriented toward external locus of control, depression, bottling up tension; denying hostility; admitting to perfectionism and strong control of self; having moods of sadness and egotism; and having a limited tendency to physical exercise. (A nonsignificant trend occurred toward higher cholesterol in the MI group, also.) In agreement with the patients' reports, the relatives of MIs re-ported patients to bottle up tension, to be external in locus of control, and to have little physical exercise, as compared to reports of relatives of non-MIs.

Other differences are consequent to the acute lesion. Among the acute MI pa-tients, as opposed to non-MI patients, the severity of coronary-related symptoms was higher, low rate monitor alarms were more frequent, blood pressure was lower, and a number of indices indicated a somatic lesion or body stress (i.e., distinctive steroid and NEFA pattern, high sedimentation rate, high SGOT, high LDH, high WBC, and a prolonged temperature elevation). In addition, physical weakness was reflected in the MI group by less TV watching, fewer trials attempted and fewer trials correct on the control task, moods of low surgency and high sadness and skepticism upon leaving the coronary unit, and a longer period before returning to work. These findings, while not predictive of future difficulty, could be used to help make the difficult distinction between the acute MI and the suspected but negative case.

PART TWO

PSYCHOLOGY AND NURSING MANAGEMENT IN CORONARY CARE

Chapter **8**

PSYCHOLOGICAL ASSESSMENT AND MANAGEMENT OF CORONARY PATIENTS

The importance of research to the nurse and physician is in direct proportion to how fully its results can be translated into patient care. The purpose of this and the following chapters is to translate research findings into the broad art and science of patient care. The present chapter presents some important psychological assessment concepts. These concepts will no doubt raise questions about what to do once the assessment is made. In the latter part of the chapter are certain approaches to psychological management that follow from the assessment concepts previously described. We do not include techniques for assessment and treatment of the physical condition, but the level of severity of the heart condition and whether the diagnosis is acute myocardial infarction will have a direct bearing upon these clinical activities. Needless to say, the concerns for physical survival and recovery of the patient will take precedence in all clinical decisions. The foregoing research chapters have shown that psychological factors do affect heart patients' physical recoveries.

In offering the following patient care suggestions, we are not attempting to create "instant psychologists" of nurses and physicians. Rather, we are recognizing recent trends that emphasize the importance of expanded professional roles and responsibilities for those who care for patients. Thus, a psychological orientation and sophistication seems appropriate and important for nurses and physicians.

PSYCHOLOGICAL ASSESSMENT OF THE CORONARY PATIENT

Psychological assessment of the coronary patient can provide a basis for responding differentially and effectively to him. True, basic psychological support and care are appropriate for almost everyone. But much of our undifferential treatment of others is based on our own projective assimilation. Projective assimilation is the

103

tendency to attribute to others one's own attitudes and feelings, and all of us have some tendency toward it. What we say subjectively is, "He must be feeling what I would feel," or "If I were acting like that, I would be feeling this way." It is frequently appropriate to treat a patient in this empathetic way, simply because great psychological similarities exist among human beings. But there are also important differences among people, and the point of a psychological orientation is to allow an individual to go beyond projective assimilation to identify, understand, and deal with those emotional and behavioral reactions of patients that he would not have under similar circumstances.

Overcoming the self-reference

The first and perhaps most important step in assessing the psychological state of a coronary patient is to separate the objective construction of the patient from one's own psychological state. This separation is not done magically nor does it depend on an ability that "some possess and others will never possess." It is not something acquired once and retained for a lifetime, like learning to ride a bicycle or to swim. Instead, the objective construction results from procedures for weighing observations of patients' reactions and using others' judgments to separate your own needs, impulses, and fears from your interpretation of your observations. Every clinical psychologist knows that from time to time distortions and blind spots impair his assessments. Similarly, you will discover that others sometimes possess a more immediate and clear understanding than you do. This is normal. No assessor of another's personality or psychological state can play God. The procedure is to observe the patient as objectively as possible (i.e., what he says and does), listen to others' perceptions of the patient, translate various observations, especially recurrent ones, into alternative clinical hypotheses, search for the strongest among these hypotheses as the best basis for taking action, and modify the hierarchy of interpretations as more evidence emerges.

When you find yourself using this clinical method to derive formulations that do not stem from personal experience, you will know you are on your way to sound professional use of psychological assessment. If, on the other hand, you find yourself consistently disagreeing with others and depending only upon your own observations, you may very likely be in trouble. As a result of too strong a need to be independently correct (sometimes a fear of being found incorrect) or to be an effective nurse or physician "on your own," you may very likely develop a set not to use others' important observations and interpretations. This type of self-reliance may be functional in collecting objective biomedical data, because in biomedical data you usually do not have the problem of separating your own personality and need system to insure the accuracy in your observations.

From another vantage point, if you find yourself defining an authority among the clinical staff members and always yielding to him or her for a final conclusion, you are certainly in trouble. Suppose the person you choose has advanced training that gives you confidence in his experience. Advanced training helps, but it still does not prevent one from being a human being whose personal life, needs, and frustrations affect what he sees. The key, therefore, in effective psychological assessment is agreement based on the publicly shared observations and interpretations of several people.

How do you develop psychodiagnostic skill? Several techniques are important. Psychologists and psychiatrists whose professional effectiveness is highly dependent on this skill often enter group or individual psychotherapy themselves to achieve insight into their own needs. More and more people in other walks of life are realizing that such a course of self-examination in therapy is a valuable tool for enhancing personal effectiveness in life and in no way carries an assumption that one is sick, maladapted, or unable to function normally. On the other hand, therapy is not absolutely necessary, and it is usually expensive.

Another way to develop clinical assessment skill is to build feedback into professional activities. Feedback can occur naturally through staffing of cases with fellow coronary staff members, but it is sometimes inefficient because of the need to focus upon the patient's physical condition. Sometimes, too, a given staff member needs to view himself as so expert or as having so much charisma that observations of the same patient from different individuals do not get an adequate hearing. If so, you can easily initiate informal feedback to compare your perceptions to others' in an atmosphere of professional confidence.

Once you are keen enough to discover your own perceptual distortions or blind spots, it is extremely important to remain aware of what it was about yourself that gave rise to shortcomings in your observations. If you can do this, you will be able to anticipate and avoid such misperceptions more often in the future. Do not try to deny that you have needs and that these needs influence your perceptions. Acknowledge them and consciously distinguish them from publicly verified perceptions of the patient.

It is important to keep carefully written behavioral notes on the patient and, just as important, to review them. In this way, recurrent behavioral trends may be observed that will not be apparent when contacts with the patient are recorded and considered separately. Recurrent trends in behavior that distinguish one person from another by definition constitute the personality of the individual. Another chore is to remove value judgments and moral descriptions from observations and interpretations, since they are not useful for clinical purposes in coronary care.

Psychologists utilize standardized tests to objectify and separate out personal influences while making assessments. In the research reported in the earlier chapters, many problems might have developed if the psychologist had interviewed each incoming patient and then made a subjective judgment about the level of depression or anxiety. Allowances must be made, of course, for changes in the psychologist's own disposition from day to day. Psychiatrists and social workers, as well as psychologists, naturally place emphasis upon clinical interviews. Sometimes they are the only answer. In the broad search for possibly undetected or poorly understood information, for the development of a close interpersonal relationship, and for assessment of dimensions for which adequate tests do not exist, interviews become important. They become more effective when the clinician knows from experience how different people respond to the questions, but they are still not complete substitutes for objective assessment techniques.

The patient's rate of information processing (scanning)

We have discussed how the nurse or physician can and should remove idiosyncratic perceptions, but we have not explained what behavioral characteristics to look for. The research findings reported in the previous chapters indicate that the patient's rate of information processing is important. While the research study used a perceptual task of size estimation to make this assessment, other approaches exist. If an individual appears continually busy—taking it all in—he is likely to be a rapid information processor. If he is actively reading, watching television, talking to the ward staff and visitors, asking questions, preoccupied when silent; if he talks at a fast rate and if while listening to him, you are left with a feeling of being "saturated" from the number of topics or facts he has covered; if in answering your questions he starts to respond (appropriately) before you finish the question—then, you can be reasonably sure in describing the individual as a rapid information processor (a hyperscanner, if you will). You may be especially sure of your description if the patient is not propelling himself at this high rate because of anxiety. On the other hand, if the patient is slow and deliberate in his response to you and if you must repeat questions or instructions more slowly, the patient may be a slow information processor. This would especially be true if you can rule out fatigue or weakness as the reason for his slow rate of responsiveness. Precoronary state, as reported by relatives and the patient, can help accurately assess rate of information processing.

Remember, our terms rapid and slow processors are labels for the poles of a normally distributed continuum. Most people are in the middle, near the average, and only a few people in the population fall at the extremes.

Locus of control

Another dimension of importance in the management of coronary patients is locus of control. As mentioned previously, locus of control is the personality variable indicating whether an individual is primarily oriented to perceive the outcome of events as a result of his own control as opposed to attributing them to fate or control by other individuals or external circumstances. In the research presented here, external versus internal control was measured by the Rotter locus of control scale (Appendix D; Rotter, 1966). Again, this variable represents a normally distributed continuum with most people falling in the middle. A clinical judgment may be made about a patient's locus of control by discussing with him what he thinks controls his life. Patients oriented to an external locus of control (ELC) will talk about fate, external circumstances, or other people determining what happens to them. However, some patients describing an external orientation for themselves are "defensive externals." That is, they proclaim an external locus of control to avoid dealing with a more subtle feeling that the outcome of events in their lives is really up to them. This type of ELC person would best not be categorized with other externals, since internal components with which he cannot deal may exist in his personality. The ILC (internal locus of control) personality will show evidence that he sees outcomes of events as his responsibility. He will take actions effecting positive outcome, even that of getting out of the hospital and getting well. If he fails in a goal-directed effort in his life situation, he will on some level, covertly if not overtly, feel that the failure results from his wrong decision.

Paranoid behavior

Occasionally, the life circumstances of an ILC personality will be so immediately and traumatically negative that he cannot keep his usual feeling of control. This may occur with a mental illness that renders him incapable of conducting his own affairs; an acute injury to his brain; brain surgery that limits his internally oriented and goal-directed problem-solving ability; a sensory handicap, such as a loss of hearing, which prevents easy communication with people around him; the realization that aging has made him a different person from what he wants to view himself to be; an acute drug intoxication (e.g., amphetamines) that temporarily impairs his ability to conceptualize cause-effect relationships; a sexual experience or obsession that is interpreted as a violation of his own self-image; or some other severe, usually abrupt, somatically or psychologically handicapping condition. In some cases, though not frequently, a heart attack is interpreted in this way.

A severe and immediate loss in maintaining the goals of self-image can produce a paranoid reaction. The individual develops delusional feelings of persecution or, less often, grandeur. Ideas of reference may occur, in which he feels erroneously that other people are talking about him or that events are intended to have some special or symbolic significance for him. It is as if the individual, in yielding his previous ILC attitudes, can nevertheless not accept an ELC, fatalistic, "go to hell" attitude. Consequently, in a state of emotional stress from the loss of control, the individual's concept system manufactures explanations that are not in line with reality, that is, are not the publicly shared perceptions of cause-effect held by others about him. Thus, an acute paranoid state may occur. This state is often misinterpreted as schizophrenia, usually a hazardous misdiagnosis. On the other hand, it is indeed emotionally based and will usually occur when an individual has already lost other psychological resources or support systems that have been important to his self-esteem. Even though a myocardial infarction can be a subtle and socially acceptable way to "get out of the rat race," it may precipitate a paranoid reaction in some patients.

Anxiety (chronic arousal, sensitization)

Arousal, tension, anxiety, and sensitization are terms that have not been completely distinguished in the psychological literature. Yet an assessment of these factors is quite important in dealing with coronary patients. Arousal has to do with readiness to be responsive. Sleep illustrates the lowest stages of arousal, but an awake person who is performing sluggishly and inefficiently would also be described as low in arousal. Moderate arousal, whether due to increased motivation, stimulants, or other factors, can be inferred from efficient task performance. With higher levels of arousal, the individual attends to irrelevant cues and feels jumpy and uptight. His performance is inefficient and inaccurate, but he cannot be characterized as sluggish. Clearly, a person's arousal varies widely, but some people can be characterized as having predominantly high arousal level. Thus, anxiety is typically viewed as a chronically heightened state of arousal resulting from learned fear responses. Notice the distinction between "state" and "trait" anxiety. State anxiety is a transient high arousal that is debilitating except when the person is performing simple tasks. Trait anxiety is a chronic and sustained level of heightened arousal. Sensitization is synonymous with "trait" anxiety.

How can anxiety be assessed? Besides scales like the one we used in this research (see Appendix C), anxiety may be clinically observed. It may be inferred from (1) the presence of environmental or life situations that ordinarily make anyone anxious; (2) verbal reports by the patient that he is fearful, upset, worried, and so on; and (3) observations of autonomic nervous system activity (increased heart rate, breathing rate, perspiration; somatic fidgeting or tremulous behavior; voice quality becoming shaky or loud and fast). It should also be recalled from the results reported in Chapter 4 that the lipids, 17-hydroxycorticosteroids and free fatty acid are elevated in the bloodstream during stressful arousal.

Depression and hostility

There is a close psychological relationship between depression and hostility. This can be seen by thinking of the patient as having a goal that is blocked by some barrier. If the patient believes (realistically or not) that he might still reach his goal, he may attack the barrier or display other forms of discontent that can be described as anger or hostility. If, on the other hand, he concludes that the goal cannot be reached, he will retreat, show despair, and in some cases become "fogged in," that is, think too unclearly for efficient problem solving activity. This we call depression. The goal need not be tangible. For example, an important goal for most people is the preservation of a positive self-image. If this is lost through public attack or embarrassment, the individual may direct an attack on the person or thing he feels is responsible for the loss. Or if expectancies are low, he may become helpless, immobilized, and depressed.

Another example is death of a loved one. People often report that their first reaction to such an unexpected loss is anger. Some bring malpractice suits against the attending physician as hostile reactions. The more common reaction is grief, which is a reaction to the recognition that the loved person will never return. Working through grief, hostility, revenge, and related manifestations may take a considerable amount of time.

Other significant life events, such as divorce, loss of job, handicap, an offspring gone astray, are all additional examples that can precipitate a depressed or hostile response. A heart attack itself may provoke one of these two reactions; on the other hand, it may serve as the unexpected shock to release a preexisting depression or hostile preoccupation. Some individuals are so conditioned to view hostility as uncivilized and unacceptable that they can show nothing but depression, even in situations that would ordinarily provoke hostility. Others may swing from one reaction to the other. An immediate, unchecked acting out, based upon abrupt feelings of hostility, is possibly the most removed from coronary proneness, even though it is considered least couth.

The relevance of depression and hostility to myocardial infarction, as may be recalled from the present or other research findings, is provocative, yet not all the research results are in. Grief and depression are associated with elevation of lipids in the bloodstream. High lipid levels have been hypothesized to be a major cause of the development of atherosclerosis. Atherosclerosis is a breaking down of the walls of medium-sized arteries in association with deposits of lipid. Without question, atherosclerosis plays a role in the etiology of myocardial infarction. Thus, depression may contribute to the etiology of myocardial infarction. In fact, among patients in mental hospitals, myocardial infarctions occur primarily to those over 40 with a diagnosis of depression.

Denying hostility is more characteristic of MI patients than of non-MI patients. While not a good predictor of how soon a second MI will occur, denial may prolong the elevated levels of blood lipids. Beyond this, the role of denial of hostility is not well understood.

How does one detect depression and hostility? Depression is perhaps the more difficult, since it may be confused with apathy, hypoactive mental retardation, the flatness of affect shown in schizophrenia, toxic conditions leading to inactivity, and weakness or fatigue leading to inactivity. We invite you to review Appendix M, which presents some MMPI Depression scale items that elicit distinctive responses from depressed individuals. Going beyond information from this scale, the verbal admissions of the patients that they are in a state of despair and the motor and thought retardation associated with this state are probably of paramount clinical importance.

Hostility is easy to detect, even in its disguised forms. Detecting denial of hostility is more difficult. When hostility is completely controlled by lowering behavioral expectancies, only depression will occur. If hostility is overtly denied but unsuccessfully controlled, it may take the form of disguised and indirect hostile acts. Coronary proneness is often thought to be associated closely with the unsuccessful control and denial of hostility. Hostility denial can be inferred when the patient declares that he is not angry but simultaneously grimaces, shows signs of internal turmoil, or actually becomes overtly angry in contradiction to his declarations.

Obsessive rumination

Closely linked to depression and possibly also to hostility is the tendency to continue to respond to a frustrating event after it has passed. Blood levels of 17-

hydroxycorticosteroids continue to go up in depressed psychiatric patients after a stressful event. This does not occur among mental patients without depression. Among coronary patients (Chapter 4), steroid level continues to rise for 70 minutes following a frustrating task, whereas it falls within 70 minutes among non-MI patients. These steroid elevations probably result from obsessive rumination about the frustrating event. It therefore seems important for nurses and physicians to assess obsessive rumination. This may be done by listening carefully to the content of patients' conversations. If the patient talks about events, people, and objects largely from the recent past, you should suspect him of rumination. If a patient's comments are limited to the here and now, you may conclude no evidence exists for continued rumination. Patients concerned only with the immediate things of the here and now will respond to things such as the medication you have just handed them, the flowers they have received, the discomfort they feel at the moment, how you are feeling today, and so on. Others will make a comment about the breakfast or doctor's visit earlier in the morning or yesterday, a visitor from a previous day, what's going on at home or work (this, too, is conceptually remote and not part of their immediate physical environment), or similar matter. The well-known coronary-prone characteristic, deadline consciousness (Freedman and Rosenman, 1974), is an example of rumination. The individual who is conscious of deadlines is one who will recurrently reflect and look on an unfinished task and the time frame available to complete it regardless of his here and now environment. When such comments occur, the patient may also reveal in some way that some frustration, problem or uncompleted task has continuously or repeatedly crossed his mind. If patients do not reveal this on their own, you may ask them. With continuing interaction with the patient you can get a picture of the balance of his focus on the here and now as opposed to things remote to the coronary unit at that moment. And, among these latter things, you may also get an understanding of whether one idea occurs repetitively or continuously. If such is the case, you may conclude the patient is susceptible to obsessive rumination. Perhaps it is no accident that the relevant psychological dimensions to be assessed in heart disease are often adaptive and beneficial in a productive and civilized society. A goal-directed orientation and control over impulsive feelings have obvious positive value for most people in society. Perhaps this is partly why the incidence of coronary heart disease is so high in advanced cultures.

Socioeconomic status

Sociologists know that people from different socioeconomic levels act differently. In terms of behavior recorded in a coronary care unit, these differences are fairly easy to understand. Patients of lower socioeconomic status (SES) generally will complain less. The degree of individualized care from coronary unit staff, the food, the bed comfort, and other personal conveniences will often be beyond that to which the low SES individual is accustomed. They may less frequently summon help—even when they need it. Individuals from higher SES will have greater expectancies of food, care, personal conveniences, and freedom from discomfort. Thus, higher SES individuals generally will complain more about "smaller things" and will summon help more often. A psychologically sophisticated nurse or physician will realize that emotional reactions that appear irrational, uncooperative, unmotivated, unreasonable, "bitchy," or spoiled are symptoms of distress. Such symptoms need treatment in the same sense as the physical illness itself. Taking offense betrays a lack of sophistication.

SES concerns education and income. The gradation is usually done on a 5-point scale developed by Hollingshead (1957). In the United States the facilities of coronary unit care are more often afforded only by the upper SES and by stable workers whose companies have good health insurance plans. Thus, coronary units usually have a biased sample of the total population.

Peeling off socialized defenses

An acute illness is taxing to the socialized defenses and controlled conduct of any person. The more the distress, the greater the strain on the defenses. On the other hand, people differ in the development of these social defenses. One of the problems on a coronary unit is to discriminate the extent to which the traumatic effects of the illness causes the patient to peel off his socialized defenses from the extent to which they were never there to begin with.

The well-integrated individual with strong socialized defenses will express concern about the people around him. He will wonder whether his requests are too much to ask of the nurse or aide or whether he is conducting himself so that he is not offensive or burdensome to the people around him. As these defenses are peeled off through the stress of acute illness or if they are not there to begin with, the patient will act in ways that will be annoying or offensive to nurses and others caring for him. When this happens, the nurse or other caregiver is faced with a major challenge not to become defensive, angry, frightened, or rejecting, but instead to diagnose the situation adequately and respond compassionately. A patient may be demanding and selfish, want to be taken care of first, fly into temper tantrums, insult the staff, or even throw things. The major assessment problem here is to get an understanding of whether this is a person with immature and maladaptive socialized defensive structures to begin with or whether the behavior is primarily due to the temporary and acute crisis of the illness. Usually, observation of the patient's behavior will not resolve the problem, but a conversation with close relatives may. Ask about what the patient was like before becoming ill. When the answers indicate that the patient's current behavior is like his regular responses to minor upsetting experiences, the inference is that the individual's socialized defenses have not been unduly lowered by his illness. If the patient's current behavior is rare and unusual to those who know him well, you can gauge the temporariness of "peeling off" resulting from the stress of illness itself.

In certain instances a patient whose MI is not severe enough to cause weakness during the first 24 hours on the unit will make amends and feel guilty about some of his early behavior. This change is an indication that the individual was responding directly to the stress of the physical illness and that he is more intact, socialized, and civilized under ordinary life circumstances.

Seeking additional psychological assessment

Occasionally, the coronary care team will want consultation on a psychological assessment or management problem. In such cases a referral may be made to a clinical psychologist, psychiatrist or psychiatric nurse specialist. It is important to make this referral carefully to get optimal results. A general request for psychological evaluation is usually not advisable. Faced with a general request, the psychologist or psychiatrist will probably not focus on issues in which you are interested. It is also unwise to request specific tests or procedures. If you simply request projective tests, an MMPI depression scale, a Wechsler intelligence test or a psychodiagnostic interview, more appropriate techniques may be available to answer your question. You run the risk of the psychologist or psychiatrist telling you much you do not want to know and little concerning the specific problem you face. Therefore, it is usually wise to state the question you want answered or the problem you want solved. State the problem clearly. In one instance you may want to know more accurately the level of depression. In another, you may want to know whether a behavioral deviancy represents an ongoing problem or is an acute temporary response to the situation. The presence of anoxia and brain damage calls for an intellectual or neuropsychological evaluation to identify an appropriate approach to rehabilitation. A more specific assessment of locus of control or scanning (information processing) level may be sought. Experience will probably show that some clinicians are more psychosomatically oriented than others. Those who are will probably provide more help and understanding of coronary patients.

Expanding assessment skills

Opportunities are increasingly available to develop skills in the assessment and management of the psychological aspects of coronary and other physical illnesses. First, there are didactic opportunities to extend and systematize your knowledge of psychological concepts and how these concepts are used clinically. There are also opportunities in individual or group psychotherapy to understand more clearly how you function and what effect your background has upon your clinical judgments. Both routes can be valuable, but efforts to improve effectiveness in the psychological aspects of caregiving will not be effective if they are limited to skills for psychological assessment. You must be able to translate observations and leading clinical hypotheses into interventions. Otherwise, you will only be able to give fancier labels or explanations and will not have improved your effectiveness in coronary *care*.

THE MANAGEMENT OF PSYCHOLOGICAL PROBLEMS: EFFECTIVE PSYCHOLOGICAL CARE

Support

All nurses and physicians should be able to give emotional support to their patients. Emotional support consists of responses that positively reinforce the patient and assure him that he is well cared for. Supportive therapy refers to a relationship in which the therapist's comments are intended to build up the patient's esteem and defenses rather than uncover underlying problems. Because of the stress of coronary illness, support should be given to all coronary patients. It may be expressed in different ways to different patients, but the more support the patient senses he is getting, the more comfort he will feel and the more cooperative he will be with efforts to promote his physical well-being.

Setting the level of information to be processed

Another role of the nurse and other caregivers in the coronary unit is to set the level of information to be processed. The staff can judge needs for lower levels by listening to the patient. When the patient himself says that he does not want diversional stimulation, frequent visitors, extensive information about heart disease, the task of dealing with leftover decisions from home or work, they should take him at his word and reduce his inputs. Conversely, when his discomfort or agitation seems to increase when left alone, they should intervene to increase input. In so doing, the first choice is to intervene with, for example, pleasant conversation, which will allow the staff to determine which input might be most beneficial. In some cases it may be a visit from a close relative; in other cases, it may be reading material or other diversion.

The greater problem is to assess demands for great amounts of informational input. Some patients' precoronary activity levels may be so high that they overextend themselves and keep their levels of stress too high. The patients may wish to have a telephone at bedside, to call meetings, and to continue activities from which he should be temporarily removed. To discourage this it is sometimes wise to advise him that there is enough "work" on the coronary unit, namely, attending to his illness and learning the self-care procedures important to his recovery when he leaves. In other words, helping him reconstrue his hospital stay as preparation for resuming a full life may remove the threat he feels from "lying there and doing nothing."

Restricting input too greatly in the hyperscanning, information-demanding individual may have its negative consequences. Remember, when external input is not available, some individuals will generate their own internally. They may become preoccupied with muscle tensions, chest pains, other symptoms, or pessimistic thoughts about their fate. In these cases the reintroduction of input, especially in the forms of things to do to aid recovery, may reduce tension and symptoms.

To manage the level of input it is advisable to have a coronary unit with good acoustical control (carpeting, draperies, acoustical ceiling), various appliances that can be installed or removed (television, radio, canned music, newspapers, magazines, outside window shades, telephone), and some control over visitors' traffic. It is especially important to control or at least to know when unfavorable news has been given the patient about his diagnosis or the seriousness of his condition in order to follow through accordingly with things he can do.

As a final note, the patient's information processing rate is in some respects a permanent personality characteristic. To expect to make permanent modifications in it or to tell the patient to do so would be unrealistic. Thus, the major goal is to keep the input level where the patient is not overtaxed (by too much or too little); to keep the stressful content of the information low; and when stressful input does indeed occur, to follow it up with an increase in self-help activity or diversion rather than with deprivation.

Providing anticipatory structure for the highly anxious

Everyone is anxious sometimes, and some people are chronically anxious. Anxiety often results when people do not understand what is happening to them. Explanations can lower anxiety. The patient may need explanations of the monitor and other coronary unit equipment and how he will experience them. He may need advance warning and explanations of procedures, such as the installing of a pacemaker. Special focus should be placed on instructions he is to carry out during his convalescence after he leaves the hospital.

Observation or suspicion of another patient's death

Handling the concerns of patients who witness or suspect death of another patient is an important part of coronary care. One should provide a view of the deceased patient that will help differentiate the deceased patient from the inquiring patient in a number of ways. Thus the patient will not identify himself as a "similar soul" who is next in line. For example, truthfully pointing out the greater severity of the other patient's condition, the differences between his pattern of symptoms and past history and the inquiring patient's, or that this particular patient was not expected to live can be helpful. For the patient who has cardiac distress himself, saying that such episodes are routine for patients on the unit is reassuring, as is explaining that the coronary unit is set up expressly to deal with such episodes. This will help patients accept such events without attaching undue anxiety to them.

Do not try to give misleading information or be untruthful to patients in your attempt to alleviate their concerns and anxiety.

As a matter of routine, disquieting information should be coupled with self-treatment activities. There should be a routine focus on what the patient must continue to do for himself when he gets out of the hospital. Even patients who seek to complete their wills or otherwise put their personal affairs in order should be encouraged and assisted because of the wisdom of preparing adequately for their futures.

As in the foregoing section, the level of anxiety and scanning of the patient is an important consideration in deciding how much information to give. The nonanxious, slow scanning patient may need only a few brief words. The anxious patient will need and probably demand more extensive attention. It is better to give and even rehearse with him things he can do for himself than to leave him isolated without information about what will happen to him or what to do about it.

When to let the patient be anxious

Not all anxiety is detrimental. Only when it interferes with problem solving can anxiety be called psychologically detrimental. Certain of our research findings suggest that patients who do not show some anxiety about their condition or their doctor's orders do not fare well when they leave the hospital. Anxiety may encourage the patient to change major aspects of his life style, such as smoking, diet, exercise, stressful work, or home situation. It may motivate patients (1) to comply with instructions and (2) to replace their unfavorable habits with new ones without a sense of loss. In this limited respect, anxiety can be beneficial in motivating the patient toward appropriate actions.

When support and explanations fail to abate great anxiety, the possibility of appropriate medication should be considered.

Self-participation and control versus complete care by others

As was documented in the foregoing chapters, it is crucial to manage the extent to which the patient views himself as participating in and controlling the outcome of his treatment. The patient with an internal locus of control needs to participate in his treatment more than others do. He will progress faster when he is able to see himself and his own decisions as instrumental in the outcome of events, including his own recovery. At the other end of the continuum, the external-locus-of-control personality may find it threatening to participate in his own treatment. For him, it is better to leave the care and decisions in the hands of others.

It is no simple matter to generate self-help activities and procedures for severely ill coronary patients. On the other hand, nontaxing, self-help procedures that may appear contrived to the coronary nurse may have remarkable psychological impact on unsophisticated and very ill patients. As noted from Chapter 2, self-participation activities used in our research project were (1) control over the printout of the patient's ECG recordings, (2) remembering and reporting of symptoms to the physician, and (3) mild exercises.

Listening

Listening is a treatment as well as an assessment tool. Sometimes just listening to what a patient says in order to assess a problem more fully makes the problem evaporate. This indicates only that the need to be listened to and attended to was more important than what was said. Filling this need often makes the listener-caregiver more instrumental and effective in influencing the patient's behavior and cooperativeness because the listener becomes personally more important to the patient.

When to prevent the unloading of feelings

Sometimes patients will want to pour out their problems at length. This calls for careful judgment. The staff member's need to serve others and to give tender care might prompt him to listen at length and let the patient unload his troubles. Also, getting to know another person's life intimately can be intriguing. Contrarily, you may feel insufficiently experienced to deal with complex personal information, or you may feel that your own personal problems make it difficult to deal with those of others. The patient's needs, not the clinician's personal motivations, should determine how to handle emotional unloading.

Judgment is critical in these situations because the response should be determined by the kind of emotions being unloaded. Attempted suicide can follow depression. This risk increases during recovery from the depression and can be heightened by talking about personal problems. Much repression of guilty feelings and of threatening subjects occurs during depression. If these guilty feelings and threatening thoughts are allowed to surface and become the objects of extensive and belabored introspection, the patient's negative feelings about himself may become too much for him to handle. Introspection is facilitated by the opportunity to talk about oneself. Consequently, it is important to prevent the depressed patient from unloading personal material for more than a few minutes. This may be done by changing the topic to nonpersonal matters, by leaving to perform duties elsewhere, or by telling the patient that it is not good for him in his present condition to talk so much about personal problems and negative feelings. Unloading should be curtailed too when its content suggests the imminence of psychosis, as when the patient's ideas do not appear to fit together logically or if references are made to sexual, religious, or other topics that are grossly inappropriate for the time, place, and other content of the conversation.

A different approach will be required with the patient who has denied all anger and hostility. Unloading anger and hostile feelings is better than restraining these and ruminating obsessively. Moreover, it is important for the nurse or physician to let the patient elaborate on the feelings sufficiently in order to be more fully able to understand the nature of the frustration. Very often, when a simmering frustration is fully understood, steps can be taken to eliminate it. In other instances, where the frustration is not correctable and elaboration about it can help the patient understand it better, the patient may discover that the high expectancies associated with the frustration are unrealistic or out of date or that not all facts were taken into consideration. In any case the nurse, in playing a listening and understanding role, will be in a position to help the patient examine his priorities and determine whether the goal or need at the source of the frustration is really still important in his current system of priorities.

Likewise, the patient displaying anxiety about his state of affairs should also be given the opportunity to unload or elaborate. Anxiety is closely associated with the inability of a patient to anticipate the future course of events in his life situation. When a nurse allows the anxious coronary patient to elaborate his fears and negative preoccupations, she gains an opportunity to provide more information with which the patient can anticipate his future. Insofar as anxiety is concerned, even the anticipation of an unfavorable outcome is anxiety reducing when it allows the patient to plan and take action to deal with the future. In fact, when the patient is not relieved by being able to anticipate events, anxiety is probably not the problem, unless some margin of uncertainty remains. Instead, anger or fear is the likely culprit.

An interesting conflict for nurses arises when a patient complains without apparent justification. It is tempting to disregard such complaints as "needless bitching" or to admonish the patient like a child. But it is important to remember that frustration has a direct effect upon blood lipid levels, which in turn affect coronary conditions. Patients who are unusually anxious, who have high expectancies for personal care and attention, and who are prone to frustration and anger when their expectations are not satisfied should be viewed as needing special psychological care from the nurse.

Need/goal and priority analysis in depression and hostility

After the assessment of depression and hostility in coronary patients, other treatment techniques are open. Depression and hostility may be usefully construed as results of the blocking of goal-directed behavior, but the depressed or hostile patient may not perceive the need or goal that is frustrated. Nurses and physicians may be highly instrumental in helping identify these underlying unmet goals or needs—an important step of clarification that can then allow the patient, with the help of a nurse or physician, to evaluate whether these needs or goals are any longer appropriate. Sometimes the goal satisfactions expected from maturing children, from the job, from the home, or from some other aspect of life are no longer appropriate. Priorities should change so that these goals are no longer held. Functionally interchangeable goal satisfactions should be sought instead. Consequently, with this type of psychological assistance, the patient can emerge from a temporary hospitalization with a new and better adjusted view of what is important and where he is going.

Shortcutting obsessive rumination

Once one has determined that a coronary patient is a victim of his own obsessive rumination, definitive action can be taken. Since obsessive rumination sustains itself, the first step is to get the patient to talk about his problem. Sometimes he must be encouraged to talk even about problems that appear small and insignificant. Second, if some overt action cannot resolve the problem directly, a redirecting of the patient's focus upon other less stressful matters may be important. It may be important simply to point out to the patient what he is doing (for example, stewing or simmering about a problem without letting it go) and that it is not good for him. This may dispel any particular rumination cycle, but little can be done in the transient treatment of the coronary care unit to change a lifelong propensity for this behavior.

Information coupling and intermediate input

In the earlier research chapters, the importance of information, information coupling, and intermediate input was described. The hyperscanning and anxious patient will inevitably feel stress until he is given extensive relevant information. Others, with low anxiety and scanning, will not wish to deal with the information. A firm diagnosis of a myocardial infarction, especially the first one, is extremely likely to be stressful information to the patient, even though he shows no overt sign of this stress. Accordingly, it is invariably important to give self-treatment or diversional activities following such instances of "heavy" information. Yet, moderation in terms of total input to the patient should be observed so that any psychological or medical intervention does not overload him with stress.

What chance for success?

It is important to remember that coronary unit workers cannot solve all their patients' psychological problems. Greatest success may be expected with disturbances that result directly from illness and removal from daily routine. There should be little expectancy for success in disturbances that are long-term manifestations and independent of the coronary illness itself. Instead, the best one can typically expect is management of the acute psychological aspects of the disturbance during the period of acute care and perhaps an orienting of the individual toward longer term help after the acute phase of illness.

Seeking more advanced interventions

As in the case of psychological assessments, the nurse or physician may often see need for intervention by a specialist in psychological problems. Sometimes the problem is acute enough to require chemotherapy. If so, the pharmacologic regime should be worked out carefully between cardiologically and psychiatrically skilled persons. In other cases, it will be evident that the long-term working through of a problem will require continued sessions with a clinical psychologist or psychiatrist. In such cases it is most advantageous to have a psychotherapist who is experienced in the interrelation of psychological problems and physical disease.

Chapter 9

PREVENTING CORONARIES
special comments on exercise programming

No one knows for sure how to prevent coronaries. Our best understandings of their etiology are incomplete. Our best understanding of how to induce behavioral change is not good. How does one help another stop smoking, lose weight, or worry less? Still, we know more now than a decade ago. The problem is to act as wisely as we can on what is known now without foreclosing the possibility of improving prevention as we learn more. The solution is to base preventive planning on clearly stated premises. Thus, as new knowledge calls for changing any premise, it will be apparent that prevention programs should be changed too.

PREMISES FOR PREVENTION

This chapter's premises are straightforward. Acute myocardial infarction results from atherosclerosis of the coronary arteries. This atherosclerosis builds up over a number of years. It results in part from chronically high blood levels of lipids and lipoproteins, which are yet to be identified precisely. The atherosclerosis results in part from lack of adaptability of the walls of coronary vessels to major changes in dilation-constriction and pulse volume. Once the atherosclerosis builds up, violent exercise without proper prior conditioning and warm-up increases the risk of an ischemic attack. Regular endurance exercise "burns off" and eliminates excess lipids and lipoproteins and probably increases the muscle blood flow.

Lipid blood level is determined partly by diet, and lipid levels are generally higher among the obese. Besides diet and obesity, anxiety, depression, and environmental stress increase lipid levels. In the case of depression and grief, lipid levels do not subside quickly but remain high for a prolonged period. Chronic anxiety and stressful events cause cardiovascular changes, the significance of which are not well understood.

119

The type A personality is properly viewed as an anxious person, since type A symptoms (impatience, competitiveness, deadline consciousness, emphatic expression, poorly controlled hostility, and so on) are ways anxiety is dealt with in our culture. Regardless of whether type A behavior is viewed as a defense against anxiety, its relevance to coronary proneness is not to be overlooked. Type A behavior is associated with coronary proneness (Freedman and Rosenman, 1974). Our premise is that this association is mediated through biological factors. We also assume that beneficial changes in diet, exercise, and living patterns can combat the proneness without necessarily requiring personality reorganization as through psychotherapy.

Our final premise, which is as revisable as all the rest, is that no pharmacologic or other medical procedure presently exists to prevent atherosclerosis and subsequent infarctions directly. No procedure exists to enliven necrotic tissue in the myocardium when an infarct occurs nor to benignly modify lipid levels or cardiovascular factors directly. Thus, changing the behavior and long-term habit structure of the coronary-prone individual is the main current way to prevention. Advice is seldom sufficient to change behavior. For this reason, management of the behavior change is as important in preventing coronary disease progression as knowing what behavior to change.

DO-IT-YOURSELF APPROACH VERSUS OUTSIDE HELP

Many coronary-prone individuals will immediately prefer to do it themselves, instead of seeking assistance from a person trained in behavior management. Seeking assistance makes the job of behavior change easier and more effective. Suppose one wants to quit smoking, permanently modify his diet, acquire better exercise habits, or all of these. Failure is likely unless one has a great personal and social commitment, understands the environmental circumstances that cause people to break and fail to break habits, and creates a feedback and support system from family and close friends who will notice, enjoy, and reinforce changes as they occur. Most human beings are "team players" in life, not hermits. They depend upon other people at home, at work, and in daily activities. Even an effective and well-adjusted loner will have a better chance of modifying personal habits if given the proper procedures. The advantage to the patient of a nurse, physician, psychologist, or other person trained in behavioral management is the same as the advantage to an athlete of a coach. It may be possible for an athletic team to succeed without a coach, but how likely is it?

BEHAVIOR MANAGEMENT

As mentioned previously, knowing what to change is not enough. One must know how to manage behavior. This chapter cannot present fully the art of behavior management, but it does summarize the basic steps. We encourage you to refer to other sources on coronary risk, behavior management, behavior modification, and behavior therapy. As you read these steps, try to think about how you would apply them to a specific behavior change, such as smoking, exercise, weight loss, or diet.

Identifying the behaviors to change

Before initiating the program, there should be an agreement between the client (patient) and the helper (trainer, therapist) that the patient wants to change specific behaviors and wishes help in changing and that the therapist wants to assist. This agreement may come when the client is advised that one or more of his behaviors increases his risk of heart disease or some other negative outcome, or it may come later. In any event, the client must want help.

Pinpointing the controlling situational stimuli

The major reason for pinpointing stimuli and situations that give rise to the target behavior is that the client often has not noticed them himself. The stimuli and situations are important. An underlying assumption of most behavior management approaches is that the controlling forces for a habit are not in the client himself but in the environmental stimuli that control the behavior. Control the environmental stimuli bonded to the behavior and you can control the behavior. This helps a person avoid situations in which undesirable behavior occurs by distinguishing them clearly from situations in which he seldom has the behavior. For example, if an individual usually smokes over coffee, then the modifying of his coffee drinking will help modify his smoking behavior.

Careful counting and written records should be kept on the frequency and settings of the behavior to be changed. These records help diagnose the problem, and they also alert the client to influences of environmental factors. It is important that these records be discussed regularly, so that the behavior and the environmental factors can be further pinpointed. A client who lacks confidence to change a given behavior will gain confidence if he can control the situational determinants and antecedent behaviors. Counting and recording often convinces the client he can control his behavior. Discussion provides the occasion for the helper to reinforce the client, and it shows the client that someone else does care.

On some occasions it is appropriate for a spouse or other family member or friend to keep parallel and independent records on the behavior. This can help the client detect distortions in his own records. It involves other people in the change program, thereby providing more reinforcement opportunities and less opportunity to back out of the program.

Executing the modification program

Modification plans vary, depending on what is to be changed, but the components of a plan are (1) to eliminate or avoid situations and stimuli that facilitate the undesirable behavior, (2) to provide reinforcement for the client's efforts to eliminate these stimuli, (3) to provide alternative stimuli and situations that could allow development of substitute behaviors, (4) to provide for reinforcements for carrying out these alternative behaviors, and (5) to provide a schedule of reinforcement for the recorded decrease in rate of the undesired behavior. These strategic steps are included in a contract or prior agreement between the client and helper or sometimes between the client and others in his environment. The contract specifies new responses to be made to old stimuli, careful recording of frequencies of the behaviors to be acquired and avoided, and specific reinforcements.

Much emphasis should be given to the feedback of information from the client to the helper. Regular meetings are scheduled between client and helper, usually several during the first two or three weeks. Telephone calls are arranged for reporting, both from client to helper and from helper to client. Most clients do not expect success. Otherwise, they would not be seeking or agreeing to help. One outcome of the feedback of behavioral and environmental analysis is that the client's attention is shifted from the ultimate goal to more immediate implementing goals. As these "subgoals" are achieved, the client may become more motivated because he begins to expect to reach his ultimate goal.

Stabilization and phaseout of help

As the undesired behavior decreases to the desired frequency, attention is given to whether the rewards for alternative behavior are strong enough to perpetuate it. The client should not see himself in a situation of self-punishment, self-sacrifice, or self-deprivation. Instead, he should see himself as having taken part in the enjoyable process of developing a new and more satisfying life style, and he should value the rewards of that style.

The helper phases himself out of the picture when it seems that family, friends, and the subject himself will provide the necessary reinforcing conditions for the new behavior to be maintained.

EXERCISE

More and more physicians are recognizing that exercise may help prevent the progression of coronary disease. Studies show that sedentary people are more at risk for coronaries than those whose occupations or habits involve physical activity. Blackburn (1975) reviewed the management of coronary risk factors and concluded that exercise is broadly important to good health, mental well-being, and weight control. Stuart and Davis (1972) view exercise as an integral part of a weight control program. Independent of weight problems, exercise should directly affect heart and lung conditioning.

An important distinction should be made between endurance and explosive intermittent exercise activities. Endurance activities, such as distance running, jogging, distance swimming, and bicycling are viewed as useful for heart and lung conditioning. The more explosive or abrupt types of activities, such as baseball, bowling, golf, football, short sprints, shoveling snow, fixing a flat tire, and heavy moving, are looked upon as less beneficial or even dangerous. Endurance activity requires a continuous output of energy past the time when perspiration and circulation reach a maximum level. When an individual's maximum level is reached, he is often described as having his "second wind." Oxygen is more efficiently transported and utilized than when circulation is below its peak. In the explosive activities, this peak level is typically not reached. Periods of abrupt activity are interrupted by periods of rest or inactivity. The abrupt actions tax both the musculoskeletal and cardiovascular systems. Such activities can be dangerous for a person whose body is not very well conditioned. Consider snow shoveling. The sedentary person should approach the shovel only after a slow standing run (about 15 minutes) that brought him to full perspiration. Then snow shoveling would not be as great a shock to his system. If, after reaching this state of perspiration, he feels too tired or exhausted to shovel snow, then it is dangerous for him to be shoveling snow in the first place.

The major obstacles to starting an exercise program are (1) the belief that it takes too much time, (2) worry that one will be uncomfortable and look awkward in public with more athletic or well-conditioned people, (3) the attitude that earlier prowess as an athlete leaves nothing to prove, and (4) lethargy that makes exercise more work than enjoyment. Because of such obstacles, several steps are often required before a client will undertake an exercise program.

The client should be asked to discuss his views on whether he wants to live a longer life with better physical and mental well-being and whether this is more important than the competing interests of job, family, and other activities. If he makes the decision in favor of exercising to better health, the nurse or physician should help him plan toward a concerted commitment. Wearing apparel, equipment, and setting should be the best the client can afford. There may be the tendency for the client not to invest heavily or not to tell others of his plans, for fear of losses or embarrassment if he changes his mind. If the client is to make a major change in his life style, he should commit himself as fully as he can afford. Depending upon which exercise he chooses to pursue, he should invest in a way that is attractive and reinforcing to him: high quality distance running shoes; membership in YMCA or YWCA, Jewish Community Center, or private club with an opportunity for attractive locker room and shower facilities; opportunity for companions with the same interests; well-chosen bicycle or tennis rackets, depending on the exercise, exemplify choices in this preparatory phase. It is also important that the equipment be for him personally, rather than shared with others, though this is not always possible or appropriate. A sharing of paraphernalia with spouse or offspring may give the client an excuse to back out of the commitment. On the other hand, the sharing of the activities can increase their attractiveness to some clients. As plans develop, the client should be encouraged to share the intention to become more physically active with family and friends. Then, as he does get involved, he should be encouraged to share with them the various targets he sets for each step in his fitness program.

After the decision and the commitment, a routine schedule should be established. This schedule should be written down, and it should be feasible. Close examination should be made of the situations that lead to departures from the schedule, which should be revised accordingly. Optimally, there should be a given time for exercise each day. The client need not give up an exercise schedule, however, if he can free himself only two or three times per week. The important thing is to meet the exercise sessions once they are scheduled. A predesignated reward should be prescribed for keeping the schedule faithfully for one full week (thereafter for two full weeks, and later for longer periods of time). A rank order should be made of the various things and activities he would enjoy. This may be, as he chooses, a steak dinner, a concert, a new acquisition for home or hobby, or other personally desired things. Whatever the reward, he must agree to forego it if he violates his schedule for any reason. In addition, should he violate his schedule without acceptable reason, he should agree in advance on some predesignated penalty, such as make-up sessions or some chore at home or work that he would prefer to avoid even more than exercise.

The reasons for not exercising that should remain unpenalized are distinct physical tiredness, exhaustion, or muscular soreness. Although no research evidence exists, clinical observation indicates that even in physically fit individuals over 40 the muscles take longer to restore themselves after a strenuous workout. Thus, the exercise program will progress more successfully if a session is skipped and the schedule modified.

The exercise schedule itself should be planned session by session. The major danger for the client is to try to accomplish too much too fast. Excellent resources on exercise schedules are available: American College of Sports Medicine's *Guidelines for Graded Exercise Testing and Exercise Prescription for College Sports Medicine* (Philadelphia: 1975, Lea & Febiger); *Official Royal Canadian Air Force Exercise Plans for Physical Fitness* (New York, 1962, Pocketbooks); and the American Heart Association's *Exercise Testing and Training of Apparently Healthy Individuals: a Handbook for Physicians* (New York, 1972). In the beginning, if the client exercises until he feels he has had enough, he has already had too much. The joy of getting back into the swing of exercise, the revival of the spirit of competitive sport, or impatience to perform better are all hazardous. In the beginning the client should quit while he clearly feels he has energy left.

To set the initial level of exercise is difficult if the client has not exercised regularly and recently. The following suggestions, used flexibly, might be helpful to the client who wants to jog, swim, or bicycle. Recommend a mild workout for five to ten minutes the first day. Do not exceed ten minutes. Make sure the pace is comfortable and far below the client's fastest possible pace. On the first day it is important to stop before feeling the need to. Stop before five to ten minutes if necessary. Then a couple of minutes should be taken to walk slowly about, to observe his breathing and how he feels. If he is not breathing heavily (for example, easy breaths through the nose with mouth closed), then one probably could have set a longer period or perhaps a slightly faster but still mild pace. If breathing is heavy but comfortable with the mouth open to get more air, yet not panting ("out of breath") or exhausted, then the pace and amount of time have been set well. If there is uncontrollable panting, nausea, lightheadedness, or headache, then the time should be cut in half and the pace greatly reduced next time.

Once the starting level has been set appropriately, the goal should be set to increase time by one minute each session. If the client has rated himself well on the first ten-minute workout, the time could be increased by two minutes rather than one on each subsequent session. As the time is increased for each session, the physical state of the client should be observed closely between sessions. If tiredness or soreness is observed, the time should be kept the same at least for one or two sessions. If the client is exhausted or ill, sessions should be skipped. If the client begins an exercise session and discovers an extreme lack of energy, exercise should be terminated instantly. This is most frequently the result of an emerging virus infection rather than lack of sleep or other reasons. All these recommendations are made with the assumption that the patient is in adequate physical health or else is having his exercise program monitored closely by a physician.

As the sessions lengthen, the pace should not be increased. When the graduated program has reached 20 minutes or longer, the client will probably begin noticing a change in circulatory functioning. If indoors or in a warm climate, he will perspire heavily. The experienced athlete will notice that his performance pace can be adjusted or increased more easily. If outside in weather cold enough to ordinarily require gloves, the jogger or bike rider will notice that he no longer needs gloves and that his breathing has slowed down without his pace being slowed. The swimmer may feel more smoothly coordinated and relaxed even though he has not slowed his pace. All these are indications that circulation has reached a better level of efficiency. The increased oxygen transport is now helping produce maximum energy for motion and minimum accumulation of lactate and fatigue. As the training schedule is continued beyond 30 minutes (and if the pace has not been increased to the point where the client is pressing himself), the client will see that the drudgery of the exercise was only during the first 20 minutes or so while he was "warming up." After the warm-up comes a period of exhilaration and euphoria. This continues until one is near the end of his physical conditioning limit. Then he will feel body fatigue or, if pressed too hard, overwinded and nauseous. Obviously, as the time of workout is expanded, this period of exhilaration from the exercise will be longer and more clearly identified before the final period of fatigue starts.

In the beginning, time of exercise is far more important than speed of pace. If the graduated program can reach 45 to 60 minutes of constant endurance exercise, then good physical fitness may be assumed. Increase in speed should not be attempted until the endurance goal of 45 to 60 minutes has been reached. Then if the client wants to work on speed, the pace should not be increased until after warming up. All experienced distance athletes know that ill-founded self-confidence may lead to a faster pace or sprinting before peak circulation has been reached. The resulting oxygen debt causes premature buildup of lactate, inability to establish a nonwinded pace later on, a performance flop, and sometimes even cramps or a pulled muscle.

After a heavy workout, warm-up clothes should be kept on so that perspiration can continue. The client should move around for at least three to five minutes. After this the client should reserve time to sit down with companions or by himself for 15 minutes or even longer for rest and fluid intake. Orange juice, coffee, or tea are acceptable. Scientifically balanced "athlete's ades," which restore sodium and potassium balance, are commercially available and recommended. It is this period that athletes and exercise buffs describe as their maximum point of euphoria. Sauna, massage, and double martinis have been described less favorably in comparison to the "high" serene feeling during this period. Once the client has reached this state of physical fitness, he is probably "addicted" to some adequate level of physical exercise for the rest of his life. He will no longer be in need of behavior management services.

Further comments about distance running

To exemplify other important details about exercise programming further comments will be made about jogging and distance running. However, much of what is said will concern other endurance exercises as well.

Part of the attraction of distance running is that it is easily accessible and good for the heart and lungs. Many joggers agree that a good distance for fitness and well-being is about 6 miles. Once 45 to 60 minutes of continuous exercise has been reached, the 6-mile run is a realistic goal.

Almost every area of the country now has a road runners or track club with inexpensive dues. These allow the jogger to participate competitively, to participate in "run for fun" or untimed events, and to meet other people interested in keeping themselves physically fit. The beginner will be surprised how much respect and admiration is offered to the individual who is just starting, the individual who is slow but working on an overweight problem, or the individual who comes in last. The experienced runners know what takes extra guts and persistence. Competitive events are usually separated by age when awards are made. Those over 40 (called the masters' level) are awarded separate ribbons and medals for achievement. Sometimes even further separations are made by sex and age levels. In this way, there is always some award that can be sought realistically.

After doing 6-mile, 10-mile, 10-kilometer (6.2 miles), and 20-kilometer (12.4 miles) races, many distance runners become interested in the marathon (26.2 miles). The American Medical Joggers' Association has helped popularize marathon running. Medical reports have claimed that the completion of one marathon is protective against a myocardial infarction for 6 years. Other reports have claimed there is no evidence that a marathon runner has ever died from coronary heart disease. Even if these claims are correct (and they are difficult to affirm), the obvious danger is not in the marathon but in the strenuous conditioning period to increase distance. If an individual has a structural defect or extensive atherosclerosis, this progressive buildup may be hazardous. On the other hand, a group of postcardiac patients from a Toronto rehabilitation center have regularly run the Boston Marathon in recent years with typical times between four and six hours. Marathoning and other distance running, like golf, is a sport of competing against one's own previous record. Research indicates that maximal performance on a marathon comes after the already experienced competitive distance runner practices about three months, averaging 9 miles running per day. No one runs a full 26-mile distance for practice, since after about 20 miles the muscle cells run low on carbohydrate and become increasingly weak. In order to run to finish but not make good time, one should be able to run 18 or 20 miles on at least two different days in the same week. Otherwise, one should not participate in a marathon at all. In distance running and in other distance sports, the increase in graduated training schedule must be handled carefully. If goals are increased too often and too much, fatigue and muscle or joint problems will occur. Hot weather may cause dehydration and hyperthermia, leading to nausea and dizziness. However, on still other occasions the runner may be feeling very bad physically and then discover even within five or ten minutes of workout that his energy reserve and performance level is even higher than average. Many aches and pains go away during a period of exercise; however, if an ache or pain increases rather than decreases, he should stop the exercise immediately. The important thing is to meet the appointed exercise schedule and give it one's best for that day. Meeting the performance goal on each particular day is not as important.

For the person supervising or getting involved in distance running as an exercise program, several aspects should be observed in order that the activity may become enjoyable and safe. *Runners World* (Mountain View, California) is a periodical that presents lay and popular articles by physicians, exercise physiologists, and coaches. The following is a checklist of items on which the distance runner should keep himself informed:

1. Full-chest breathing and full exhalation are important to avoid oxygen debt and rid lungs of carbon dioxide.

2. Requirements in rate of breathing should be established for each individual. As a rule of thumb, one complete inhalation and exhalation with each four steps (two strides) will avoid excessive oxygen debt.

3. Many runners hyperventilate in order to expel carbon dioxide while warming up and while ascending hills.

4. The point when the individual should speed up to his best distance pace should be established. Starting prematurely (before reaching peak circulation) will involve premature fatigue from oxygen debt; starting too late will cause a slower race.

5. In addition to the mileage one runs per week, interval training should be considered to prepare leg muscles for more power and faster pace. Interval training involves sprinting at top speed to the point of getting winded (usually 25 to 50 yards), running at regular pace for approximately the same distance until regular breathing for distance running is restored, and repeating this cycle continuously throughout the run. As training continues, the sprinting distance should be continually lengthened and the regular running distance should be shortened.

6. The "final kick," that is, the increase in speed or sprinting at the end of a race, should be learned cautiously. Human beings cannot estimate precisely what resources they will have left near the end of a race; consequently, some reserve is usually left that can be expended for an improved time. The practice of a final kick prepares the individual psychologically to run at top speed while feeling exhausted and, like intervals, will condition the muscles for future runs.

7. Gait is important to consider for energy conservation and to avoid injuries. Inexperienced distance runners can often detect an improper gait when running alongside an experienced runner. The head may bob up and down because the runner springs off the ground with each stride, raises knees too high, lands stiff-legged and heavy, stays on only the balls of the feet or a combination of these. What is appropriate for leaning into a full sprint is inefficient for distance running. Level ground calls for smooth heel-to-toe running without excessive stride. The runner should lengthen stride and coast downhill and shorten stride and run on balls of the feet only while going up hill. If hamstring or calf problems develop, he should insert heel pads to raise the heel. If joint or arch problems develop, he should add insole cushioning or get better supported, cushioned running shoes. If feet are well accustomed to exercise, light running shoes are recommended. One pound on the feet is equal in work load to four pounds on the back.

8. Fluid intake is important in avoiding dehydration. While very little weight is lost warming up, a half pound of fluid per mile is commonly lost in steady-state running. Beyond 6 miles on a hot day and 10 miles on any day, the runner should not wait until the end of the race to replenish with fluid intake. The sphincter allowing water out of the stomach does not allow the body to restore fluid at the rate it is lost while running. Therefore, fluid should be taken before, during, and after a run. Solutions containing sugar should be avoided. The runner should walk briefly while drinking during a race unless he has learned to drink while running. If he waits until he is thirsty to drink during a long race, it is already too late.

9. Diet is important to attain maximal performance. Carbohydrates during the 72 hours before a race build up muscle energy, but an all-carbohydrate diet for several weeks before a race is deteriorating to both health and performance. Protein is needed to rebuild muscle and other body cells. Controlled research has shown that a noncarbohydrate (all protein and fat) diet starting 11 days before a race, culminated by a strenuous workout, then an all carbohydrate diet for the final three or four days with moderate training provides optimal endurance in an event or on treadmill tests.

10. The importance of body weight may be recognized through remembering that 4 pounds of excess fat carried in a 6-mile run is equivalent in work to carrying a 24-pound weight on a mile run or a 48-pound weight on a half-mile run. Weight loss is ill-advised just before a racing event, however, since one loses protein and carbohydrate proportionately to fat, and the former two substances are vital to build and sustain muscle cells. Carrying excess fat requires energy. The excess fat must be lost over weeks and months.

11. Tolerance for high body heat must also be examined for each individual. The carbohydrate and oxygen resources produce heat as well as kinetic energy. Excess fatty tissue and closed pores due to lack of warm-up will retard heat from being expelled. Ice water and ice, loose white clothing, billed or brimmed caps, fishnet shirts, or spray from garden hose while running are all important to avoid nausea from overheating.

The importance of a helper in the behavior management of a major life-style change is evident from the preceding paragraphs. It is also evident that the helper's role must consist of more than giving such health advice as "Get more exercise" if preventive health care is to be achieved. Most of all, it is apparent that a successful major life-style change requires extensive utilization of positive reinforcers, along with removal of negative reinforcers and hazards. To be successful, these must become well established in the client's life. The following sections on other life-style changes, while extremely important, will not be as extensive. The very important behavior management procedures may be generalized from the foregoing comments on exercise. Other acceptable resources on the different content areas are already available.

ANXIETY

Anxiety has often been characterized as a generalized fear-and-avoidance response. Unlike phobias, anxiety is not linked to specific fear-provoking stimuli. It is associated with high autonomic nervous system and exocrine glandular activity. It is often thought to reflect intrapsychic unresolved conflicts and is also closely associated with type A behavior of the coronary-prone personality and high-rate information processing (hyperscanning).

The type A pattern of coronary risk was first described by Freedman and Rosenman (1974). The pattern has been described by Caffrey as aggressive, impatient, hurried, competitive, and driven by a sense of time urgency. Bortner (1969), in the development of a brief rating scale, has used additional descriptions such as never late, anticipates, rushed, impatient, goes all out, does many things at once, emphatic expression, seeks recognition, fast, hard driving, many interests, and ambitious. Jenkins (1971) has presented an extensive review of research on type A behavior and other psychosocial factors. Rosenman and co-workers (1970) have shown type A behavior to be independent of other risk factors in coronary heart disease. Kenigberg and others have shown type A behavior to be associated with heart attacks in females as well as males. Meanwhile, Thiel (1973) has shown the broader concept of anxiety to be a risk factor with or without the presence of depression. Our own study has emphasized the importance of anxiety along with hyperscanning in the prediction of early recurrence of a myocardial infarction.

Intensive individual psychotherapy has been the treatment of choice for anxiety. This follows from the assumption that unresolved conflicts cause the anxiety. For example, needs for personal power, recognition, or affection may be in continual conflict with needs for passive comfort, decorum, or dependence. Repression or inadequate conceptualization of the conflict has prevented alternatives of action from being examined so that all needs are satisfied equally well. The typical goal of psychotherapy has been to gain insight into conflicts and to resolve them. Other goals have been to build more adequate skills by which to construe events and to anticipate their outcomes.

A second treatment of choice for anxiety is pharmacologic. Muscle relaxants and minor tranquilizers are often used in addition to psychotherapy or as a temporary substitute for it. There is no evidence that the pharmacologic intervention will modify coronary proneness even when it reduces anxiety.

More recently, behavior management techniques have been focused on the problems of anxiety, depression, and hostility. Meichenbaum and Turk (1976) have proposed three phases in the management of anxiety. In the first phase the client should be trained toward a conceptual framework that allows the development of a plan for what to do. The patient is urged to stop attending to the actual feelings of anxiety and to concentrate instead on the specific situational factors that give rise to the anxiety. It is the feelings that distract him from a plan of what to do in response to the anxiety-provoking situation. This plan may involve self-statements, self-imposed relaxation instructions, a rating of level of anxiety on a ten-point scale before, during, and after some particular problem solving action. Past responses to the anxiety are compared with new and alternative responses.

The second phase consists of the rehearsal of the coping skills to be carried out. This may be done with real, practiced, or imagined stimuli that have been anxiety provoking. The therapist and patient choose the type of rehearsal that best fits the patient and the problem.

In the third phase, the patient reports back to the therapist (trainer) about anxious and potentially anxious events. The presence, length, and intensity of anxiety is evaluated quantitatively and discussed. Alternative self-instruction procedures and reinforcement are discussed. The short-term goal is for the patient to put himself voluntarily into increasingly anxiety-provoking situations. The final goal is for the anxiety to be prevented by self-instructed strategies.

DEPRESSION

Depression is generally described as a sustained state of negative mood that in advanced stages will be associated with physical lethargy, psychomotor slowing, and even slowing of the cognitive processes. Liljefors and Rahe (1970) have described life dissatisfaction, no doubt associated with depression, to be a major risk factor. However, Jenkins (1971) has pointed out that depression, as measured by the Minnesota Multiphasic Personality Inventory (MMPI), has not been consistently identified as a risk factor in various studies of coronary proneness. In our own study on recurrence, reported earlier, depression was a borderline predictor that fell from significance as further data was collected.

Lebovitz and others (1967) found MMPI depression scores to be especially high among nonsurvivors of coronary attacks. Bartle and Bishop (1974) found that those who survive in good health from heart attacks were low in depression. These findings suggest that while depression may not be a strong risk factor for the initial coronary attack, it may indeed affect the severity and recurrence factors that cause death from the first heart attack or soon after.

As with anxiety, depression has typically been treated with intensive individual psychotherapy. Tricyclic antidepressants have been found to be effective in the endogenous, as opposed to the reactive, form of depression. The latter is distinguished from the former by being precipitated by clearly identifiable life events. Recent work on genetics has helped differentiate between unipolar and bipolar depression, the latter having periods of euphoria or mania in between depressive attacks. No evidence exists that pharamacologic intervention has any effect upon the coronary proneness and survival implications associated with depression.

In a behavioral view of depression, Gnepp (1975) describes it as an unconditioned (unlearned, reflexive) reaction to failure. Conditioning occurs when a demand stimulus leads to a conditioned response to anticipate failure and subsequent depression. The purpose of treatment from this view would be to extinguish this conditioned reaction.

Meichenbaum's cognitive behavior management approach is now being applied to depression as well as to anxiety. Rush, Khatami, and Beck (1975) also describe a behavioral approach to depression. They believe that the unfounded generalization of negative mood and the selective remembering of negative events tend to perpetuate the depression. Consequently they launch programs for the patient to become physically active, to keep schedules of his own daily activity between meetings for the first three visits, to rate each activity separately on scales of pleasure and of mastery. Then, in the therapy session, these schedules are discussed to pinpoint areas of unwarranted generalization. Some periods are viewed as all bad, and enjoyable activity during the period is not discriminated. In addition, they recommended separate and parallel lists be kept by the spouse. These separate lists tend to rate the patient higher in mastery than the patient himself does. Also more periods are discriminated as enjoyable versus unenjoyable. Within this context of greater hedonistic discrimination and mastery satisfaction, more physical activities are encouraged.

The behavioral approach by Lazarus (1974) puts slightly more focus upon the reinforcement of positive thinking and evaluations. Development of new skills are emphasized. The future is discussed to project and formulate rewarding activities yet to come. Enjoying, self-asserting, and uninhibited responses are reinforced. Self-depreciating responses are negatively reinforced and eliminated.

McLean (1976) has summarized six models of depression: lack of behavioral reinforcement, cognitive distortion, life stress events, interpersonal disturbance, learned helplessness, and a "variable causes" model. From this summary, he has integrated a behavioral therapy approach that emphasizes various goals and reinforcers to be used in the treatment of depression within a time limited 12-week program. The goals include communication, production of successful behavior, social interaction, assertiveness, decision making, problem solving, and cognitive self-control.

Lewinsohn and co-workers (1976) have described an extensive 3-month limited behavior therapy program based on a central assumption that depression results directly from a history of lack of positive reinforcement. Although the program of treatment overlaps with others in terms of pleasant activities, social behavior, and involvement of others, a broad range of other features are also considered. Among these are response costs (depositing money with the therapist) for failing to attend appointments, home visits by the therapist to better assess home social interaction, sleep disturbance, and suicidal risk.

GENERAL STRESS

Independent of what reaction may occur, such as anxiety or depression, Theorell and Rahe (1971) have found the number of life changes to be high during the period just before a myocardial infarction as compared to other baseline periods before and after the MI. Jobs and family are often referred to as major sources of life stress. Moreover, recommending that an individual change jobs or make major modifications in his living situation can be hazardous. While some sources of stress may be removed, the advantages of removal must be weighed against the probability that any life change demands new and unexpected coping responses. Consequently, intervention to prevent coronaries would not ordinarily be conducted at this level if the individual is already at critically high risk. On the other hand, the individual at critically high risk may be advised to avoid making major life changes wherever possible until other risk factors are under control. Emotional support should be provided in dealing with those life problems that do have to be coped with.

SMOKING

Cigarette smoking has been widely emphasized and discussed as a risk factor (Kannel, 1973; Rosenman and others, 1970; Jenkins, 1971; Thiel and others, 1973; Theorell and Lind, 1973; Blackburn, 1975). Smoking is a difficult habit to extinguish and to replace with alternative satisfying behaviors. Behavior modification approaches so far have been the most effective. Any procedure to help an individual quit smoking should utilize the behavior management procedures described earlier. The *Journal of Abnormal Psychology* has featured a series of articles on mastering the termination of smoking. Evidence indicates that aversion therapy is a useful technique to help highly motivated subjects. Puffing a cigarette every six seconds in a hot steamy smoky room until the subject feels discomfort and wishes to stop is usually the basis of this procedure. These sessions, if continued repeatedly, will yield a negative association to the taste of tobacco. The expected outcome is that the client is unable to complete a cigarette or declines to take one puff. On the other hand, rare cases occur where individuals sustain their smoking behavior under these negative circumstances and build up tolerance. If so, the aversion therapy should be terminated. Recent techniques by Suedfeld and Ikard (1974) emphasize putting the subject into a stimulus-deprived chamber for a period of time before giving him reeducation treatment or aversion therapy. This approach is a benign application of "brain washing" principles, since the deprivation of stimulation increases the permanence of attitude changes. With all therapeutic approaches, motivation of the patient is important. Individuals who have a high certainty that smoking is affecting their health have the greatest success in quitting smoking. If health problems do exist, their physical status should be monitored closely during the therapy.

BLOOD PRESSURE

Recent biofeedback techniques have been developed to modify blood pressure in essential hypertension. Biofeedback involves presenting information to the subject about his own physiological responses so that he can learn to use subjective techniques to control and modify them. Blood pressure has represented a challenge to biofeedback researchers because of the problem of continuous monitoring of blood pressure. The reader is referred to the journal *Psychophysiology* for further references on biofeedback control of blood pressure.

DIET

In the history of approaches to heart disease, early emphasis was placed upon cholesterol as a risk factor. This led to diet as a major preventive approach. Later it was learned that metabolic factors relatively independent of diet were important in maintaining high cholesterol levels in the blood stream. Still later, other lipids, such as triglycerides, were emphasized as potential risk factors. A major distinction has been made between saturated and unsaturated lipids. Blackburn (1975) emphasizes that the presence of saturated lipids (typically solid at room temperature), not the substitution of unsaturated lipids (maize oil, olive oil), is the crucial factor in coronary risk. Based upon current knowledge, it appears that the elimination of saturated fats from the diet should be the major target for behavior management in diet. The reader is referred to Stuart and Davis (1972), also discussed in the following section, for behavioral management programs to control obesity.

OBESITY

Weight control and treatment of obesity have represented major areas where behavior management techniques have been highly successful. Stuart and Davis (1972) outline an extensive three-pronged approach to weight control: (1) identify and control the environmental factors that influence the amount, kind, and regularity of eating behavior; (2) regulate the nutritional input so that a new set of balanced, calorie-restricted food choices may be enjoyed; and (3) increase physical exercise to raise the individual's calorie ceiling for weight control. The latter step, aside from other advantages of exercise, serves to make the diet less restrictive. Stuart and Davis focus upon the assumption that the environment rather than the individual actually controls eating behavior. The controlling environmental stimuli that lead to excessive, inappropriate, and irregular eating should be identified. Availability of the stimuli should be decreased. The availability of reinforcing events that follow and strengthen the undesirable eating behavior should also be eliminated. Contrarily, environmental events that control desirable eating should be increased. The events that follow and reinforce the desirable eating behavior are also to be identified and increased. Crash diets and abrupt weight losses are strongly discouraged. Through careful programming the authors demonstrate that weight can be lost with only a minimal reduction of calories in the three-part program.

PREMATURE VENTRICULAR BEATS (PVBs)

Much emphasis has been placed upon the existence of premature ventricular beats as a risk factor in cardiographic data. No evidence yet exists that psychosocial factors well known to influence coronaries have a direct influence upon PVBs. The factors that mediate between PVBs and atherosclerosis are likewise little understood.

Whether the elimination of PVBs would constitute an amelioration of coronary risk is unknown. Thus, additional research is needed to examine whether other risk factors are important antecedents of PVBs and whether and when infarcts will occur through some other route. Such research would help advance the understanding of coronary risk and may shed light on when prevention measures will be successful.

FAMILY HISTORY

It has long been known that a history of coronary heart disease in the family background represents a factor of increased risk. However, it is a weak indicator. The great majority of people who are the victims of coronary heart disease have no immediate blood relatives with coronary heart disease. While individuals with a positive family history have a slightly higher incidence of heart attacks, a great number escapes the disease. The person who does have a positive family history is alerted to avoid the more major risk factors. In this way, the presence of heart disease in the family can work to the advantage of the individual and to the nurse practitioner or physician working with the individual in effective preventive care.

GENERAL PREVENTION

For further information on the general prevention of coronary heart disease, the reader is referred to Blackburn (1975); to the report of the Inter-Society Commission for Heart Disease Resources (1970); and to "Primary Prevention of the Atherosclerotic Diseases" (Circulation **42**:A-39, 1971). Also of value is a publication of the Scientific Meeting on Cardiac Rehabilitation of the International Society of Cardiology: *Myocardial Infarction: How to Prevent, How to Rehabilitate* (Boehringer-Mannheim, 1973).

REFERENCES

American Heart Association, Committee on Exercise: Exercise testing and training of apparently healthy individuals; a handbook for physicians, New York: 1972, The Association.

Bartle, S. H., and Bishop, L. F.: Psychological study of patients with coronary heart disease with unexpectedly long survival and high level function, Psychosomatics 15:68-69, 1974.

Blackburn, H.: Coronary risk factors: how to evaluate and manage them, Eur. J. Cardiol. 273:249-283, 1975.

Bortner, R. W.: A short rating scale as a potential measure for pattern A behavior, J. Chronic Dis. 22:87-91, 1969.

Brown, C.: The techniques of plethysmography. In Brown, C., editor: Methods of psychophysiology, Baltimore, 1967, The Williams & Wilkins Company, pp. 57-74.

Cooper, K. W.: Aerobics, New York, 1968, M. Evans and Co., Inc.

Cromwell, R. L.: Stimulus redundancy and schizophrenia, J. Nerv. Ment. Dis. 146:360-375, 1968.

Davidson, P. O., editor: The behavioral management of anxiety, depression, and pain, New York, 1976, Brunner/Mazel, Inc.

Duncombe, W. C.: The colorimetric microdetermination of long-chain fatty acids, Biochem. J. 88:7-10, 1963.

Ebbinghaus, H.: Das Gedachtnis: untersuchungen experimentellen Psychologie, Leipzig, 1885, Duncker & Humblot. Ruger, H. A., and Bussenias, C. E., translators: Memory: a contribution to experimental psychology, New York, 1913, Columbia University Teachers College.

Freedman, M., and Rosenman, R. H.: Type A behavior and your heart, Greenwich, Conn., 1974, Fawcett Publications.

Gnepp, E. H.: Principles of learning and depressive neurosis, Psychology 12:1-7, 1975.

Harris, J. G.: Size estimation of pictures as a function of thematic content for schizophrenic and normal subjects, J. Pers. 25:651-671, 1957.

Hathaway, S. A., and McKinley, J. C.: Minnesota multiphasic personality inventory, Minneapolis, 1943, University of Minnesota.

Hollingshead, A. B.: Two-factor index of social position, New Haven, Conn., 1957, Yale University Press.

Hunt, W. A., editor: New approaches to behavioral research on smoking, J. Abnorm. Psychol. (special issue) 81, no. 2, 1973.

Jenkins, C. D.: Psychological and social precursors of coronary disease. I and II. N. Engl. J. Med. 1971, 284:244-255; 284:307-317.

Kannel, W. B.: The natural history of myocardial infarction: the Framingham study, Leiden, The Netherlands, 1973, Leiden University Press.

Kenigberg, D., Zyzanski, S. J., Jenkins, C. D., Wardwell, W. J., and Licciardelio, A. T.: The coronary prone behavior pattern in hospital patients with and without coronary heart disease, Psychosom. Med. 36:344-351, 1974.

Kohout, M., Kohoutova, B., and Heimberg, M.: The regulation of hepatic triglyceride metabolism by free fatty acids, J. Biol. Chem. 246:5067-5074, 1971.

Lacey, J. I.: Psychophysiological approaches to the evaluation of psychotherapeutic process and outcome. In Rubenstein, A., and Parloff, M. B., editors: Conference on research in psychotherapy, Washington, D.C., 1958, National Publishing Company, pp. 160-208.

Lazarus, A. A.: Multimodal behavioral treatment of depression, Behav. Therapy 5:549-554, 1974.

Lazarus, R. S., Speisman, J. C., and Mordkoff, A. M.: The relationship between autonomic indicators of psychological stress: heart rate and skin conductance, Psychosom. Med. 25:19-30, 1963.

Lebovitz, B. Z., Shekelle, R. B., Ostfeld, A. M., and Paul, O.: Prospective and retrospective psychological studies in coronary heart disease, Psychosom. Med. 24:265-272, 1967.

Lewinsohn, P. M., Biglan, A., and Zeiss, A. M.: Behavioral treatment of depression. In Davidson, P. O., editor: The behavioral management of anxiety, depression, and pain, New York, 1976, Brunner/Mazel, Inc.

Liljefors, I., and Rahe, R. H.: One identical twin study of psychosocial factors in coronary heart disease in Sweden, Psychosom. Med. 32:523-542, 1970.

McCormick, W. K.: Cardiac rate and size estimation in schizophrenic and normal subjects, Ph.D. thesis. Madison, 1974, University of Wisconsin.

McLean, O.: Therapeutic decision-making in the behavioral treatment of depression. In Davidson, P. O., editor: The behavioral management of anxiety, depression, and pain, New York, 1976, Brunner/Mazel, Inc.

Meichenbaum, D., and Turk, D.: The cognitive-behavioral management of anxiety, anger, and pain. In Davidson, P. O., editor: The behavioral management of anxiety, depression, and pain, New York, 1976, Brunner/Mazel, Inc.

Mueller, E. F., Kasl, S. V., Brooks, G. W., and Cobb, S.: Psychosocial correlates of serum urate levels, Psychol. Bull. 73:238-257, 1970.

Nowlis, V.: Research with the Mood Adjective Checklist. In Tomkins, S., and Izard, C. E., editors: Affect, cognition, and personality, New York, 1965, Springer Publishing Co., Inc.

Official Royal Canadian Air Force exercise plans for physical fitness, New York, 1962, Pocket Books (revised U.S. edition).

Rosenman, R. H., Freedman, M., Straus, R., Jenkins, C. D., Zyzanski, S. J., and Wurm, M.: Coronary heart disease in the Western Collaborative Group Study, J. Chronic Dis. 23:173-190, 1970.

Rotter, J. B.: Generalized expectancies for internal vs. external control of reinforcement, Psychol. Monographs 80, no. 609, 1966.

Rush, A. J., Khatami, M., and Beck, A. T.: Cognitive and behavior therapy in chronic depression, Behav. Ther. 6:398-404, 1975.

Schmale, A.: Object loss, "giving up," and disease onset. Symposium on medical aspects of stress in the military climate, Washington, D.C., 1964, Walter Reed Army Institute of Research, pp. 433-448.

Silber, R. H., and Porter, C. C.: Determination of 17, 21-hydroxy-20-ketosteroids in urine and plasma, Methods Biochem. Anal. 4:139, 1957.

Silverman, J.: The problem of attention in research and theory in schizophrenia, Psychol. Rev. 71:352-379, 1964.

Stuart, R., and Davis, B.: Slim chance in a fat world, Champaign, Ill., 1972, Research Press.

Suedfeld, P., and Ikard, F. F.: Use of sensory deprivation in facilitating the reduction of cigarette smoking, J. Clin. Consult. Psychol. 42:888-895, 1974.

Theorell, T., and Lind, E.: Systolic blood pressure, serum cholesterol, and smoking in relation to sociological factors and myocardial infarction, J. Psychosom. Res. 17:327-332, 1973.

Theorell, T., and Rahe, R. H.: Psychosocial factors and myocardial infarction: an inpatient study in Sweden, J. Psychosom. Res. 15:25-39, 1971.

Thiel, H. G., Parker, D., and Bruce, T. A.: Stress factors and the risk of myocardial infarction, J. Psychosom. Res. 17:43-57, 1973.

Ullmann, L. P.: An empirically derived MMPI scale which measures facilitation-inhibition of recognition of threatening stimuli, J. Clin. Psychol. 18:127-132, 1962.

Warner, D. C.: Cardiac rate responses in two groups of schizophrenics during performance on a size estimation task, M. A. thesis. Madison, 1973, University of Wisconsin.

Wehmer, G. M.: The effects of a stressful movie on ratings of momentary mood, experienced anxiety, and plasma 17-hydroxycorticosteroid level in three psychiatric groups, Ann Arbor, Mich., 1966, University Microfilms.

TRANSCRIPT OF LOW INFORMATION TAPE

This recording has been prepared to acquaint you with the specially developed coronary care unit at Holy Cross Hospital.

By now you have probably noticed, and may be wondering about, some of the features of your hospital room. You are not sharing it with anyone; still, yours is not what you would call a private room. You are constantly visible to the nurses and doctors and they often look to see how you are doing. Also, there are other patients near you in rooms similar to yours. These rooms—the one you are in, and five similar ones near you—form a special part of our hospital and are referred to as the coronary care unit or the CCU. You have been placed in the coronary care unit rather than in a regular hospital room or ward because your doctor believes you may have had a coronary or heart attack or because you have some of the symptoms of a heart attack.

The doctors here at Holy Cross, and at many other hospitals as well, have learned from experience that patients who are suspected of having had heart attacks can be treated much more effectively in a unit like this than in the regular hospital area. The CCU is especially designed and staffed with highly trained nurses to provide the most rapid possible treatment if an emergency arises. We know that otherwise serious problems may be easily treated and with excellent results when they are promptly recognized. That is why we have arranged the rooms in the coronary care unit as we have.

There are always at least two nurses or nursing aides present in the unit. Many times there are additional medical personnel present, and much of the time a resident physician is here. All of the nurses, the aides, and other personnel here have had extensive and special training in the treatment of heart disease. In the past, when patients with heart problems were placed in rooms all about the hospital and were being cared for by nurses with a variety of training, it was not always possible to treat them as soon as problems developed. Their difficulties may have gone unnoticed for a longer period of time or their nurses might not have recognized the exact nature of the problem as quickly as your present nurses.

You may have noticed that almost the first thing done when you arrived in the unit was to have some electrodes attached to your chest. These electrodes do not cause any discomfort or pain other than some occasional irritation of the skin. Most patients don't have any irritation of the skin. Most patients don't have any irritation at all, but if you do, just let us know about it. The discomfort can be cleared almost immediately by simply moving the electrodes to another location on your chest. The electrodes conduct the electrical activity of your heart to a monitoring unit, a machine that is one of the great advances of medical science. You may see your heart's electrical activity, the electrocardiogram, on the display panel of the unit. The monitoring unit automatically records your electrocardiogram so that your nurses and doctors will have a record of your heart's activity. In addition to the hourly recordings, your nurse and doctor may take readings at any time they need to check on the performance of your heart. Besides these things, each heartbeat is indicated by a flashing light and beeping tone, which may be seen and heard from any part of the nursing station. Consequently, any irregularity of your heartbeat may be detected instantly. All patients have some irregularities, and most of them are unimportant. Your nurses have been thoroughly trained in how to recognize the significant irregularities in your heartbeat. The machine is also set to detect very low and very high heart rates and to signal the nurse when they occur. Like all mechanical warning systems, this one may sometimes give false alarms. It will signal the nurse if you move about in certain ways or if an electrode becomes loosened from your chest. These types of alarms are easily distinguished. Furthermore, the monitoring unit is constructed so that a nurse must come to your bedside to correct it even if she is certain that it is a false alarm. Because of special devices like this, and because of the high quality of our nurses, we expect your recovery to be smooth and uneventful.

In order to help you recover, the number of visitors you may have, your use of the telephone, and the number of flowers you may have at your bedside will be restricted. Our observations are that sometimes patients recover more quickly if they are not visited too much. Of course, we know that your relatives are concerned about your condition and want to be as near to you as is possible. In order to accommodate them when they are unable to be at your bedside, there is a room just outside the unit where they may wait. In addition, we will telephone any member of your family if they are not here at the hospital.

Please feel free to discuss any problems you may have with any of the CCU staff. We are here to help you. We wish to do whatever we can to make your stay comfortable and beneficial.

TRANSCRIPT OF HIGH INFORMATION TAPE

In a previous recording you were told something about the coronary care unit and the nurses who will be caring for you during your stay here. Now I would like to give you some information about your heart.

In order to function properly, every part of your body needs a constant supply of fresh oxygen. That fresh oxygen is carried from your lungs to the various parts of the body by your blood. The main job of your heart is to pump your blood and its supply of fresh oxygen from your lungs to the rest of your body. It does that by contracting rhythmically and forcing the blood through your arteries and veins.

Your heart is made of many muscle bundles. The technical term for these muscles is myocardium. Like all of your other muscles, your myocardium or heart muscle also needs fresh oxygen. It receives that oxygen from its own blood supply coming through your coronary arteries to all parts of the heart. If one of these coronary arteries is blocked, the heart muscle in the area served fails to receive oxygen, and the muscle cells die. The dead heart muscle which results from the blockage of a coronary artery is called a myocardial infarction. Infarct means tissue which has died because of lack of oxygen and myocardial refers to heart muscle, hence the term myocardial infarction for heart muscle which has died because of a lack of oxygen.

When one of the coronary arteries is blocked, some of the heart's blood supply is cut off and pain results. In most people, the pain or pressure sensation is felt in the chest generally under the breast bone, but it may also be felt in one or both arms or up in the jaw. Pains of this type are frequently accompanied by sweating, nausea, and shortness of breath and are often a person's first indication that he is having a myocardial infarction or, in more common language, a coronary, or heart attack. All myocardial infarctions are not accompanied by pain, and pains of this type are not always signs of a myocardial infarction. Some people develop partial, rather than complete, blockage of their coronary arteries. In cases of partial blockage of a coronary artery, some blood does get to the heart and the muscle tissue does not actually die; it is just generally taxed. In such cases, chest, arm, or jaw pains appear only after unusual physical exertion, after eating, or in cold weather. Pain of this type is called angina pectoris. The pain of angina pectoris is less intense, though still often severely uncomfortable, than the pain associated with myocardial infarction and is usually not accompanied by sweating and nausea. Furthermore, angina pectoris is quickly relieved by stopping exertion or by placing nitroglycerin under the tongue. Nitroglycerin and the stopping of exertion do not usually stop the pain of myocardial infarction.

Remember you were told that your monitoring unit measures and records the electrical activity of your heart and that the obstruction of a coronary artery results in the death of heart muscle, that is, results in myocardial infarction. Part of the value of measuring and recording the electrical activity of the heart stems from the fact that dead muscle tissue does not conduct electricity. Therefore, the electrical activity of the hearts of persons who have had myocardial infarctions and the conduction of that electricity is often different from that of persons who have not had myocardial infarctions. Consequently, monitoring units of the type to which you are connected may assist your doctor in assessing the degrees, if any, of heart damage which you may have suffered. While the monitoring unit may *assist* your doctor in assessing the degree of damage to heart muscle, it is not possible for any single monitoring unit to assess the electrical activity of the entire heart. Therefore, it is possible for a person to have heart damage which is not detected at all or is only partially detected by the monitoring unit. It is necessary, therefore, for the doctors to learn more about your heart, so that while you are here a more detailed electrocardiogram will be taken with another machine from time to time. The *main* purpose, however, for attaching you to a monitoring unit while you are in this unit is not to assess the extent of any possible myocardial infarction but rather to show the regularity and speed with which your heart beats.

People are often concerned about how well their heart will work after they have had a myocardial infarction. As surprising as it may seem, a heart frequently pumps as much blood and functions just as efficiently after a myocardial infarction as it did before the infarction. There are several reasons for this. For one thing, the body begins to act to restore a blood supply to the heart through other arteries as soon as a coronary artery becomes obstructed. In this way, the extent of the infarction, that is, the amount of heart muscle that actually dies, is minimized. More importantly, healing and time tend to overcome any functional weakness which may result from an infarction. It is possible to see why time and healing make so much difference by realizing that dead heart muscle turns into a scar very much like the scar that results from surgical incision which a doctor makes in the abdominal muscle when he removes an appendix. Right after an appendectomy, the abdominal muscle is weak. Gradually, scar tissue forms, and the abdominal muscle wall becomes as strong as it was before the operation. It is the same way with the dead heart muscle—the heart may be as strong as it ever was.

Since dead heart tissue does not conduct electricity and the electrocardiogram remains abnormal even after the heart has regained its full functioning power, other devices or diagnostic techniques must be used to help assess the heart's recovery. One simple and extremely easy way to assess the functioning of the heart is to measure blood pressure. You will recall that the main function of the heart is to force blood through the arteries and veins to all parts of the body. By measuring the pressure of the blood as it moves through your arteries and veins, it is possible to determine how forcefully your heart is working.

Immediately after a myocardial infarction, the pumping power of the heart is often diminished, and that is why a person who is suspected of having had a myocardial infarction must at first remain relatively inactive. If the heart's power is diminished, it can less readily meet and may be damaged trying to meet the extra demands for pumping blood which result from exertion. The time after an attack and during which a heart's pumping power may be diminished varies from patient to patient and depends upon the size of the infarct. In general, the most critical period is the first five to ten days after the infarct occurs. Accordingly, patients usually leave the CCU and go to a regular hospital unit within ten days after their admission to CCU.

A question which is uppermost in the minds of many patients is, "Will I be able to return to work?" The answer is that the great majority of patients return to their regular work without any restrictions whatsoever. At this particular time, even your physician may not know when you will be able to work again, but he will appreciate your telling him any of your fears or concerns and will answer your questions to the best of his ability.

Many patients are also worried about whether they will have another heart attack. You may know that statistics clearly indicate that people who have had one heart attack are more prone to have another. Statistics also show very definitely that if weight and diet are controlled, and particularly regular, moderately strenuous exercise is performed, the likelihood of having a second heart attack is greatly lessened. Let me tell you more about the relationships between exercise, diet, weight, and the likelihood of heart attacks.

There appears to be a definite relationship between being grossly overweight and having heart attacks. It has been clearly established that heart function is impaired in the obese individual. For that reason, physicians often recommend that heart patients reduce their weight by diet. A crash diet is not recommended. Simply leaving a few items such as bread, potatoes, milk, and desserts out of a regular day's meal is usually sufficient. Eating serves to relieve tension, and a very strict diet will frequently make you more nervous. Weight reducing diets are not the only types of diet which heart patients may be urged to use. It is clearly established that the presence of increased blood level of triglycerides and cholesterol are *related* to increased risk of heart attack. Because of this relationship, and even though there may be some disagreement about its significance, heart patients are often urged to reduce their intake of animal fats and of dairy products such as butter, cream, milk, and cheese.

Animal fats contain more saturated fats and are more closely associated with the high risk of having a heart attack than are vegetable or polyunsaturated fats. Of all of the fatty substances, cholesterol seems to be the most closely associated with high risk of heart disease. Eggs, shell fish, and organ meats, as for example, liver, are particularly high in cholesterol and for that reason heart patients are often urged to reduce their intake of them. While it is often important to reduce the amount of saturated fat and cholesterol which is ingested, it is also important to maintain a well-balanced diet. For example, moderate amounts of fat are essential to good health so that one should not completely eliminate fats from the diet. For reasons like these, the heart patient should not change his eating habits except under the direction of a physician. Your doctor will be glad to tell you about the foods which you should and should not eat. Pamphlets are also available from the local heart association describing these diets.

Exercise is perhaps the most important factor in preventing coronary disease. There are several reasons for this. One of the reasons is illustrated by the fact that even patients who are on a high cholesterol diet do not have high levels of cholesterol in their blood if they exercise regularly and keep their weight down. Another reason is that since the heart is a muscle, it is strengthened and its blood flow increased by exercise. Consequently, exercise can condition the heart so that unusual amounts of exertion or other taxing events will be much less likely to damage it. For reasons like these, some doctors actually have heart patients gradually increase the amount of vigorous exercise they take. On the other hand, unusually strenuous exercise in an unconditioned person may aggravate a heart problem. We are all familiar with the fact that many men have heart attacks while shoveling snow. Here we are dealing with multiple factors of work and environment. The secret to benefiting from exercise is to take the proper amount of the proper kind. The surest way to do this is to rely upon your physician for guidance. Among other things, he will tell you that isometric exercises, those in which you simply oppose one group of muscles against another or against an immovable object, are largely useless in preventing heart disease. They simply improve the general muscle strength. Running and stair climbing are among the more beneficial and readily available exercises. Still, no heart patient should undertake any program of exercise without first consulting his physician.

Two other factors have been related to increased risk of heart disease; they are smoking and emotional strain. Heavy cigarette smoking is statistically associated with heart disease. Pipe and cigar smoking seem less harmful. There is also evidence that within months or, at most, a few years after a person, even a heavy smoker, quits smoking, his chances of having a heart attack have been reduced to the level of similar persons who have never smoked. For that reason, heart patients are often advised not to smoke.

It has been observed that many heart patients are overly conscientious. They take their work and financial obligations extremely seriously. This makes it seem advisable for a person with a heart condition not to accept responsibilities outside of his necessary home duties and work. It is also advisable to avoid those situations which seem particularly upsetting and to attempt to slow the psychological pace of one's life. It is often not necessary to drastically reduce the number of things which one does but rather just to change the intensity or haste with which one does them.

Let me conclude by saying that I hope you have found this recording to be interesting and informative. If you would like to hear it again, just ask the young lady who brought it to you or ask your nurse. If you would like to have a written copy of the material on this recording, you need also just ask the young woman who played the tape for you or ask your nurse. Also, there are other written materials about heart attacks and their treatment available upon request. Just ask your nurse for them. Finally, please feel free to ask questions of anyone in the CCU anytime you are curious about something. We are all here to help you.

Appendix C

ULLMANN SCALE OF INHIBITING VERSUS FACILITATING ANXIETY *

The following scale has often been referred to in this book as a measure of anxiety as such, as well as a measure of repression-sensitization. This is because the objective measures of these various constructs are so highly correlated that it is not justifiable to treat them as separate constructs. Also, our results did not support the notion that low sensitization (anxiety) reflected repression.

The instructions and a small sample of the items are as follows:

OPINION SURVEY

This inventory consists of a number of statements. Read each statement to yourself and decide whether it is *true as applied to you or false as applied to you.*

Remember to give YOUR OWN opinion of yourself. Try to answer all of them.

F   1. I am certainly lacking in self-confidence.

F   2. I do many things that I regret afterwards. (I regret things more or more often than others seem to.)

F   3. I sometimes keep on at a thing until others lose their patience with me.

F   4. Someone has it in for me.

---

*Acknowledgment is made to the Psychological Corporation and to Leonard Ullmann for permission to quote these sample items.

ROTTER LOCUS OF CONTROL SCALE*

NOTE: The "a" or "b" choice is italicized according to which item should be scored in the direction of internal locus of control. If neither choice is italicized, the item is a filler that should not be scored. The reader should note that in much of the research literature the alternative scoring procedure is used where external locus of control is scored in the high direction.

I more strongly believe that: (Choose "a" or "b" in each item.)

2.   a. Many of the unhappy things in people's lives are partly due to bad luck.
     b. People's misfortunes result from the mistakes they make.
3.   *a.* One of the major reasons why we have wars is because people don't take enough interest in politics.
     b. There will always be wars, no matter how hard people try to prevent them.
4.   *a.* In the long run people get the respect they deserve in this world.
     b. Unfortunately, an individual's worth often passes unrecognized no matter how hard he tries.
5.   a. Without the right breaks one cannot be an effective leader.
     b. Capable people who fail to become leaders have not taken advantage of their opportunities.
6.   a. No matter how hard you try some people just don't like you.
     b. People who can't get others to like them, don't understand how to get along with others.

---

*Acknowledgment is given to the author, Julian B. Rotter, and the American Psychological Association for permission to quote these sample items.

SEVERITY INDEX

Definition	Severity I* (Most severe condition manifested within first 24 hours after admission to unit. Check only one.)	Severity II* (Most severe condition manifested at any *other* later time while on unit. To be filled out at end of patient's stay. Check only one.)
Mild. No evidence of cardiac failure apart from a transient rise in the jugular venous pressure.		
Severe. Definite evidence of circulatory embarrassment, including prostration, hypotension, or evidence of cardiac failure.		
Cardiogenic shock or cardiac arrest. Systolic arterial pressure below 80 mm Hg, pallor, cyanosis, sweating cold skin, oliguria, and failure to improve within half an hour after relief of pain and the administration of oxygen. Or severe arrhythmia.		

*A check for mild = 1; a check for severe = 2; a check for shock = 3.

146

Appendix F

COMFORT INTERVIEW*

COMFORT KEY: 4 = definite yes
              3 = qualified yes
              2 = qualified no
              1 = definite no

1. Have you been bored during your stay in CCU? (yes) How much of the time? What would
   have made your stay less boring for you? (no) What kept you from being bored?
2. Have you been comfortable during your stay? (yes) All of the time? Can you tell me some
   specific things that have made you comfortable? (no) How much of the time have you been
   uncomfortable? What would have made you more comfortable?
3. Have the nurses been reassuring? (yes) Were they reassuring all of the time? In what ways
   have they been reassuring? Is there something the nurses *say* that is reassuring? Something
   in their attitude? (no) What was it that makes you say that? How often did it happen?
4. How do you feel about having been attached to the monitoring unit? Do you wish you had
   not been attached to it? Have you been aware of the monitoring unit? Are there particular
   times when you were more aware of it than usual? Has the monitor disturbed you and how?
   Has its presence affected the way you feel about CCU? How?
5. If you knew someone who had a heart attack, would you urge him to come to this unit?

*SCORING: For each of the five items use the comfort key to score how the patient described his com-
fort level.

NOWLIS MOOD ADJECTIVE CHECKLIST*†

Each letter, A, B, C, D, E, F, G, H, I, J, and K, represents a separate mood category for aggression, anxiety, surgency, elation, concentration, fatigue, social affection, sadness, skepticism, egotism, and vigor respectively.

KEY: vv = very valid description = 3
v = valid description = 2
? = uncertain = 1
no = not valid = 0

A	angry	vv	v	?	no
B	clutched up	vv	v	?	no
C	carefree	vv	v	?	no
D	elated	vv	v	?	no
E	concentrating	vv	v	?	no
F	drowsy	vv	v	?	no
G	affectionate	vv	v	?	no
H	regretful	vv	v	?	no
I	dubious	vv	v	?	no
J	boastful	vv	v	?	no
K	active	vv	v	?	no
A	deviant	vv	v	?	no
B	fearful	vv	v	?	no
C	playful	vv	v	?	no
D	overjoyed	vv	v	?	no

*Acknowledgment is given Vincent Nowlis and Springer Publishing Company for permission to quote items from the Mood Adjective Checklist.
†SCORING: Use the key to assign weight to each response, and compile a separate score for the A items, B items, and so on.

148

E	engaged in thought	vv	v	?	no
F	sluggish	vv	v	?	no
G	kindly	vv	v	?	no
H	sad	vv	v	?	no
I	skeptical	vv	v	?	no
J	egotistical	vv	v	?	no
K	energetic	vv	v	?	no
A	rebellious	vv	v	?	no
B	jittery	vv	v	?	no
C	witty	vv	v	?	no
D	pleased	vv	v	?	no
E	intent	vv	v	?	no
F	tired	vv	v	?	no
G	warmhearted	vv	v	?	no
H	sorry	vv	v	?	no
I	suspicious	vv	v	?	no
J	self-centered	vv	v	?	no
K	vigorous	vv	v	?	no

Appendix **H**

COOPERATION INTERVIEW

When patients with heart conditions leave the hospital, their physicians invariably tell them that they must change many of their ways of living to guard against future heart attacks. People react very differently to these instructions.

Some people feel that their mode of living is so central to their happiness and satisfaction that they would rather continue to live as they did before their heart attack and for a shorter time than change any part of their way of living and live longer. These people will usually not change anything about the way they live.

Other people feel that the most important thing of all is to live as long as possible. They feel that they can accommodate to any way of living and enjoy it and that the most sensible thing to do is to change their lives in whatever way will allow them to live longer. These people usually change their lives in whatever ways the physician suggests.

Still other people feel that some aspects of their way of living, for example, working one's hours, are too important to change, even if not changing will cause them to die sooner. These same people feel that other things, for example, what they eat, are relatively unimportant. These people usually change some of their ways of living, but others do not.

Look at this card. Each word (none, a few, many, most, every) could be an answer to the question, "In how many ways would you change your life if your doctor told you that it was necessary to change COMPLETELY in order to assure you that you would not have a fatal heart attack in the near future. Now I want you to think about the idea of changing *completely*.

1. Did you smoke? (If no, go to 3.) How many cigarettes a day? Do you think even if your doctor told you that if you did not stop smoking completely you would have another heart attack, you would actually stop smoking completely?

2. If your doctor told you to spend 15 minutes three times a day or 45 minutes doing specific exercises, do you think you'd do them? How regularly?

150

3. If your doctor told you that you were to eat *no sweets,* no foods with starch in them, and that you were to lose 15 pounds and maintain that loss, do you believe you'd do it? How sure are you that you'd take it off and keep it off? Remember, now, no sweets and no starches.

Appendix I

GUIDELINES FOR UNDERSTANDING RESEARCH AND STATISTICAL ANALYSES

Individuals unaccustomed to dealing regularly with research and research findings will find the following guide helpful in reviewing the research and statistical data presented here.

An experiment

Much of the research presented here has employed the experimental method. Stated simply, in an *experiment* something is done to something else to see what happens. This definition may be analyzed to its three parts: (1) Do something, (2) to something else, (3) to see what happens. In the first part, the something that is done, the experimenter changes the state of a variable so that two or more states or conditions of the variable may be studied. Traditionally, this variable is referred to as the *independent variable*. In psychometrics, it is also called a *predictor variable*. In the second part of the definition, the "something else" is the *subject sample*, the objects or people being observed. The number of cases observed contribute to the stability of the results, and the symbol N is used to refer to the sample size. The third part, "to see what happens," is the outcome or result of the experiment. Traditionally, these dimensions of outcome are referred to as the *dependent variables*. Some experiments have only one dependent variable; only one result or dimension of outcome is of interest. Others have more. In the language of psychometrics, dependent variables are also referred to as criterion variables.

In the research study presented here, a number of independent variables were studied: high information (X) versus low information (M), high diversion (D) versus low diversion (Q), high participation (P) versus low participation (R), high anxiety or sensitization (S) versus low anxiety (R), hyper- or overscanning (O) versus hypo- or underscanning (U), internal locus of control (I) versus external locus of control (E),

152

acute MI patients on coronary unit versus coronary unit (on-ward) non-MI patients versus off-ward non-MI patients. No matter how many independent variables there are, the research design must allow each one to be varied separately and independently of the others, so that its individual effects may be studied. It will be noted that independent variables may be divided into stimulus variables (environmental conditions created by the researcher) and organismic variables (those conditions already inherent in the subjects at the beginning of the experiment).

The subject sample of the present study demands less explanation. This was the group of patients under 60 years of age consecutively admitted to the coronary care unit, except where practical external reasons prevented their study. There were also control patients from elsewhere in the hospital.

The dependent variables fell into three classes: recovery-related, cooperation-related, and comfort-related. There were 21 variables, mostly recovery-related. Recurrence of an acute MI, death, length of stay in the coronary unit, and length of stay in the hospital represent examples of the dependent variables.

No matter how simple or complex the experiment, its design should be viewed primarily in terms of the independent and dependent variables. In scientific journal articles the independent and dependent variables are often revealed in the title of the article: "The effect of _____ upon _____" or "_____ as a function of _____." If for a moment we think of the independent variable as X and the dependent variable as Y, these two common title formats would be translated as "The effect of X upon Y" and "Y as a function of X." When research is done on the effect of a new treatment drug versus placebo upon rate of improvement in a disease, drug versus placebo is the independent variable and rate of improvement is the dependent variable. Can you identify the independent and dependent variables in our stress experiment, where steroid levels, free fatty acid levels, digital pulse amplitude, digital blood volume, and heart rate were studied as a function of solvable task versus unsolvable task versus baseline activity?

A controlled experiment

Scientists have invented the controlled experiment as the most precise method yet devised for making observations and drawing conclusions. In a controlled experiment, as the scientist sets the different levels or conditions of the independent variable and the measure of outcome in the dependent variable, he keeps all other variables inoperative that might also influence the dependent variable. For a given experiment the scientist categorizes all of the variables of the universe into five categories: independent variables, dependent variables, controlled variables, extraneous (uncontrolled) variables, and parameter (irrelevant) variables. A *controlled variable* is a variable that potentially influences the dependent variable but whose effects have been removed from the experiment. An *extraneous variable* is one that affects the dependent variable but whose effects have not been removed from the experiment. A *parameter variable* is one whose variation will not have any effect upon the outcome of the experiment.

Variables may be controlled in different ways: keeping the variable constant, using exclusion criteria, counterbalancing, insuring that the changes in the variable occur randomly so that its effects are averaged out, using control groups that differ from each other in the magnitude or state of the variable in known ways, or allowing the variable to vary freely but recording its magnitude so that its effects may be removed statistically after the experiment by partial correlation or analysis of covariance.

Controlling a variable by holding it constant is illustrated in the present study by the diagnostic procedure. Different physicians use different criteria for diagnosing acute myocardial infarction. These criteria were kept constant by having all diagnoses performed by the same cardiologically trained physician who used a single set of U.S. Public Health Service criteria.

Controlling a variable through an exclusion criterion is illustrated in the present study by the age criterion. Complicating factors in addition to acute MI are more prominent in people over 60 years of age. Thus this variable was controlled simply by eliminating these older subjects.

Controlling a variable through randomization is illustrated by the assignment of subjects to the eight different nursing care conditions. The personality and physical status of the subject represent major variables determining recovery, cooperation, and comfort. While studying the effects of nursing care approaches, the personality and severity variables, of course, cannot be held constant. Therefore, subjects are assigned to different nursing care conditions without prior knowledge of their personality or physical status. In this way it is assumed that the latter variables are randomly distributed so that one personality or level of severity does not get overrepresented in any one nursing care group. In other words, the differences among subjects attributable to personality or severity of illness get averaged out.

Counterbalancing as a method of controlling a variable may be illustrated by consumer research that compares two different products, such as the quality of wine or the performance of a vacuum cleaner or lawn mower. In making a judgment, the sequence of comparison is an important variable to control. That is, a given judge may have a tendency to choose the first (or else last) product examined no matter what it is. To control the variable of sequence, half the judges examine product A first, then B. The other half are given B, then A. In the present study counterbalancing was considered but rejected with respect to the sequence of the solvable and unsolvable tasks in the stress experiment. If counterbalancing had been applied, half of the patients would have received the solvable task first, then unsolvable. The other half would have received the reverse. Counterbalancing was not used here because the effects of a frustrating and failed performance upon the subsequent solvable task performance would be greater than and different from the effects of the reverse sequence.

Control groups may also be used to control variables. Some people erroneously conclude that controlled research occurs when a control group has been used. This is a naive assumption. A control group is simply one of many methods by which to control a variable. Use of a control group in the present study is illustrated by the on-ward and off-ward non-MI groups. We are interested in studying acute myocardial infarction, but this variable is confounded since all acute MI patients being studied are also coronary unit patients. Therefore, to determine what results to attribute to the acute MI and what to attribute to coronary unit treatment, non-MI patients were studied on and off the coronary unit.

When a particular variable in need of control varies in a separate way from the independent variable and if this separate variation can be recorded, then the variable may be controlled through statistical procedures following the experiment. Analysis of covariance and partial correlation are the most important among these statistical procedures. For example, if we are interested in the effect of the different nursing care conditions upon length of stay in the coronary unit but we know that severity of illness has an important effect upon length of stay, then we could obtain better answers to our research question if we covaried out the effects of severity of illness while examining the effect of the nursing care conditions upon hospital stay. As another example, if we are interested in the level of a patient's anxiety upon his degree of cooperation with nurses but we know that socioeconomic status also has an effect upon cooperation, then we could partial socioeconomic status out of the correlation between anxiety and level of cooperation.

Descriptive tables and graphs

Descriptive tables and graphs are much easier to read if you first note from the title or caption what are the independent and dependent variables. (For tables presenting p values and correlation matrices this suggestion does not apply.) In tables the conditions of the independent and sometimes controlled variables are usually designated in the titles of the columns of numbers and also along the left side in the titles of the rows of numbers. The magnitude of the dependent variable will typically be found in the body of the table. The purpose of the table is to assist the reader in comparing various magnitudes of the dependent variable in relation to various conditions of the independent variable. For example, length of stay in the hospital may be the dependent variable in question, and this would be examined as a function of the eight different nursing care conditions that constitute the independent variables.

Sometimes research results are better understood if they are visualized rather than set down in numbers. If so, a graph will be used instead of a table. In a line graph, the vertical axis usually designates the magnitude of the dependent variable, for example, the amount of steroids in the bloodstream. The horizontal axis will usually designate some condition of the independent variable, say, for example, before, during, and after the stressful task. Thus, if the line of the graph goes up, steroid level is higher during the time or experimental condition designated below on the horizontal axis; likewise, if the line of the graph goes down, the level of steroids has dropped at that time designated below.

In a bar graph the dependent variable is designated by the length of the bar, and a separate bar is drawn for each condition of the independent variable. Unlike the line graph, the length of the bar, designating the amount of the dependent variable, may be horizontal or vertical. A bar graph, for example, may designate length of hospital stay under given treatment or personality conditions.

Other scientific methods

What has been described here is the experimental method of controlled research. Other scientific methods also exist. The *clinical method* involves first observing one or more cases and building a set of testable hypotheses about what is taking place. A testable hypothesis is a hunch or proposition that can definitely be confirmed or disconfirmed by subsequent data. Then, as the next step, one intervenes in some way, as by asking additional questions or applying a treatment; then, further observations are made. The hypotheses are then revised into a hierarchy according to level of support the data has given to each. This cycle of scientific activity is repeated until some hypotheses have reached a confidence level so high that they can be viewed as conclusions. This clinical method has advantages over the experimental method in that new thinking and hypotheses are more often generated and compared; however, its serious limitations concern observer bias, inability to determine whether some extraneous variable is accounting for the results, and less quantification upon which to base the final conclusions.

Another scientific approach, the *test and measurements* (T and M) *method* involves measuring every conceivable variable that might be important in a situation and then analyzing all of the interrelationships through multivariate statistics. Human beings do not have the capacity to discern immediately the relationships among variables they are experiencing. For this reason it took several years to discover that retrolentalfibroplasia, a cause of blindness in premature infants, was related specifically to the variable of excessive oxygen shortly after birth. The great advantage of the T and M approach is that relationships among variables may be uncovered that would otherwise go undetected. The disadvantages, compared to the experimental method, are that the cause-effect relationship among variables cannot be discerned and the effects of variables that always covary together cannot be separated. Compared to the clinical method, the T and M approach has the disadvantage that initial measures thought relevant at the beginning of the study cannot be changed or modified until the project is completed.

From this brief review each of the different scientific methods can be seen to have advantages and disadvantages. However, the relationship between a given independent and dependent variable becomes the focal question, and more can be learned with greater certainty through the experimental method than through any other.

Descriptive and inferential statistics

Once measurements have been taken and scores recorded on all the relevant variables, conclusions can usually not yet be drawn. The amount of data may be large and perplexing. The final hurdle before drawing sound conclusions from data must be the application of logic and mathematics. Statistics is a branch of mathematics that allows the drawing of conclusions when numerous observations have been made.

The purpose of statistics may be separated into two categories: descriptive and inferential. *Descriptive statistics*, as the name implies, refers to the procedures of direct description of a sample of observations. No regard is given as to whether these observations are biased or may be generalized to other representatives of the same population. In the present research, for example, descriptive statistics would concern the characteristics of the subject sample, not whether the findings are to be judged significant for all people who have acute MIs.

A set of observations or scores from a sample of subjects may be described in only a finite number of ways. We learn early in elementary school that they may be described in terms of central tendency. For our purposes, the *mean* or *average* is the most useful descriptor of central tendency. For example, length of stay in the coronary unit for each nursing care group was described in terms of means. A mean will often be symbolized as $\overline{X}$.

Second, a set of scores may be described in terms of dispersion, that is, the amount of scatter or deviation of each score from a central point such as the mean. Most useful here is the *standard deviation*, sometimes symbolized as SD, *s*, or sigma. For purposes of interpreting research, the important thing is not to know the formula for standard deviation but to compare the various values of standard deviation in a table to determine whether certain groups of scores have greater scatter than others.

Third and fourth, groups of scores may also be described in terms of skewness and kurtosis. *Skewness* refers to a lopsided distribution of scores. Normally, the major cluster of scores, such as for body weight, fall in the middle of the distribution with a few people being extremely high and equally few people being extremely low. A normal distribution fits these characteristics. A skewed distribution occurs where the major cluster of scores are on the high side or low side rather than in the middle. A distribution of SGOT or white blood cell count would be skewed if people were in the normal range except for a disproportionate number with abnormally high scores. *Kurtosis* refers to how peaked or flattened out a distribution is, regardless of its skewness. People who are interested only in interpreting research reports typically need not be concerned about kurtosis.

A fifth measure in descriptive statistics is *correlation*. Types of correlation differ according to whether the scores are continuous, rank ordered, or dichotomized; however, the most common type of correlation is the Pearson (product-moment) correlation, symbolized as *r*. It is designed primarily to deal with continuous normal distributions of scores but under certain conditions may be applied to other types of data. Correlation is the description of relationship between two variables. An *r* may vary from -1.00 through zero to $+1.00$. If two variables are positively correlated, such as height and weight, the correlation will be greater than zero but not greater than the perfect correlation $+1.00$. This means that the greater an individual's height, the greater his weight will tend to be, and vice versa. Yet we know that the correlation is not perfect, that is, $+1.00$. If it were, we could determine everybody's weight exactly if we knew their height, and vice versa. If we square a correlation coefficient, this gives us the percentage of variance that the two variables share in common. Thus, as already indicated, a perfect correlation squared (1.00×1.00) gives us a value of 1.00, i.e., 100% of the variance shared between the two variables. The correlation between the intelligence of parents and their offspring is $r = +.50$. This tells us that a positive relationship exists. The greater the parent's intelligence, the greater the child's is likely to be. If we square .50 $(.50 \times .50)$, we get .25. This tells us that 25% of the variance in children's intelligence is accounted for by the intelligence of their parents. This means, of course, that 75% of the variance of intelligence in the offspring is accounted for by other factors including fortuitous and chance circumstances.

A negative correlation is illustrated by the relation between patient anxiety and the level of cooperation with nurses. If, for example, a correlation of $r = -.30$ exists, then as a small tendency the higher the anxiety, the less the cooperation, the lower the anxiety the greater the cooperation. The square of .30 is .09, indicating that only 9% of the variance of cooperation with nurses can be accounted for by the patient's anxiety.

Inferential statistics

The purpose of *inferential statistics* is to designate how likely a given finding is simply the result of chance. Stated a different way, if we repeat the experiment over and over again, with subjects drawn from the same population—for example, all acute MI patients everywhere—what are the chances that a given finding of ours would represent a mere chance fluctuation of the data from which we should not conclude statistical significance?

Two types of questions are put to the test of inferential statistics: questions concerning difference and questions concerning relationship.

Questions concerning difference occur when we have two or more groups of scores and want to know whether real variables or chance accounted for the group differences. When we are comparing only two groups of scores, such as the levels of MI patients and non-MI patients on a variable in Chapter 6, the t test is the most common statistical technique. If we wish to compare more than two groups, *analysis of variance* (ANOVA) is the most common. For example, in Chapters 2 and 3 the three dimensions of nursing care (high versus low information, high versus low diversion, high versus low participation) were arranged in a $2 \times 2 \times 2$ design, illustrated by a three-dimensional cube (see Fig. 2-2). Group comparisons and analyses of variance may be flexibly arranged, just as one can arrange children's blocks along different dimensions. A t test is illustrated by two blocks sitting side by side for comparison. An analysis of variance may be done by comparing two, three, four or more blocks (sets of scores) in a row, each block (cell) representing a different condition of the independent variable along a single dimension. Or we may have two dimensions of the independent variable, such as high versus low participation and internal versus external locus of control. In Table J-8 such an ANOVA is done for each of the 21 dependent variables. In such an example, we would have a 2×2 design. We could have more than two conditions along each dimension, such as a

3×2 design, a 4×8 design, and so on. Or, we could have more than two dimensions, as illustrated in the three-dimensional design in Fig. 2-2. A four-dimensional design might be illustrated by two of the nursing care designs in Fig. 2-2 sitting side by side, say one for male patients and the other for female patients. This, of course, would be a $2 \times 2 \times 2 \times 2$ design. And so on. As one increases the number of dimensions and the number of cells (conditions) within a dimension—no matter how complex the design—the reader is reminded that the same simple question is being asked: Do differences occur among the cells (sets of scores)?

The reader will sometimes note that a given t test is for correlated means or, in other cases, independent means. In analysis of variance the reader will sometimes note that a given dimension is designated a "within" or a "between" dimension. In each instance this refers to whether the scores in the different cells are from separate groups of unmatched subjects. If they are, the t test would be for independent means, and the analysis of variance would be for a "between" dimension. If, on the other hand, the scores in different cells are from the same group of subjects measured under repeated but different conditions (or from different groups of subjects who have been matched pairwise, tripletwise, and so on), the t test would be for correlated means and the analysis of variance would be for a "within" dimension respectively. While different statistical formulas should be used in each case, the reader need not regard these distinctions as important so long as the statistics are used correctly.

The great advantage of analysis of variance is that one can analyze in a single experiment not only the differences between two groups of scores, not only several different levels or conditions of an independent variable, not only two or more independent variables (dimensions) at the same time, but also how two or more independent variables may interact to bring about a result that could not be accounted for by each independent variable alone.

Let us again take as an example the nursing care study. Three dimensions were studied as independent variables: high versus low information (XM), high versus low diversion (DQ), high versus low participation (PR). Analysis of variance separates the amount of variance and significance of the *main effects*, the *interactions*, and the variance within cells *(error variance)*. That is, for a given dependent variable, let us say, length of stay in the coronary unit, the amount of variance and significance attributable to a patient's receiving high versus low information (XM) would be the first main effect. The other two main effects would be the diversion (DQ) and participation (PR) variables, each also yielding a separate statistical result.

Next would be the different possible two-way interactions: information × diversion $(XM \times DQ)$, information × participation $(XM \times PR)$, and diversion × participation $(DQ \times PR)$. If an interaction has an amount of variance significant enough to be interpretable, the difference between high and low found along one dimension varies according to what level exists along the other dimension. For example, if a significant interaction exists between information and diversion, then we can make either of the following statements: The difference between high and low information depends upon whether diversion is high or low in a given subject, or the difference between high and low diversion depends upon whether information is high or low.

Finally, we have the possibility of a three-way interaction: information $\times$ diversion $\times$ participation $(XM \times DQ \times PR)$, which, incidently, was actually found to be significant in the present study. A significant three-way interaction may be interpreted in either of the following ways: one cell is out of line (deviantly high or low) with its row, column, and layer membership or how one variable differs depends upon the status of the other two variables. With any interaction, two way or three way, one must do further simple analyses to determine the direction of the interaction. For example, the three-way interaction among the nursing care conditions resulted from high information, low diversion, and low participation being a combination that yielded an unusually long stay in the coronary unit and in the hospital.

Analysis of variance has the mathematical feature of all these sources of variance adding up precisely to the total variance. Thus, in a three-dimensional design examining independent variables A, B and C, the variances for A, B, C, $A \times B$, $A \times C$, $B \times C$, $A \times B \times C$, and the error variance should add up to the total variance. Significance is tested through an F ratio where a main effect (e.g., A) or an interaction $(A \times B)$ variance is in the numerator and appropriate error term is the denominator.

The other application of inferential statistics concerns questions of significance of relationship. Correlation, you will recall, is the most typical measure of relationship. Here we are simply asking the question: is a given correlation coefficient attributable to chance fluctuation of the data, or, contrarily, can chance be ruled out? The size of the sample (N) and the magnitude of the correlation coefficient (r) are used to compute the statistical significance of the correlation. In this computation, we are asking the following questions: if there were no relationship between the two variables and we were dealing only with random members, then what percentage of the time would we expect to get a correlation this large or larger?

The significance level and the degree of relationship reflected in a correlation are separate but important considerations. The larger the sample size, the greater the possibility that a small correlation, say $r = .15$, will be statistically significant. While this means that chance factors are unlikely to account for the relationship, it also means that barely over 2% of the variance is accounted for. Thus, a given relationship may be discarded as inconsequential even though it is stable and statistically significant. Significance level and degree of relationship answer two separate questions: is anything there at all that can be described as a stable relationship? If some relationship is in fact there, how strong is the degree of relationship?

The p value

The p value describes the probability of a given result being attributable only to chance. You have already noticed that many scientists choose an arbitrary criterion that a p value must be .05 or less in order to conclude a given finding is significant. In some cases, where the alternative of being wrong is costly, such as in cases of life or death, the p value will be set at lower levels, such as .01, .001, or some other level. This will also depend on the cost of assuming the results are not significant when they really are.

You have probably discovered that inequality signs are often used with p values. For example, $p < .05$ means the probability is less than 5%. A $p > .05$ means the probability is greater than 5%, and the result is usually considered not statistically significant (NS). These inequality signs help convey that the results have met at least a given level of confidence and that a more precise p value is unnecessary or unavailable.

You have also probably discovered that the lower the p value the greater the significance of the results, that is, the less likely they may be attributed to chance. If you are already cognizant of these aspects of the p value, you may have asked yourself the question: why do scientists and statisticians make life difficult by having the index of significance (the p value) inverse to the positiveness of the result? Why not say the data is significant at the 95% level rather than the 5% level, at the 99% level instead of the 1% level?

The answer to this question directly reflects the relativity of all scientific knowledge. In the beginning of these guidelines, you will recall, an experiment was defined as doing something to something else to see what happens. An experiment is when you manipulate or change the conditions of an independent variable to see what happens with respect to a dependent variable. A controlled experiment is when you have varied the conditions of your independent variable and kept other variables controlled that might also affect the dependent variable. The problem is that the scientist who has a significant result is never absolutely sure that the result is to be attributed to the independent variable he manipulated. The result may instead be due to another variable—one he failed to control as adequately as he had wished or an extraneous variable he could not control or an extraneous variable of which he was not even aware. The tool of statistics can take the scientist only so far in answering his research question, and no further. All that inferential statistics can do is tell the scientist the likelihood that chance alone is accounting for the results. If we set for ourselves the null hypothesis that no difference between groups (or no correlation) exists, we can say with a measurable level of confidence that the null hypothesis has been rejected. But, as far as the concluding of positive results is concerned, that the independent variable has indeed affected the dependent variable, every scientist is on his own. Statistics does not help him take that final step. The probability is not .95 or greater that the independent variable has affected (or bears a relationship to) the dependent variable. Instead, the probability is 5% or less that chance alone can account for the observed result.

TABLES OF RESULTS OF THE NURSING CARE STUDY

Table J-1. Summary of analyses of variance of recovery, comfort, and cooperation factors as a function of nursing care dimensions (information, diversion, and participation) in MI patients

Dependent variable title	Information (*X* vs *M*): direction/*N*/*p*	Diversion (*D* vs *Q*): direction/*N*/*p*	Participation (*P* vs *R*): direction/*N*/*p*	Interactions *p*
Recovery-related variables				
Days in CCU	NS	NS	NS	*DQ* × *PR*; .10 *DQ* × *PR* × *XM*; .01
Days in hospital	NS	NS	NS	*DQ* × *PR*; .02 *DQ* × *PR* × *XM*; .02
Low alarms	NS	NS	NS	*DQ* × *XM*; .07 *RP* × *XM*; .05
High alarms	NS	NS	NS	*DQ* × *XM*; .06 *PR* × *XM*; .06 *XM* × *DQ* × *PR*; .08
Sedimentation rate	NS	NS	NS	NS
Uric acid	NS	NS	NS	NS
Cholesterol	*M* > *X*; 44, 50; .07	NS	NS	NS
SGOT	NS	NS	NS	NS
LDH	NS	NS	NS	NS
WBC	NS	NS	NS	NS
Highest temperature	NS	NS	NS	NS
Return to work	*X* > *M*; 55, 55; .06	NS	NS	*XM* × *DQ*; .06
Subsequent MIs	NS	NS	NS	NS
Death	NS	*D* > *Q*; 56; .08	NS	NS
Severity change	NS	NS	NS	NS
Temperature change	NS	NS	NS	NS
Comfort-related variables				
Comfort interview	NS	NS	NS	*XM* × *PR*; .07

Table J-1. Summary of analyses of variance of recovery, comfort, and cooperation factors as a function of nursing care dimensions (information, diversion, and participation) in MI patients—cont'd

Dependent variable title	Information (X vs M): direction/N/p	Diversion (D vs Q): direction/N/p	Participation (P vs R): direction/N/p	Interactions p
Depression change	NS	NS	$R > P$; 43, .04	NS
Mood change	NS	NS	NS	NS
Cooperation-related variables				
Cooperation interview	NS	NS	$R > P$; 52, 57; .01	NS
Nurses' cooperation rating	NS	NS	NS	NS

Table J-2. Length of stay in coronary care unit and hospital of MI patients as function of nursing care dimensions

Information	Diversion	Participation	Summary code	Length of stay in CCU	Length of stay in hospital
High	Low	Low	QRX	7.8	28.0
High	High	High	DPX	7.5	25.3
Low	Low	High	QPM	6.9	22.1
Low	High	Low	DRM	6.3	23.1
Low	High	High	DPM	6.2	22.3
Low	Low	Low	QRM	5.9	22.7
High	High	Low	DRX	5.7	19.5
High	Low	High	QPX	5.5	20.9

Table J-3. Summary of analyses of variance of recovery, comfort, and cooperation factors as a function of nursing care dimensions (information, diversion, and participation) in non-MI patients

Dependent variable title	Information (X vs M): direction/N/p	Diversion (D vs Q): direction/N/p	Participation (P vs R): direction/N/p	Interactions p
Recovery-related variable				
Days in CCU	NS	D > Q; 30, 38; .05	NS	NS
Days in hospital	NS	D > Q; 30, 38; .05	NS	NS
Low alarms	NS	NS	NS	NS
High alarms	NS	NS	NS	NS
Sedimentation rate	NS	NS	NS	NS
Uric acid	NS	NS	NS	XM × DQ; .06
Cholesterol	NS	NS	NS	NS
SGOT	NS	D > Q; 29, 38; .06	NS	NS
LDH	NS	NS	NS	NS
WBC	NS	NS	NS	NS
Highest temperature	NS	NS	NS	NS
Return to work	NS	NS	NS	NS
Subsequent MIs	NS	NS	NS	NS
Death	NS	NS	NS	NS
Severity change	NS	NS	NS	NS
Temperature change	NS	NS	NS	NS
Comfort-related variable				
Comfort interview	NS	NS	NS	NS
Depression change	NS	NS	NS	NS
Mood change	NS	NS	NS	DQ × PR; .04
Cooperation-related variable				
Cooperation interview	NS	NS	NS	NS
Nurses' cooperation rating	NS	D > Q; 22, 29; .05	NS	NS

Table J-4. Summary of analyses of variance of recovery, comfort, and cooperation indices as function of nursing care (high versus low information) and personality (repression-sensitization) in MI patients

Dependent variable title	Nursing care variable: high vs low information (X vs M): direction/N/p	Personality variable: represser vs sensitizer (R vs S): direction /N/p	Interaction (X vs $M \times R$ vs S): p
Recovery-related variable			
Days in CCU	NS	NS	NS
Days in hospital	NS	NS	NS
Low alarms	NS	NS	NS
High alarms	NS	NS	.05 (see text)
Sedimentation rate	NS	NS	NS
Uric acid	$X > M$; 47, 50; .07	NS	NS
Cholesterol	NS	NS	NS
SGOT	NS	NS	NS
LDH	NS	NS	NS
WBC	NS	NS	NS
Highest temperature	NS	NS	NS
Return to work	$X > M$; 55, 54; .06	NS	NS
Subsequent MIs	NS	$S > R$; 57, 55; .01	NS
Death	NS	NS	NS
Severity change	NS	$R > S$; 58, 57; .05	NS
Temperature	NS	NS	NS
Comfort-related factors			
Comfort interview	NS	NS	NS
Depression change	NS	NS	NS
Mood change	NS	NS	NS
Cooperation-related factors			
Cooperation interview	NS	NS	NS
Nurses' cooperation rating	NS	$R > S$; 55, 55; .06	.02 (see text)

Table J-5. Summary of analyses of variance of recovery, comfort, and cooperation indices as function of nursing care (high versus low information) and personality (repression-sensitization) in non-MI patients

Dependent variable title	Nursing care variable: high vs low information (X vs M): direction/N/p	Personality variable: represser vs sensitizer (R vs S): direction/N/p	Interaction (X vs $M \times R$ vs S): p
Recovery-related variable			
Days in CCU	NS	NS	.0086 (see text)
Days in hospital	NS	NS	NS
Low alarms	NS	NS	NS
High alarms	NS	NS	NS
Sedimentation rate	NS	NS	NS
Uric acid	NS	NS	NS
Cholesterol	NS	NS	NS
SGOT	NS	NS	NS
LDH	NS	NS	NS
WBC	NS	NS	NS
Highest temperature	NS	NS	NS
Return to work	NS	NS	NS
Subsequent MIs	NS	NS	NS
Death	NS	NS	NS
Severity change	$M > X$; 13, 5; .03	$S > R$; 9, 9; .03	.0254 (see text)
Temperature change	NS	NS	NS
Comfort-related factors			
Comfort interview	NS	NS	NS
Depression change	NS	$S > R$; 23, 25; .001	NS
Mood change	NS	NS	NS
Cooperation-related factors			
Cooperation interview	NS	NS	NS
Nurses' cooperation rating	NS	NS	NS

Table J-6. Summary of analyses of variance of recovery, comfort, and cooperation indices as function of nursing care (diversion) and personality (scanning) in MI patients

Dependent variable title	Nursing care variable: high vs low diversion (D vs Q): direction/N/p	Personality variable: over vs under scanners (O vs U): direction/N/p	Interaction (DQ × OU): p
Recovery-related variable			
Days in CCU	NS	NS	NS
Days in hospital	NS	NS	NS
Low alarms	NS	NS	NS
High alarms	NS	$U > O$; 45, 32; .05	.002 (see text)
Sedimentation rate	NS	$O > U$; 50, 44; .09	NS
Uric acid	NS	NS	NS
Cholesterol	NS	NS	NS
SGOT	NS	NS	NS
LDH	NS	NS	NS
WBC	NS	NS	NS
Highest temperature	NS	NS	NS
Return to work	NS	NS	NS
Subsequent MIs	NS	NS	NS
Death	$D > Q$; 51, 53; .10	NS	NS
Severity change	NS	NS	NS
Temperature change	NS	NS	NS
Comfort-related factors			
Comfort interview	NS	NS	.04 (see text)
Depression change	NS	NS	NS
Mood change	NS	NS	NS
Cooperation-related factors			
Cooperation interview	NS	NS	NS
Nurses' cooperation rating	NS	NS	NS

Table J-7. Summary of analyses of variance of recovery, comfort, and cooperation indices as function of nursing care (diversion) and personality (scanning) in non-MI patients

Dependent variable title	Nursing care variable: high vs low diversion (*D* vs *Q*): direction/*N*/*p*	Personality variable: over vs under scanners (*O* vs *U*): direction/*N*/*p*	Interaction (*DQ* × *OU*): *p*
Recovery-related variable			
Days in CCU	NS	NS	.0634 (see text)
Days in hospital	*D* > *Q*; 25, 33; .04	NS	NS
Low alarms	NS	NS	NS
High alarms	NS	NS	NS
Sedimentation rate	NS	NS	NS
Uric acid	NS	NS	.0548 (see text)
Cholesterol	NS	*U* > *O*; 22, 25; .04	NS
SGOT	*D* > *Q*; 24, 33; .02	NS	NS
LDH	*D* > *Q*; 24, 31; .02	NS	NS
WBC	NS	NS	.0276 (see text)
Highest temperature	NS	NS	NS
Return to work	NS	NS	.0256 (see text)
Subsequent MIs	NS	NS	NS
Death	NS	NS	NS
Severity change	NS	NS	NS
Temperature change	NS	NS	NS
Comfort-related factors			
Comfort interview	NS	NS	NS
Depression change	NS	NS	NS
Mood change	NS	NS	NS
Cooperation-related factors			
Cooperation interview	NS	*U* > *O*; 20, 23; .04	NS
Nurses' cooperation rating	*D* > *Q*; 18, 28; .07	NS	NS

Table J-8. Summary of analyses of variance of recovery, comfort, and cooperation measures as function of nursing care (participation in self-treatment) and personality (locus of control) in MI patients

Dependent variable title	Nursing care variable: high vs low participation (P vs R) direction/N/p	Personality variable: locus of control (I vs E): direction/N/p	Interaction (PR × IE): p
Recovery-related variable			
Days in CCU	NS	$E > I$; 61, 58; .04	NS
Days in hospital	NS	NS	NS
Low alarms	NS	NS	NS
High alarms	NS	NS	NS
Sedimentation rate	NS	NS	NS
Uric acid	NS	NS	NS
Cholesterol	NS	NS	NS
SGOT	NS	NS	NS
LDH	NS	$E > I$; 59, 56; .03	NS
WBC	NS	NS	NS
Highest temperature	NS	$E > I$; 61, 58; .01	NS
Return to work	NS	NS	NS
Subsequent MIs	NS	NS	.0606 (see text)
Death	NS	NS	.0571 (see text)
Severity change	NS	NS	NS
Temperature change	NS	NS	NS
Comfort-related factors			
Comfort interview	NS	NS	NS
Depression change	NS	NS	NS
Mood change	NS	NS	NS
Cooperation-related factors			
Cooperation interview	$R > P$; 51, 59; .08	$I > E$; 56, 54; .06	NS
Nurses' cooperation rating	NS	NS	NS

Table J-9. Summary of analyses of variance of recovery, comfort, and cooperation measures as function of nursing care (participation in self-treatment) and personality (locus of control) in non-MI patients

Dependent variable title	Nursing care variable: high vs low participation (*P* vs *R*) direction/*N*/*p*	Personality variable: locus of control (*I* vs *E*): direction/*N*/*p*	Interaction (*PR* × *IE*): *p*
Recovery-related variable			
Days in CCU	*P* > *R;* 31, 37; .08	NS	NS
Days in hospital	*P* > *R;* 31, 37; .08	NS	NS
Low alarms	NS	NS	NS
High alarms	NS	NS	NS
Sedimentation rate	NS	NS	NS
Uric acid	NS	NS	NS
Cholesterol	NS	NS	NS
SGOT	NS	NS	NS
LDH	NS	NS	NS
WBC	NS	NS	NS
Highest temperature	NS	NS	NS
Return to work	NS	*E* > *I;* 10, 4; .07	NS
Subsequent MIs	NS	NS	NS
Death	NS	NS	NS
Severity change	NS	NS	NS
Temperature change	NS	NS	NS
Comfort-related factors			
Comfort interview	NS	NS	NS
Depression change	NS	NS	NS
Mood change	*I* > *E;* 21, 27; .03	NS	NS
Cooperation-related factors			
Cooperation interview	NS	NS	NS
Nurses' cooperation rating	NS	NS	NS

TABLES OF RESULTS FROM PREDICTION STUDY

Table K-1. Significant correlations in split-half samples and total sample for MI patients

Variable	Sample 1			Sample 2			Total sample		
	r	*N*	*p*	*r*	*N*	*p*	*r*	*N*	*p*
Locus of control (LC)									
17-OH-CS scan 6	.57	12	.05	.46	15	.05	.50	27	.005
Total Coronary Proneness (CP) scale	.21	62	.05	.21	62	.05	.21	124	.025
Repression-sensitization (R-S)									
Education	.30	61	.025	.35	61	.005	.32	122	.0005
Salary	.35	59	.005	.25	58	.05	.28	117	.005
Depression I	−.30	54	.025	−.26	53	.05	−.28	107	.005
Mood II: sadness	−.32	50	.025	−.41	50	.005	−.36	100	.0005
Denial: dissatisfaction	.23	61	.05	.46	50	.0005	.34	111	.0005
Denial: anxiety	.39	61	.005	.52	60	.0005	.46	121	.0005
CP Scale I, R-S	−.35	63	.005	−.22	62	.05	−.28	125	.005
CP Scale III, perfectionism	−.29	63	.01	−.32	62	.005	−.30	125	.005
Total CP scale	−.46	63	.0005	−.36	62	.005	−.41	125	.0005
Relatives' Ullmann	.83	16	.0005	.62	15	.01	.72	31	.0005
Size estimation (SE)									
Depression I	−.40	48	.005	−.35	49	.01	−.37	97	.0005
Sedimentation rate	−.30	45	.025	−.27	49	.05	−.28	94	.005
Subsequent MIs	−.35	51	.01	−.41	52	.005	−.39	103	.0005
Sex									
Salary	−.26	61	.025	−.23	59	.05	−.24	120	.01
Uric acid	−.25	53	.05	−.48	55	.0005	−.38	108	.0005
Age									
Mood II: elation	.25	51	.05	.27	50	.05	.21	101	.025
Denial: sexuality	.35	63	.005	.29	60	.025	.33	123	.0005
Education									
R-S	.30	61	.025	.35	61	.005	.32	122	.0005
Salary	.50	61	.0005	.30	59	.025	.37	120	.0005

Continued.

Table K-1. Significant correlations in split-half samples and total sample for MI patients—cont'd

Variable	Sample 1			Sample 2			Total sample		
	r	N	p	r	N	p	r	N	p
Mood I: elation	−.24	62	.05	−.32	61	.01	−.26	123	.005
Mood I: egotism	−.33	62	.005	−.25	61	.05	−.28	123	.005
Denial: self-interest	−.24	61	.05	−.34	59	.005	−.29	120	.005
Denial: sexuality	−.27	61	.025	−.32	59	.01	−.29	120	.005
Anticoagulants	.23	63	.05	.28	61	.025	.25	124	.005
Religion									
Salary	.22	61	.05	.27	59	.025	.25	120	.005
Salary									
R-S	.35	59	.005	.25	58	.05	.28	117	.005
Sex	−.26	61	.025	−.23	59	.05	−.24	120	.01
Education	.50	61	.0005	.30	59	.025	.37	120	.0005
Religion	.22	61	.05	.27	59	.025	.25	120	.005
Mood I: elation	−.36	60	.005	−.25	58	.05	−.29	118	.005
Mood II: elation	−.25	50	.05	−.31	46	.025	−.29	96	.005
Denial: self-interest	−.30	60	.025	−.25	56	.05	−.27	116	.005
Denial: sexuality	−.49	60	.0005	−.34	56	.01	−.41	116	.0005
Relatives' CP V, exercise	−.44	16	.05	−.53	14	.025	−.47	30	.01
Anticoagulants	.28	61	.025	.22	58	.05	.24	119	.01
TV time									
None									
Cardiac information test									
Uric acid	.35	44	.025	.29	45	.05	.32	89	.005
Information	.40	54	.005	.33	52	.01	.37	106	.0005
Nonesterized fatty acids (NEFA) solvable 10:45	.51	15	.025	.49	19	.025	.47	34	.005
NEFA solvable 11:00	.54	15	.025	.44	18	.05	.41	33	.01
NEFA unsolvable 11:00	.51	15	.025	.44	19	.05	.41	34	.01
NEFA unsolvable 12:10	.78	10	.005	.68	10	.025	.64	20	.005
Familial heart disease (FHD)									
None									
Previous MIs									
Heart history	.59	65	.0005	.49	64	.0005	.54	129	.0005
False alarms									
None									
Lie score									
Denial: self-interest	.47	61	.0005	.39	60	.005	.43	121	.0005
Denial: dissatisfaction	.40	61	.005	.27	60	.025	.33	121	.0005
Denial: dependence	.37	61	.005	.23	60	.05	.29	121	.005
Denial: hostility	.46	61	.0005	.41	60	.005	.43	121	.0005
Denial: anxiety	.37	61	.005	.28	60	.025	.32	121	.0005
Denial: sexuality	.54	61	.0005	.35	60	.005	.45	121	.0005
Relatives' CP III, perfectionism	.56	16	.025	.68	15	.005	.64	31	.0005
Days CCU									
Days hospital	.26	65	.025	.48	66	.0005	.36	131	.0005
Days before testing	.55	63	.0005	.28	66	.025	.43	129	.0005
Severity I	.43	60	.0005	.42	62	.0005	.43	122	.0005
Severity II	.35	60	.005	.27	62	.025	.30	122	.005
High alarms	.30	44	.025	.36	46	.01	.33	90	.005

Table K-1. Significant correlations in split-half samples and total sample for MI patients—cont'd

Variable	Sample 1			Sample 2			Total sample		
	r	*N*	*p*	*r*	*N*	*p*	*r*	*N*	*p*
Number days temperature over 99° F	.42	40	.005	.35	41	.025	.38	81	.0005
SGOT	.51	63	.0005	.27	65	.025	.41	128	.0005
Lactate dehydrogenase (LDH)	.47	61	.0005	.21	64	.05	.36	125	.0005
Highest temperature	.30	65	.01	.35	66	.005	.32	131	.0005
Severity total	.44	60	.0005	.38	62	.005	.41	122	.0005
Days hospital									
Days CCU	.26	65	.025	.48	66	.0005	.36	131	.0005
Number days temperature over 99° F	.28	40	.05	.30	41	.05	.31	81	.005
Highest temperature	.33	65	.005	.29	66	.01	.31	131	.0005
Relatives LC	−.54	16	.025	−.58	15	.025	−.57	31	.005
17-OH-CS solvable 12:10	.49	21	.025	.49	23	.01	.48	44	.005
Heart history									
Previous MIs	.59	65	.0005	.49	64	.0005	.54	129	.0005
Days before testing									
Days CCU	.55	63	.0005	.28	66	.025	.43	129	.0005
Severity I	.32	60	.01	.42	62	.0005	.35	122	.0005
Severity II	.39	60	.005	.21	62	.05	.30	122	.005
SGOT	.43	61	.0005	.36	65	.005	.41	126	.0005
Highest temperature	.28	63	.025	.29	66	.01	.29	129	.0005
Severity total	.41	60	.0005	.35	62	.005	.37	122	.0005
Comfort interview									
Temperature change	.35	56	.005	.24	56	.05	.29	112	.005
Cooperation interview									
NEFA solvable 3:30	−.90	5	.025	−.91	5	.025	−.89	10	.0005
Nurses' cooperation									
Mood I: aggression	−.29	55	.025	−.27	57	.025	−.27	112	.005
Mood I: egotism	−.22	55	>.05	−.30	57	.025	−.24	112	.01
Severity I									
Days CCU	.43	60	.0005	.42	62	.0005	.43	122	.0005
Days before testing	.32	60	.01	.42	62	.0005	.35	122	.0005
Severity II	.54	60	.0005	.64	62	.0005	.59	122	.0005
Number days temperature over 99° F	.37	40	.025	.33	41	.025	.36	81	.005
SGOT	.34	58	.005	.32	62	.01	.32	120	.0005
Highest temperature	.36	60	.005	.48	62	.0005	.42	122	.0005
Severity total	.87	60	.0005	.90	62	.0005	.89	122	.0005
Severity change	.45	60	.0005	.42	62	.0005	.44	122	.0005
Severity II									
Days CCU	.35	60	.005	.27	62	.025	.30	122	.005
Days before testing	.39	60	.005	.21	62	.05	.30	122	.005
Severity I	.54	60	.0005	.64	62	.0005	.59	122	.0005
Number episodes CCU	.58	40	.0005	.63	41	.0005	.60	81	.0005
Number arrhythmias CCU	.54	40	.0005	.40	40	.01	.47	80	.0005
SGOT	.23	58	.05	.25	62	.025	.22	120	.025
Severity total	.88	60	.0005	.90	62	.0005	.89	122	.0005
Severity change	−.51	60	.0005	−.43	62	.0005	−.47	122	.0005

Continued.

Table K-1. Significant correlations in split-half samples and total sample for MI patients—cont'd

Variable	Sample 1			Sample 2			Total sample		
	r	N	p	r	N	p	r	N	p
Depression I									
R-S	−.30	54	.025	−.26	53	.05	−.28	107	.005
SE	−.40	48	.005	−.35	49	.01	−.37	97	.0005
Depression II	.81	45	.0005	.87	45	.0005	.85	90	.0005
Denial: anxiety	−.23	54	.05	−.56	51	.0005	−.42	105	.0005
Depression change	−.46	45	.005	−.24	45	.05	−.35	90	.0005
Depression II									
Depression I	.81	45	.0005	.87	45	.0005	.85	90	.0005
Surgency mood II	−.27	46	.05	−.27	46	.05	−.28	92	.005
Denial: anxiety	−.25	49	.05	−.56	45	.0005	−.43	94	.0005
Low alarms									
Denial: self-interest	−.30	43	.025	−.37	42	.01	−.32	85	.005
Denial: hostility	−.28	43	.05	−.27	42	.05	−.22	85	.025
High alarms									
Days CCU	.30	44	.025	.36	46	.01	.33	90	.005
Mood I: aggression									
Nurses' cooperation	−.29	55	.025	−.27	57	.025	−.27	112	.005
Mood I: anxiety	.28	63	.025	.46	64	.0005	.36	127	.0005
Mood I: sadness	.51	63	.0005	.31	64	.01	.42	127	.0005
Mood I: skepticism	.58	63	.0005	.45	64	.0005	.52	127	.0005
Mood I: egotism	.55	63	.0005	.55	64	.0005	.55	127	.0005
Mood II: aggression	.35	51	.01	.59	48	.0005	.45	99	.0005
Mood II: sadness	.28	51	.05	.47	48	.0005	.36	99	.0005
Phenothiazines	.25	63	.025	.25	62	.025	.25	125	.005
Mood change	.40	51	.005	.36	48	.01	.38	99	.0005
Mood I: anxiety									
Mood I: aggression	.28	63	.025	.46	64	.0005	.36	127	.0005
Mood I: fatigue	.35	63	.005	.35	64	.005	.34	127	.0005
Mood I: sadness	.37	63	.005	.53	64	.0005	.44	127	.0005
Mood I: skepticism	.33	63	.005	.39	64	.005	.36	127	.0005
Mood I: egotism	.23	63	.05	.37	64	.005	.29	127	.0005
Mood II: sadness	.26	51	.05	.44	48	.005	.34	99	.0005
Denial: anxiety	−.24	61	.05	−.30	58	.025	−.27	119	.005
17-OH-CS unsolvable 7:30	.38	25	.05	.43	18	.05	.40	43	.005
Mood I: surgency									
Mood I: elation	.66	63	.0005	.54	64	.0005	.62	127	.0005
Mood I: social affection	.60	63	.0005	.51	64	.0005	.56	127	.0005
Mood I: vigor	.59	63	.0005	.50	64	.0005	.56	127	.0005
Mood II: surgency	.54	51	.0005	.50	48	.0005	.51	99	.0005
Mood II: elation	.48	51	.0005	.46	48	.0005	.47	99	.0005
Mood II: vigor	.27	51	.05	.41	48	.005	.33	99	.0005
Denial: anxiety	.33	51	.025	.22	58	.05	.27	109	.005
Mood I: elation									
Education	−.24	62	.05	−.32	61	.01	−.26	123	.005
Salary	−.36	60	.005	−.25	58	.05	−.29	118	.005
Mood I: surgency	.66	63	.0005	.54	64	.0005	.62	127	.0005
Mood I: concentration	.30	63	.01	.21	64	.05	.27	127	.005
Mood I: social affection	.58	63	.0005	.39	64	.005	.50	127	.0005
Mood I: egotism	.30	63	.01	.40	64	.0005	.35	127	.0005

Table K-1. Significant correlations in split-half samples and total sample
for MI patients—cont'd

Variable	Sample 1			Sample 2			Total sample		
	r	*N*	*p*	*r*	*N*	*p*	*r*	*N*	*p*
Mood I: vigor	.49	63	.0005	.54	64	.0005	.51	127	.0005
Mood II: elation	.50	51	.0005	.57	48	.0005	.53	99	.0005
Mood I: concentration									
Mood I: elation	.30	63	.01	.21	64	.05	.27	127	.005
Mood I: social affection	.35	63	.005	.22	64	.05	.28	127	.005
Mood I: vigor	.26	63	.025	.27	64	.025	.27	127	.005
Mood II: anxiety	.27	51	.05	.28	48	.05	.26	99	.005
Mood II: concentration	.43	51	.005	.56	48	.0005	.49	99	.0005
NEFA scan 2	−.63	9	.05	−.85	7	.01	−.76	16	.0005
Mood I: fatigue									
Mood I: anxiety	.35	63	.005	.35	64	.005	.34	127	.0005
Mood I: sadness	.23	63	.05	.40	64	.0005	.33	127	.0005
Mood II: fatigue	.32	51	.01	.53	48	.0005	.44	99	.0005
17-OH-CS scan 1	.49	13	.05	.79	7	.025	.63	20	.005
CP scale I, R-S	.40	61	.005	.34	60	.005	.37	121	.0005
Phenothiazines	.30	63	.01	.23	62	.05	.25	125	.005
17-OH-CS solvable 10:45	.46	22	.025	.62	23	.005	.58	45	.0005
17-OH-CS solvable 11:00	.44	22	.025	.62	22	.005	.56	44	.0005
17-OH-CS solvable 3:30	.40	27	.025	.67	25	.0005	.51	52	.0005
17-OH-CS unsolvable 7:30	.33	25	>.05	.53	18	.025	.40	43	.005
17-OH-CS unsolvable 10:45	.43	24	.025	.52	24	.005	.47	48	.0005
17-OH-CS 11:00	.39	23	.05	.61	24	.005	.50	47	.0005
17-OH-CS 12:10	.38	23	.05	.52	23	.01	.39	46	.005
Mood I: social affection									
Mood I: surgency	.60	63	.0005	.51	64	.0005	.56	127	.0005
Mood I: elation	.58	63	.0005	.39	64	.005	.50	127	.0005
Mood I: concentration	.35	63	.005	.22	64	.05	.28	127	.005
Mood I: vigor	.54	63	.0005	.30	64	.01	.44	127	.0005
Mood II: surgency	.28	51	.05	.49	48	.0005	.38	99	.0005
Mood II: elation	.30	51	.025	.37	48	.005	.34	99	.0005
Mood II: social affection	.35	51	.01	.62	48	.0005	.48	99	.0005
Mood I: sadness									
Mood I: aggression	.51	63	.0005	.31	64	.01	.42	127	.0005
Mood I: anxiety	.37	63	.005	.53	64	.0005	.44	127	.0005
Mood I: fatigue	.23	63	.05	.40	64	.0005	.33	127	.0005
Mood I: skepticism	.54	63	.0005	.43	64	.0005	.49	127	.0005
Mood I: egotism	.44	63	.0005	.32	64	.005	.38	127	.0005
Mood II: anxiety	.24	51	.05	.36	48	.01	.30	99	.005
Mood II: sadness	.42	51	.005	.46	48	.0005	.44	99	.0005
Mood II: skepticism	.24	51	.05	.46	48	.0005	.33	99	.0005
Mood change	.30	51	.025	.34	48	.01	.32	99	.005
Mood I: skepticism									
Mood I: aggression	.58	63	.0005	.45	64	.0005	.52	127	.0005
Mood I: anxiety	.33	63	.005	.39	64	.005	.36	127	.0005
Mood I: sadness	.54	63	.0005	.43	64	.0005	.49	127	.0005
Mood I: egotism	.53	63	.0005	.33	64	.005	.44	127	.0005
Mood II: sadness	.26	51	.05	.48	48	.0005	.35	99	.0005
Mood II: skepticism	.37	51	.005	.60	48	.0005	.47	99	.0005
Phenothiazines	.31	63	.01	.23	62	.05	.27	125	.005

Continued.

Table K-1. Significant correlations in split-half samples and total sample for MI patients—cont'd

Variable	Sample 1			Sample 2			Total sample		
	r	N	p	r	N	p	r	N	p
Mood I: egotism									
Education	−.33	62	.005	−.25	61	.025	−.28	123	.005
Nurses' cooperation	−.22	55	.05	−.30	57	.025	−.24	112	.01
Mood I: aggression	.55	63	.0005	.55	64	.0005	.55	127	.0005
Mood I: anxiety	.23	63	.05	.37	64	.005	.29	127	.0005
Mood I: elation	.30	63	.01	.40	64	.0005	.35	127	.0005
Mood I: sadness	.44	63	.0005	.32	64	.005	.38	127	.0005
Mood I: skepticism	.53	63	.0005	.33	64	.005	.44	127	.0005
Mood II: aggression	.50	51	.0005	.47	48	.0005	.48	99	.0005
Phenothiazines	.47	63	.0005	.23	62	.05	.39	125	.0005
Mood I: vigor									
Mood I: surgency	.59	63	.0005	.50	64	.0005	.56	127	.0005
Mood I: elation	.49	63	.0005	.54	64	.0005	.51	127	.0005
Mood I: concentration	.26	63	.025	.27	64	.025	.27	127	.005
Mood II: vigor	.42	51	.005	.64	48	.0005	.51	99	.0005
Number days temperature over 99° F	−.26	39	.05	−.27	40	.05	−.25	79	.025
Denial: complacency	.23	61	.05	.25	58	.05	.24	119	.01
Mood II: aggression									
Mood I: aggression	.35	51	.01	.59	48	.0005	.45	99	.0005
Mood I: egotism	.50	51	.0005	.47	48	.0005	.48	99	.0005
Mood II: anxiety	.54	51	.0005	.40	50	.005	.46	101	.0005
Mood II: sadness	.35	51	.01	.28	50	.025	.32	101	.005
Mood II: skepticism	.38	51	.005	.41	50	.005	.39	101	.0005
Mood II: egotism	.60	51	.0005	.29	50	.025	.47	101	.0005
Mood II: anxiety									
Mood I: concentration	.27	51	.025	.28	48	.05	.26	99	.005
Mood I: sadness	.24	51	.05	.36	48	.01	.30	99	.005
Mood II: aggression	.54	51	.0005	.40	50	.005	.46	101	.0005
Mood II: fatigue	.56	51	.0005	.38	50	.005	.45	101	.0005
Mood II: sadness	.56	51	.0005	.57	50	.0005	.56	101	.0005
Mood II: skepticism	.53	51	.0005	.60	50	.0005	.56	101	.0005
Cards turned solvable	−.36	23	.05	−.37	26	.05	−.33	49	.025
Mood II: surgency									
Depression II	−.27	46	.05	−.27	46	.05	−.28	92	.005
Mood I: surgency	.54	51	.0005	.50	48	.0005	.51	99	.0005
Mood I: social affection	.28	51	.025	.49	48	.0005	.38	99	.0005
Mood II: elation	.44	51	.005	.62	50	.0005	.54	101	.0005
Mood II: social affection	.45	51	.005	.43	50	.005	.45	101	.0005
Mood II: vigor	.48	51	.0005	.46	50	.0005	.47	101	.0005
17-OH-CS solvable 7:30	−.51	17	.025	−.42	17	.05	−.46	34	.005
Mood II: elation									
Age	.25	51	.05	.27	50	.05	.21	101	.025
Salary	−.25	50	.05	−.31	46	.025	−.29	96	.005
Mood I: surgency	.48	51	.0005	.46	48	.0005	.47	99	.0005
Mood I: elation	.50	51	.0005	.57	48	.0005	.53	99	.0005
Mood I: social affection	.30	51	.025	.37	48	.005	.34	99	.0005
Mood II: surgency	.44	51	.0005	.62	50	.0005	.54	101	.0005
Mood II: social affection	.32	51	.01	.40	50	.005	.38	101	.0005
Mood II: vigor	.33	51	.01	.56	50	.0005	.45	101	.0005

Table K-1. Significant correlations in split-half samples and total sample for MI patients—cont'd

Variable	Sample 1			Sample 2			Total sample		
	r	N	p	r	N	p	r	N	p
Mood II: concentration									
Mood I: concentration	.43	51	.005	.56	48	.0005	.49	99	.0005
Mood II: social affection	.28	51	.025	.23	50	.05	.26	101	.005
Mood II: sadness	.36	51	.005	.32	50	.01	.34	101	.0005
Mood II: skepticism	.44	51	.0005	.44	50	.005	.44	101	.0005
17-OH-CS scan 2	−.55	11	.05	−.60	9	.05	−.54	20	.01
Anticoagulants	−.25	51	.05	−.29	49	.025	−.26	100	.005
Mood II: fatigue									
Mood I: fatigue	.32	51	.01	.53	48	.0005	.44	99	.0005
Mood II: anxiety	.56	51	.0005	.38	50	.005	.45	101	.0005
Mood II: sadness	.51	51	.0005	.30	50	.025	.39	101	.0005
Mood II: skepticism	.41	51	.005	.30	50	.025	.35	101	.0005
Mood II: vigor	−.28	51	.025	−.27	50	.05	−.28	101	.005
Uric acid	.27	42	.05	.30	45	.025	.24	87	.025
Mood change	−.31	51	.025	−.37	48	.005	−.33	99	.0005
Cards wrong dry	.38	23	.05	.40	26	.025	.36	49	.01
Mood II: social affection									
Mood I: social affection	.35	51	.01	.62	48	.0005	.48	99	.0005
Mood II: surgency	.45	51	.0005	.43	50	.005	.45	101	.0005
Mood II: elation	.32	51	.01	.40	50	.005	.38	101	.0005
Mood II: concentration	.28	51	.025	.23	50	.05	.26	101	.005
Death	−.26	50	.05	−.36	49	.01	−.32	99	.005
Participation	.33	51	.01	.24	49	.05	.27	100	.005
NEFA scan 1	−.77	7	.025	−.84	5	.05	−.76	12	.005
NEFA scan 7	−1.00	4	.0005	−.73	8	.025	−.76	12	.005
Mood II: sadness									
R-S	−.36	50	.01	−.41	50	.005	−.36	100	.0005
Mood I: aggression	.28	51	.025	.47	48	.0005	.36	99	.0005
Mood I: anxiety	.26	51	.05	.44	48	.005	.34	99	.0005
Mood I: sadness	.42	51	.005	.46	48	.0005	.44	99	.0005
Mood I: skepticism	.26	51	.05	.48	48	.0005	.35	99	.0005
Mood II: aggression	.35	51	.01	.28	50	.025	.32	101	.005
Mood II: anxiety	.56	51	.0005	.57	50	.0005	.56	101	.0005
Mood II: concentration	.36	51	.005	.32	50	.01	.34	101	.0005
Mood II: fatigue	.51	51	.0005	.30	50	.025	.39	101	.0005
Mood II: skepticism	.50	51	.0005	.65	50	.0005	.57	101	.0005
Mood II: skepticism									
Mood I: sadness	.24	51	.05	.46	48	.0005	.33	99	.0005
Mood I: skepticism	.37	51	.005	.60	48	.0005	.47	99	.0005
Mood II: aggression	.38	51	.005	.41	50	.005	.39	101	.0005
Mood II: anxiety	.53	51	.0005	.60	50	.0005	.56	101	.0005
Mood II: concentration	.44	51	.0005	.44	50	.005	.44	101	.0005
Mood II: sadness	.50	51	.0005	.65	50	.0005	.57	101	.0005
17-OH-CS scan 2	−.66	11	.025	−.60	9	.05	−.59	20	.005
Mood II: egotism									
Mood II: aggression	.60	51	.0005	.29	50	.025	.47	101	.0005
WBC	.23	49	.05	.28	50	.025	.21	99	.025
Mood II: vigor									
Mood I: surgency	.27	51	.025	.41	48	.005	.33	99	.0005

Continued.

Table K-1. Significant correlations in split-half samples and total sample for MI patients—cont'd

Variable	Sample 1			Sample 2			Total sample		
	r	N	p	r	N	p	r	N	p
Mood I: vigor	.42	51	.005	.64	48	.0005	.51	99	.0005
Mood II: surgency	.48	51	.0005	.46	50	.0005	.47	101	.0005
Mood I: elation	.33	51	.01	.56	50	.0005	.45	101	.0005
Mood I: fatigue	−.28	51	.025	−.27	50	.05	−.28	101	.005
Depression change	−.37	43	.005	−.35	44	.01	−.36	87	.0005
Mood change	.32	51	.01	.41	48	.005	.35	99	.0005
17-OH-CS scan 1									
Mood I: fatigue	.49	13	.05	.79	7	.025	.63	20	.005
17-OH-CS scan 2									
Mood II: concentration	−.55	11	.05	−.60	9	.05	−.54	20	.01
Mood II: skepticism	−.66	11	.025	−.60	9	.05	−.59	20	.005
17-OH-CS scan 3									
17-OH-CS scan 4	.81	11	.005	.92	6	.005	.84	17	.0005
17-OH-CS scan 5	.89	6	.01	1.00	4	.0005	.75	10	.01
Cholesterol	.67	14	.005	.70	8	.05	.68	22	.0005
17-OH-CS unsolvable 3:30	.59	11	.05	.99	5	.0005	.64	16	.005
17-OH-CS scan 4									
17-OH-CS scan 3	.81	11	.005	.92	6	.005	.84	17	.0005
17-OH-CS scan 5	.93	5	.01	.93	5	.01	.92	10	.0005
Total CP scale	.51	13	.05	.61	9	.05	.56	22	.005
17-OH-CS solvable 10:45	.77	11	.005	.82	8	.01	.80	19	.0005
17-OH-CS unsolvable 3:30	.80	9	.005	.94	7	.005	.85	16	.005
17-OH-CS scan 5									
17-OH-CS scan 3	.89	6	.01	1.00	4	.0005	.75	10	.01
17-OH-CS scan 4	.93	5	.01	.93	5	.01	.92	10	.0005
Number days temperature over 99° F	.63	9	.05	.84	7	.01	.63	16	.005
17-OH-CS solvable 7:30	.91	9	.0005	.75	7	.025	.85	16	.0005
17-OH-CS solvable 10:45	.85	9	.005	1.00	6	.0005	.86	15	.0005
17-OH-CS solvable 11:00	.58	9	.05	.85	6	.025	.62	15	.01
17-OH-CS unsolvable 10:45	.70	10	.025	.94	.8	.0005	.72	18	.0005
17-OH-CS unsolvable 11:00	.72	10	.01	.96	8	.0005	.75	18	.0005
17-OH-CS unsolvable 12:10	.56	10	.05	.69	7	.05	.55	17	.025
17-OH-CS unsolvable 3:30	.93	9	.0005	.91	8	.005	.89	17	.0005
17-OH-CS scan 6									
LC	.57	12	.05	.46	15	.05	.50	27	.005
17-OH-CS scan 7									
Diversion	−.62	10	.05	−.57	12	.05	−.49	22	.01
17-OH-CS solvable 12:10	.65	8	.05	.54	11	.05	.49	19	.025
17-OH-CS unsolvable 10:45	.59	10	.05	.98	11	.0005	.80	21	.0005
NEFA solvable 10:45	−.99	4	.005	−.55	10	.05	−.65	14	.01
NEFA solvable 11:00	−.84	5	.05	−.61	10	.05	−.64	15	.005
17-OH-CS scan 8									
17-OH-CS solvable 10:45	.85	7	.01	.86	5	.05	.80	12	.005
17-OH-CS solvable 11:00	.79	7	.025	.96	5	.005	.78	12	.005
17-OH-CS unsolvable 10:45	.94	6	.005	1.00	4	.0005	.95	10	.0005
Number episodes CCU									
Severity II	.58	40	.0005	.63	41	.0005	.60	81	.0005
Number arrhythmias CCU	.45	40	.005	.30	41	.05	.39	80	.0005

Table K-1. Significant correlations in split-half samples and total sample for MI patients—cont'd

Variable	Sample 1			Sample 2			Total sample		
	r	N	p	r	N	p	r	N	p
Denial: complacency	−.28	39	.05	−.29	40	.05	−.28	79	.01
Severity total	.44	40	.005	.63	41	.0005	.52	81	.0005
Severity change	−.42	40	.005	−.27	41	.05	−.35	81	.005
Number arrhythmias CCU									
Severity II	.54	40	.0005	.40	40	.005	.47	80	.0005
Number episodes CCU	.45	40	.005	.30	40	.05	.39	80	.0005
Severity total	.46	40	.005	.40	40	.005	.44	80	.0005
Number days temperature over 99° F									
Days CCU	.42	40	.005	.35	41	.025	.38	81	.0005
Days hospital	.28	40	.05	.30	41	.025	.31	81	.005
Severity I	.37	40	.01	.33	41	.025	.36	81	.005
Mood I: vigor	−.26	39	.05	−.27	40	.05	−.25	79	.025
17-OH-CS scan 5	.63	9	.05	.84	7	.01	.63	16	.005
LDH	.36	38	.025	.48	41	.005	.43	79	.0005
WBC	.47	38	.005	.36	41	.01	.35	79	.005
Highest temperature	.77	40	.0005	.67	41	.0005	.72	81	.0005
Last 4:00 temperature	.30	40	.05	.30	41	.025	.31	81	.005
Severity total	.46	40	.005	.28	41	.05	.38	81	.0005
Sedimentation rate									
Size estimation	−.30	45	.025	−.27	49	.05	−.28	94	.005
First 4:00 temperature	.29	53	.025	.26	60	.025	.28	113	.005
Subsequent hospital MI	.34	47	.01	.26	54	.05	.30	101	.005
Relatives CP I, R-S	−.58	16	.01	−.52	14	.05	−.40	30	.025
Uric acid									
Sex	−.25	53	.05	−.48	55	.0005	−.38	108	.0005
Cardiac information test	.35	44	.01	.29	45	.025	.32	89	.005
Mood II: fatigue	.27	42	.05	.30	45	.025	.24	87	.025
Analgesics	−.29	53	.025	−.31	53	.025	−.28	106	.005
Cholesterol									
17-OH-CS scan 3	.67	14	.005	.70	8	.05	.68	22	.0005
17-OH-CS solvable 7:30	.71	19	.0005	.42	18	.05	.53	37	.0005
17-OH-CS solvable 10:45	.41	18	.05	.53	18	.025	.49	36	.005
17-OH-CS solvable 11:30	.59	18	.005	.49	18	.025	.51	36	.005
17-OH-CS unsolvable 7:30	.55	24	.005	.63	17	.005	.55	41	.0005
17-OH-CS unsolvable 10:45	.40	21	.05	.65	21	.005	.51	42	.0005
17-OH-CS unsolvable 3:30	.72	21	.0005	.39	21	.05	.51	42	.0005
17-OH-CS unsolvable 11:30	.71	18	.0005	.76	15	.0005	.66	33	.0005
SGOT									
Days CCU	.51	63	.0005	.27	65	.025	.41	128	.0005
Days before testing	.43	61	.0005	.36	65	.005	.41	126	.0005
Severity I	.34	58	.005	.32	62	.005	.32	120	.0005
Severity II	.23	58	.05	.25	62	.025	.22	120	.025
LDH	.69	61	.0005	.73	64	.0005	.71	125	.0005
Relatives Ullmann	.48	16	.05	.54	15	.025	.49	31	.005
Severity total	.32	58	.01	.32	62	.005	.30	120	.005
LDH									
Days CCU	.47	61	.0005	.21	64	.05	.36	125	.0005
Number days temperature over 99° F	.36	38	.025	.48	41	.005	.43	79	.0005

Continued.

Table K-1. Significant correlations in split-half samples and total sample for MI patients—cont'd

Variable	Sample 1			Sample 2			Total sample		
	r	*N*	*p*	*r*	*N*	*p*	*r*	*N*	*p*
SGOT	.69	61	.0005	.73	64	.0005	.71	125	.0005
WBC	.23	61	.05	.52	64	.0005	.33	125	.0005
Highest temperature	.24	61	.05	.48	64	.0005	.33	125	.0005
NEFA scan 2	.74	8	.025	.71	7	.05	.74	15	.005
WBC									
Mood II: egotism	.23	49	.05	.28	50	.025	.21	99	.025
Number days temperature over 99° F	.47	38	.005	.36	41	.01	.35	79	.005
LDH	.23	61	.05	.52	64	.0005	.33	125	.0005
Highest temperature	.28	63	.025	.25	66	.0005	.25	129	.005
Highest temperature									
Days CCU	.30	65	.01	.35	66	.005	.32	131	.0005
Days hospital	.33	65	.005	.29	66	.01	.31	131	.0005
Days before testing	.28	63	.025	.29	66	.01	.29	129	.0005
Severity I	.36	60	.005	.48	62	.0005	.42	122	.0005
Number days temperature over 99° F	.77	40	.0005	.67	41	.0005	.72	81	.0005
LDH	.24	61	.05	.48	64	.0005	.33	125	.0005
WBC	.28	63	.025	.25	66	.0005	.25	129	.005
First 4:00 temperature	.26	63	.025	.36	65	.005	.31	128	.0005
Severity total	.27	60	.025	.44	62	.0005	.35	122	.0005
17-OH-CS unsolvable 11:00	.50	24	.01	.39	25	.05	.45	49	.005
17-OH-CS unsolvable 12:10	.45	24	.025	.38	24	.05	.41	48	.005
First 4:00 temperature									
Sedimentation rate	.29	53	.025	.26	60	.025	.28	113	.005
Highest temperature	.26	63	.025	.36	65	.005	.31	128	.0005
Temperature change	.77	63	.0005	.65	65	.0005	.71	128	.0005
Last 4:00 temperature									
Number days temperature over 99° F	.30	40	.05	.30	41	.025	.31	81	.005
Temperature change	−.52	63	.0005	−.43	65	.0005	−.47	128	.0005
Return to work									
None									
Subsequent hospital MI									
Size estimation	−.35	51	.01	−.41	52	.005	−.39	103	.0005
Sedimentation rate	.34	47	.01	.26	54	.05	.30	101	.005
Death									
Mood II: social affection	−.26	50	.05	−.36	49	.01	−.32	99	.005
Denial: self-interest									
Education	−.24	61	.05	−.34	59	.005	−.29	120	.005
Salary	−.30	60	.01	−.25	56	.05	−.27	116	.005
Lie score	.47	61	.0005	.39	60	.005	.43	121	.0005
Low alarms	−.30	43	.025	−.37	42	.01	−.32	85	.005
Denial: dissatisfaction	.59	63	.0005	.36	60	.005	.48	123	.0005
Denial: dependence	.23	63	.05	.25	60	.025	.24	123	.01
Denial: hostility	.62	63	.0005	.44	60	.0005	.53	123	.0005
Denial: complacency	.30	63	.01	.42	60	.0005	.36	123	.0005
Denial: sexuality	.55	63	.0005	.52	60	.0005	.53	123	.0005
CP Scale III, perfectionism	.42	61	.0005	.26	60	.025	.34	121	.0005
CP Scale VI, overeating	−.24	61	.05	−.21	60	.05	−.22	121	.025

Table K-1. Significant correlations in split-half samples and total sample for MI patients—cont'd

Variable	Sample 1			Sample 2			Total sample		
	r	N	p	r	N	p	r	N	p
Denial: dissatisfaction									
Repression-sensitization	.23	61	.05	.46	60	.0005	.34	121	.0005
Lie score	.40	61	.005	.27	60	.025	.33	121	.0005
Denial: self-interest	.59	63	.0005	.36	60	.005	.48	123	.0005
Denial: hostility	.60	63	.0005	.60	60	.0005	.60	123	.0005
Denial: anxiety	.45	63	.0005	.65	60	.0005	.56	123	.0005
Denial: sexuality	.45	63	.0005	.46	60	.0005	.46	123	.0005
Denial: dependence									
Lie score	.37	61	.005	.23	60	.05	.29	121	.005
Denial: self-interest	.23	63	.05	.25	60	.025	.24	123	.01
Denial: anxiety	.28	63	.025	.30	60	.01	.29	123	.005
Denial: complacency	.47	63	.0005	.28	60	.025	.37	123	.0005
NEFA scan 2	.72	10	.01	.89	6	.01	.65	16	.005
Denial: hostility									
Lie score	.46	61	.0005	.41	60	.005	.43	121	.0005
Low alarms	−.28	43	.05	−.27	42	.05	−.22	85	.025
Denial: self-interest	.62	63	.0005	.44	60	.0005	.53	123	.0005
Denial: dissatisfaction	.60	63	.0005	.65	60	.0005	.60	123	.0005
Denial: anxiety	.50	63	.0005	.50	60	.0005	.50	123	.0005
Denial: sexuality	.54	63	.0005	.61	60	.0005	.58	123	.0005
Denial: anxiety									
Repression-sensitization	.39	61	.005	.52	60	.0005	.46	121	.0005
Lie score	.37	61	.005	.28	60	.025	.32	121	.0005
Depression I	−.23	54	.05	−.56	51	.0005	−.42	105	.0005
Depression II	−.25	49	.05	−.56	45	.0005	−.43	94	.0005
Mood I: anxiety	−.24	61	.05	−.30	58	.025	−.27	119	.005
Mood I: surgency	.33	61	.005	.22	58	.05	.27	119	.005
Denial: dissatisfaction	.45	63	.0005	.65	60	.0005	.56	123	.0005
Denial: dependence	.28	63	.025	.30	60	.01	.29	123	.005
Denial: hostility	.50	63	.0005	.50	60	.0005	.50	123	.0005
Denial: sexuality	.41	63	.0005	.35	60	.005	.38	123	.0005
NEFA solvable 11:30	−.96	4	.025	−1.00	3	.0005	−.89	7	.005
Denial: complacency									
Mood II: vigor	.23	61	.05	.25	58	.05	.24	119	.01
Number episodes CCU	−.28	39	.05	−.29	40	.05	−.28	79	.01
Denial: self-interest	.30	63	.01	.42	60	.0005	.36	123	.0005
Denial: dependence	.47	63	.0005	.28	60	.025	.37	123	.0005
CP II, scanning	.26	61	.025	.39	60	.005	.31	121	.005
CP III, perfectionism	.28	61	.025	.43	60	.0005	.36	121	.0005
CP IV, control of self	.28	61	.025	.27	60	.025	.26	121	.005
CP total	.21	61	.05	.28	60	.025	.25	121	.005
Denial: sexuality									
Age	.35	63	.005	.29	60	.025	.33	123	.0005
Education	−.27	61	.025	−.32	59	.01	−.29	120	.005
Salary	−.49	60	.0005	−.34	56	.005	−.41	116	.0005
Lie score	.54	61	.0005	.35	60	.005	.45	121	.0005
Denial: self-interest	.55	63	.0005	.52	60	.0005	.53	123	.0005
Denial: dissatisfaction	.45	63	.0005	.46	60	.0005	.46	123	.0005
Denial: hostility	.54	63	.0005	.61	60	.0005	.58	123	.0005
Denial: anxiety	.41	63	.0005	.35	60	.005	.38	123	.0005

Continued.

Table K-1. Significant correlations in split-half samples and total sample for MI patients—cont'd

Variable	Sample 1			Sample 2			Total sample		
	r	N	p	r	N	p	r	N	p
CP scale I, R-S									
Repression-sensitization	−.35	63	.005	−.22	62	.05	−.28	125	.005
Mood I: fatigue	.40	61	.005	.34	60	.005	.37	121	.0005
Total CP	.55	63	.0005	.56	62	.0005	.55	125	.0005
Participation	.23	58	.05	.32	60	.01	.28	118	.005
CP Scale II, scanning									
Denial: complacency	.26	61	.025	.39	60	.005	.31	121	.005
CP Scale III, perfectionism									
Repression-sensitization	−.29	63	.01	−.32	62	.005	−.30	125	.005
Denial: self-interest	.42	61	.0005	.26	60	.025	.34	121	.0005
Denial: complacency	.28	61	.025	.43	60	.0005	.36	121	.0005
CP Scale IV, control of self	.36	63	.005	.36	62	.005	.34	125	.0005
Total CP	.76	63	.0005	.65	62	.0005	.70	125	.0005
Relatives CP III, perfectionism	.59	16	.01	.52	15	.025	.52	31	.005
CP Scale IV, control of self									
Denial: complacency	.28	61	.025	.27	60	.025	.26	121	.005
CP Scale III, perfectionism	.36	63	.005	.36	62	.005	.34	125	.0005
Total CP	.65	63	.0005	.63	62	.0005	.63	125	.0005
CP Scale V, exercise									
Total CP	.28	63	.025	.31	62	.01	.29	125	.005
CP Scale VI, overeating									
Denial: self-interest	−.24	61	.05	−.21	60	.05	−.22	121	.025
Total CP									
LC	.21	62	.05	.21	62	.05	.21	124	.025
R-S	−.46	63	.0005	−.36	62	.005	−.41	125	.0005
17-OH-CS scan 4	.51	13	.05	.61	9	.05	.56	22	.005
Denial: complacency	.21	61	.05	.28	60	.025	.25	121	.005
CP Scale I, R-S	.55	63	.0005	.56	62	.0005	.55	125	.0005
CP Scale III, perfectionism	.76	63	.0005	.65	62	.0005	.70	125	.0005
CP Scale IV, control of self	.65	63	.0005	.63	62	.0005	.63	125	.0005
CP V, exercise	.28	63	.025	.31	62	.01	.29	125	.005
Relatives CP I, R-S									
Sedimentation rate	−.58	16	.01	−.52	14	.05	−.40	30	.025
Total relatives CP	.66	16	.005	.63	15	.01	.67	31	.0005
Relatives CP II, scanning									
None									
Relatives CP III, perfectionism									
Lie score	.56	16	.025	.68	15	.005	.64	31	.0005
CP III, perfectionism	.59	16	.01	.52	15	.025	.52	31	.005
Total relatives CP	.61	16	.01	.77	15	.0005	.70	31	.0005
Relatives CP IV, control of self									
Total relatives CP	.68	16	.005	.59	15	.01	.62	31	.0005
Relatives CP V, exercise									
Salary	−.44	16	.05	−.53	14	.025	−.47	30	.01
Relatives CP VI, overeating									
None									
Total relatives CP									
Relatives CP I, R-S	.66	16	.005	.63	15	.01	.67	31	.0005
Relatives CP III, perfectionism	.61	16	.01	.77	15	.0005	.70	31	.0005

Table K-1. Significant correlations in split-half samples and total sample
for MI patients—cont'd

Variable	Sample 1			Sample 2			Total sample		
	r	N	p	r	N	p	r	N	p
Relatives CP IV, control of self	.68	16	.005	.59	15	.01	.62	31	.0005
Relatives LC									
Days hospital	−.54	16	.025	−.58	15	.025	−.57	31	.005
Relatives Ullmann	−.47	16	.05	−.45	15	.05	−.46	31	.01
Relatives Ullmann									
Repression-sensitization	.83	16	.0005	.62	15	.01	.34	31	.05
SGOT	.48	16	.05	.54	15	.025	.49	31	.005
Relatives LC	−.47	16	.05	−.45	15	.05	−.46	31	.01
Relatives lie score									
None									
Severity total									
Days CCU	.44	60	.0005	.38	62	.005	.41	122	.0005
Days before testing	.41	60	.0005	.35	62	.005	.37	122	.0005
Severity I	.87	60	.0005	.90	62	.0005	.89	122	.0005
Severity II	.88	60	.0005	.90	62	.0005	.89	122	.0005
Number episodes CCU	.44	40	.005	.63	41	.0005	.52	81	.0005
Number arrhythmias CCU	.46	40	.005	.40	40	.005	.44	80	.0005
Number days temperature over 99° F	.46	40	.005	.28	41	.05	.38	81	.0005
SGOT	.32	58	.01	.32	62	.01	.30	120	.005
Highest temperature	.27	60	.025	.44	62	.0005	.35	122	.0005
Mood change	.24	51	.05	.28	47	.05	.26	98	.005
Severity change									
Severity I	.45	60	.0005	.42	62	.0005	.44	122	.0005
Severity II	−.51	60	.0005	−.43	62	.0005	−.47	122	.0005
Number episodes CCU	−.42	40	.005	−.27	41	.05	−.35	81	.005
Phenothiazines									
Mood I: aggression	.25	63	.025	.25	62	.025	.25	125	.005
Mood I: fatigue	.30	63	.01	.23	62	.05	.25	125	.005
Mood I: skepticism	.31	63	.01	.23	62	.05	.27	125	.005
Mood I: egotism	.47	63	.0005	.23	62	.05	.39	125	.0005
Barbiturates									
None									
Anticoagulants									
Education	.23	63	.05	.28	61	.025	.25	124	.005
Salary	.28	61	.025	.22	58	.05	.24	119	.01
Mood II: concentration	−.25	51	.05	−.29	49	.025	−.26	100	.005
Analgesics									
Uric acid	−.29	53	.025	−.31	53	.025	−.28	106	.005
Total sleep									
NEFA scan 5	.80	8	.01	.68	7	.05	.66	15	.005
Temperature change									
Comfort interview	.35	56	.005	.24	56	.05	.29	112	.005
First 4:00 temperature	.77	63	.0005	.65	65	.0005	.71	128	.0005
Last 4:00 temperature	−.52	63	.0005	−.43	65	.0005	−.47	128	.0005
Depression change									
Depression I	−.46	45	.005	−.24	45	.05	−.35	90	.0005
Mood II: vigor	−.37	43	.005	−.35	44	.01	−.36	87	.0005
Mood change	−.51	43	.0005	−.45	44	.005	−.48	87	.0005

Continued.

Table K-1. Significant correlations in split-half samples and total sample for MI patients—cont'd

Variable	Sample 1			Sample 2			Total sample		
	r	N	p	r	N	p	r	N	p
Mood change									
Mood I: aggression	.40	51	.005	.36	48	.01	.38	99	.0005
Mood I: sadness	.30	51	.025	.34	48	.01	.32	99	.005
Mood II: fatigue	−.31	51	.025	−.37	48	.005	−.33	99	.0005
Mood II: vigor	.32	51	.01	.41	48	.005	.35	99	.0005
Severity total	.24	51	.05	.28	47	.05	.26	98	.005
Depression change	−.51	43	.0005	−.45	44	.005	−.48	87	.0005
Diversion									
17-OH-CS scan 7	−.62	10	.05	−.57	12	.05	−.49	22	.01
Participation									
Mood II: social affection	.33	51	.01	.24	49	.05	.27	100	.005
CP Scale I, R-S	.23	58	.05	.32	60	.01	.28	118	.005
Exercycle	.38	60	.005	.42	60	.0005	.40	120	.0005
Information									
Cardiac information test	.40	54	.005	.33	52	.01	.37	106	.0005
Blood pressure									
None									
17-OH-CS solvable 7:30									
Mood II: surgency	−.51	17	.025	−.42	17	.05	−.46	34	.005
17-OH-CS scan 5	.91	9	.0005	.75	7	.025	.85	16	.0005
Cholesterol	.71	19	.0005	.42	18	.05	.53	37	.0005
17-OH-CS solvable 10:45	.87	15	.0005	.62	11	.025	.68	26	.0005
17-OH-CS solvable 11:00	.89	15	.0005	.61	12	.025	.69	27	.0005
17-OH-CS solvable 12:10	.52	14	.05	.80	12	.005	.65	26	.0005
17-OH-CS solvable 3:30	.78	19	.0005	.53	17	.025	.63	36	.0005
17-OH-CS solvable 11:30	.77	14	.005	.56	18	.01	.63	32	.0005
17-OH-CS unsolvable 7:30	.88	19	.0005	.56	17	.01	.68	36	.0005
17-OH-CS unsolvable 10:45	.88	16	.0005	.52	16	.025	.65	32	.0005
17-OH-CS unsolvable 11:00	.91	16	.0005	.50	16	.025	.64	32	.0005
17-OH-CS solvable 10:45									
Mood I: fatigue	.46	22	.025	.62	23	.005	.58	45	.0005
17-OH-CS scan 4	.77	11	.005	.82	8	.01	.80	19	.0005
17-OH-CS scan 5	.85	9	.005	1.00	6	.0005	.86	15	.0005
17-OH-CS scan 8	.85	7	.01	.86	5	.05	.80	12	.005
Cholesterol	.41	18	.05	.53	18	.025	.49	36	.005
17-OH-CS solvable 7:30	.87	15	.0005	.62	11	.025	.68	26	.0005
17-OH-CS solvable 11:00	.89	23	.0005	.98	21	.0005	.95	44	.0005
17-OH-CS solvable 12:10	.62	21	.005	.83	22	.0005	.68	43	.0005
17-OH-CS solvable 3:30	.67	21	.0005	.73	18	.0005	.67	39	.0005
17-OH-CS solvable 11:30	.66	14	.005	.69	11	.01	.58	25	.005
17-OH-CS unsolvable 7:30	.80	18	.0005	.74	12	.005	.60	30	.0005
17-OH-CS unsolvable 10:45	.80	19	.0005	.73	19	.0005	.71	38	.0005
17-OH-CS unsolvable 11:00	.80	19	.0005	.75	19	.0005	.73	38	.0005
17-OH-CS unsolvable 12:10	.74	19	.0005	.62	19	.005	.57	38	.0005
17-OH-CS unsolvable 3:30	.81	17	.0005	.84	17	.0005	.81	34	.0005
17-OH-CS unsolvable 11:30	.74	12	.005	.76	11	.005	.56	23	.005
17-OH-CS solvable 11:00									
Mood I: fatigue	.44	22	.025	.62	22	.005	.56	44	.0005

Table K-1. Significant correlations in split-half samples and total sample for MI patients—cont'd

Variable	Sample 1			Sample 2			Total sample		
	r	N	p	r	N	p	r	N	p
17-OH-CS scan 5	.58	9	.05	.85	6	.025	.62	15	.01
17-OH-CS scan 8	.85	7	.01	.86	5	.05	.78	12	.005
17-OH-CS solvable 7:30	.89	15	.0005	.61	12	.025	.69	27	.0005
17-OH-CS solvable 10:45	.89	23	.0005	.98	21	.0005	.95	44	.0005
17-OH-CS solvable 12:10	.70	21	.0005	.85	21	.0005	.70	42	.0005
17-OH-CS solvable 3:30	.76	21	.0005	.77	19	.0005	.72	40	.0005
17-OH-CS solvable 11:30	.80	14	.0005	.77	12	.005	.67	.26	.0005
17-OH-CS unsolvable 7:30	.88	18	.0005	.79	13	.005	.64	31	.0005
17-OH-CS unsolvable 10:45	.87	19	.0005	.72	19	.0005	.73	38	.0005
17-OH-CS unsolvable 11:00	.84	19	.0005	.72	19	.0005	.74	38	.0005
17-OH-CS unsolvable 12:10	.78	19	.0005	.64	19	.005	.59	38	.0005
17-OH-CS unsolvable 3:30	.60	17	.005	.82	17	.0005	.72	34	.0005
17-OH-CS unsolvable 11:30	.79	12	.005	.79	11	.005	.58	23	.005
17-OH-CS solvable 12:10									
Days hospital	.49	21	.025	.49	23	.01	.48	44	.005
17-OH-CS scan 7	.65	8	.05	.54	11	.05	.49	19	.025
17-OH-CS solvable 7:30	.52	14	.05	.80	12	.005	.65	26	.0005
17-OH-CS solvable 10:45	.62	21	.005	.83	22	.0005	.68	43	.0005
17-OH-CS solvable 11:00	.70	21	.0005	.85	21	.0005	.70	42	.0005
17-OH-CS solvable 3:30	.68	21	.0005	.71	19	.0005	.69	40	.0005
17-OH-CS solvable 11:30	.69	14	.005	.58	12	.025	.66	26	.0005
17-OH-CS unsolvable 7:30	.85	18	.0005	.65	13	.01	.82	31	.0005
17-OH-CS unsolvable 10:45	.76	19	.0005	.73	20	.0005	.74	39	.0005
17-OH-CS unsolvable 11:00	.49	19	.025	.74	20	.0005	.55	39	.0005
17-OH-CS unsolvable 12:10	.54	19	.01	.67	20	.005	.56	39	.0005
17-OH-CS unsolvable 3:30	.53	17	.01	.73	18	.0005	.56	35	.0005
17-OH-CS unsolvable 11:30	.87	12	.0005	.53	11	.05	.81	23	.0005
17-OH-CS solvable 3:30									
Mood I: fatigue	.40	27	.025	.67	25	.0005	.51	52	.0005
17-OH-CS solvable 7:30	.78	19	.0005	.53	17	.025	.63	36	.0005
17-OH-CS solvable 10:45	.67	21	.0005	.73	18	.0005	.67	39	.0005
17-OH-CS solvable 11:00	.76	21	.0005	.77	19	.0005	.72	40	.0005
17-OH-CS solvable 12:10	.68	21	.0005	.71	19	.0005	.69	40	.0005
17-OH-CS solvable 11:30	.83	20	.0005	.80	19	.0005	.82	39	.0005
17-OH-CS unsolvable 7:30	.82	25	.0005	.70	17	.005	.79	42	.0005
17-OH-CS unsolvable 10:45	.76	23	.0005	.82	21	.0005	.79	44	.0005
17-OH-CS unsolvable 11:00	.71	22	.0005	.80	21	.0005	.75	43	.0005
17-OH-CS unsolvable 12:10	.70	22	.0005	.67	21	.0005	.67	43	.0005
17-OH-CS unsolvable 3:30	.77	23	.0005	.84	22	.0005	.79	45	.0005
17-OH-CS unsolvable 11:30	.72	19	.0005	.80	15	.0005	.74	34	.0005
17-OH-CS solvable 11:30									
Cholesterol	.59	18	.005	.49	18	.025	.51	36	.005
17-OH-CS solvable 7:30	.77	14	.005	.56	18	.01	.63	32	.0005
17-OH-CS solvable 10:45	.66	14	.005	.69	11	.01	.58	25	.005
17-OH-CS solvable 11:00	.80	14	.0005	.77	12	.005	.67	26	.0005
17-OH-CS solvable 12:10	.69	14	.005	.58	12	.025	.66	26	.0005
17-OH-CS solvable 3:30	.83	20	.0005	.80	19	.0005	.82	39	.0005
17-OH-CS unsolvable 7:30	.81	19	.0005	.69	18	.005	.76	37	.0005

Continued.

Table K-1. Significant correlations in split-half samples and total sample for MI patients—cont'd

Variable	Sample 1			Sample 2			Total sample		
	r	N	p	r	N	p	r	N	p
17-OH-CS unsolvable 10:45	.80	16	.0005	.74	17	.0005	.77	33	.0005
17-OH-CS unsolvable 11:00	.77	16	.0005	.67	17	.005	.71	33	.0005
17-OH-CS unsolvable 12:10	.78	16	.0005	.54	16	.025	.70	32	.0005
17-OH-CS unsolvable 3:30	.74	19	.0005	.81	18	.0005	.75	37	.0005
17-OH-CS unsolvable 11:30	.85	17	.0005	.82	16	.0005	.84	33	.0005
17-OH-CS unsolvable 7:30									
Mood I: anxiety	.38	25	.05	.43	18	.05	.40	43	.005
Mood I: fatigue	.33	25	.05	.53	18	.025	.40	43	.005
Cholesterol	.55	24	.005	.63	17	.005	.55	41	.0005
17-OH-CS solvable 7:30	.88	19	.0005	.56	17	.01	.68	36	.0005
17-OH-CS solvable 10:45	.80	18	.0005	.74	12	.005	.60	30	.0005
17-OH-CS solvable 11:00	.88	18	.0005	.79	13	.005	.64	31	.0005
17-OH-CS solvable 12:10	.85	18	.0005	.65	13	.01	.82	31	.0005
17-OH-CS solvable 3:30	.82	25	.0005	.70	17	.005	.79	42	.0005
17-OH-CS solvable 11:30	.81	19	.0005	.69	18	.005	.76	37	.0005
17-OH-CS unsolvable 10:45	.84	22	.0005	.51	18	.025	.70	40	.0005
17-OH-CS unsolvable 3:30	.86	23	.0005	.59	18	.005	.78	41	.0005
17-OH-CS unsolvable 11:30	.76	20	.0005	.85	16	.0005	.79	36	.0005
17-OH-CS unsolvable 10:45									
Mood I: fatigue	.43	24	.025	.52	24	.005	.47	48	.0005
17-OH-CS scan 5	.70	10	.025	.94	8	.0005	.72	18	.0005
17-OH-CS scan 7	.59	10	.05	.98	11	.0005	.80	21	.0005
17-OH-CS scan 8	.94	6	.005	1.00	4	.0005	.95	10	.0005
Cholesterol	.40	21	.05	.65	21	.005	.51	42	.0005
17-OH-CS solvable 7:30	.88	16	.0005	.52	16	.025	.65	32	.0005
17-OH-CS solvable 10:45	.80	19	.0005	.73	19	.0005	.71	38	.0005
17-OH-CS solvable 11:00	.87	19	.0005	.72	19	.0005	.73	38	.0005
17-OH-CS solvable 12:10	.76	19	.0005	.73	20	.0005	.74	39	.0005
17-OH-CS solvable 3:30	.76	23	.0005	.82	21	.0005	.79	44	.0005
17-OH-CS solvable 11:30	.80	16	.0005	.74	17	.0005	.77	33	.0005
17-OH-CS unsolvable 7:30	.84	22	.0005	.51	18	.025	.70	40	.0005
17-OH-CS unsolvable 11:00	.86	24	.0005	.92	25	.0005	.89	49	.0005
17-OH-CS unsolvable 12:10	.79	23	.0005	.69	24	.0005	.74	47	.0005
17-OH-CS unsolvable 3:30	.64	20	.005	.75	23	.0005	.70	43	.0005
17-OH-CS unsolvable 11:30	.84	16	.0005	.77	16	.0005	.80	32	.0005
17-OH-CS unsolvable 11:00									
Mood I: fatigue	.39	23	.05	.61	24	.005	.50	47	.0005
17-OH-CS scan 5	.72	10	.01	.96	8	.0005	.75	18	.0005
Highest temperature	.50	24	.01	.39	25	.05	.45	49	.005
17-OH-CS solvable 7:30	.91	16	.0005	.50	16	.025	.64	32	.0005
17-OH-CS solvable 10:45	.80	19	.0005	.75	19	.0005	.73	38	.0005
17-OH-CS solvable 11:00	.84	19	.0005	.72	19	.0005	.74	38	.0005
17-OH-CS solvable 12:10	.49	19	.025	.74	20	.0005	.55	39	.0005
17-OH-CS solvable 3:30	.71	22	.0005	.80	21	.0005	.75	43	.0005
17-OH-CS solvable 11:30	.77	16	.0005	.67	17	.005	.71	33	.0005
17-OH-CS unsolvable 10:45	.86	24	.0005	.92	25	.0005	.89	49	.0005
17-OH-CS unsolvable 12:10	.84	23	.0005	.69	24	.0005	.76	47	.0005
17-OH-CS unsolvable 3:30	.71	20	.0005	.69	23	.0005	.69	43	.0005
17-OH-CS unsolvable 11:30	.63	15	.01	.57	16	.01	.57	31	.005

Table K-1. Significant correlations in split-half samples and total sample for MI patients—cont'd

Variable	Sample 1			Sample 2			Total sample		
	r	N	p	r	N	p	r	N	p
17-OH-CS unsolvable 12:10									
Mood I: fatigue	.38	23	.05	.52	23	.005	.39	46	.005
17-OH-CS scan 5	.56	10	.05	.69	7	.05	.55	17	.025
Highest temperature	.45	24	.025	.38	24	.05	.41	48	.005
17-OH-CS solvable 10:45	.72	19	.0005	.62	19	.005	.57	38	.0005
17-OH-CS solvable 11:00	.78	19	.0005	.64	19	.005	.59	38	.0005
17-OH-CS solvable 12:10	.54	19	.01	.67	20	.005	.56	39	.0005
17-OH-CS solvable 3:30	.70	22	.0005	.67	21	.0005	.67	43	.0005
17-OH-CS solvable 11:30	.78	16	.0005	.53	16	.025	.70	32	.0005
17-OH-CS unsolvable 10:45	.79	23	.0005	.69	24	.0005	.74	47	.0005
17-OH-CS unsolvable 11:00	.84	23	.0005	.69	24	.0005	.76	47	.0005
17-OH-CS unsolvable 3:30	.53	21	.01	.71	22	.005	.62	43	.0005
17-OH-CS unsolvable 3:30									
17-OH-CS scan 3	.59	11	.05	.99	5	.0005	.64	16	.005
17-OH-CS scan 4	.80	9	.005	.94	7	.005	.85	16	.0005
17-OH-CS scan 5	.93	9	.0005	.91	8	.005	.89	17	.0005
Cholesterol	.72	21	.0005	.39	21	.05	.51	42	.0005
17-OH-CS solvable 10:45	.81	17	.0005	.84	17	.0005	.81	34	.0005
17-OH-CS solvable 11:00	.60	17	.005	.82	17	.0005	.72	34	.0005
17-OH-CS solvable 12:10	.53	17	.025	.73	18	.0005	.56	35	.0005
17-OH-CS solvable 3:30	.77	23	.0005	.84	22	.0005	.79	45	.0005
17-OH-CS solvable 11:30	.74	19	.0005	.81	18	.0005	.75	37	.0005
17-OH-CS unsolvable 7:30	.86	23	.0005	.59	18	.005	.78	41	.0005
17-OH-CS unsolvable 10:45	.64	20	.005	.75	23	.0005	.70	43	.0005
17-OH-CS unsolvable 11:00	.71	20	.0005	.69	23	.0005	.69	43	.0005
17-OH-CS unsolvable 12:10	.53	21	.01	.72	22	.0005	.62	43	.0005
17-OH-CS unsolvable 11:30	.70	19	.0005	.72	16	.005	.71	35	.0005
17-OH-CS unsolvable 11:30									
Cholesterol	.71	18	.0005	.76	15	.0005	.66	33	.0005
17-OH-CS solvable 10:45	.74	12	.005	.76	11	.005	.56	23	.005
17-OH-CS solvable 11:00	.79	12	.005	.79	11	.005	.58	23	.005
17-OH-CS solvable 12:10	.87	12	.0005	.53	11	.05	.81	23	.0005
17-OH-CS solvable 3:30	.72	19	.0005	.80	15	.0005	.74	34	.0005
17-OH-CS solvable 11:30	.85	17	.0005	.82	16	.0005	.84	33	.0005
17-OH-CS unsolvable 7:30	.76	20	.0005	.85	16	.0005	.79	36	.0005
17-OH-CS unsolvable 10:45	.84	16	.0005	.77	16	.0005	.80	32	.0005
17-OH-CS unsolvable 11:00	.63	15	.01	.57	16	.01	.57	31	.005
17-OH-CS unsolvable 3:30	.70	19	.0005	.72	16	.005	.71	35	.0005
NEFA solvable 7:30									
None									
NEFA solvable 10:45									
Cardiac information test	.51	15	.025	.49	19	.025	.47	34	.005
17-OH-CS scan 7	−.99	4	.005	−.55	10	.05	−.65	14	.01
NEFA solvable 11:00	.98	16	.0005	.96	20	.0005	.95	36	.0005
NEFA solvable 12:10	.90	13	.0005	.95	12	.0005	.93	25	.0005
NEFA unsolvable 10:45	.47	14	.05	.77	18	.0005	.63	32	.0005
NEFA unsolvable 11:00	.90	14	.0005	.63	18	.005	.67	32	.0005
NEFA unsolvable 12:10	.70	12	.01	.93	12	.0005	.82	24	.0005
NEFA scan 6	.73	6	.05	.81	13	.0005	.80	19	.0005

Continued.

Table K-1. Significant correlations in split-half samples and total sample for MI patients—cont'd

Variable	Sample 1			Sample 2			Total sample		
	r	*N*	*p*	*r*	*N*	*p*	*r*	*N*	*p*
NEFA solvable 11:00									
Cardiac information test	.54	15	.025	.44	18	.05	.41	33	.01
17-OH-CS scan 7	−.84	5	.05	−.61	10	.05	−.64	15	.005
NEFA solvable 10:45	.98	16	.0005	.96	20	.0005	.95	36	.0005
NEFA solvable 12:10	.90	14	.0005	.93	12	.0005	.89	26	.0005
NEFA unsolvable 10:45	.55	15	.025	.88	18	.0005	.72	33	.0005
NEFA unsolvable 12:10	.76	13	.005	.87	12	.0005	.84	25	.0005
NEFA solvable 12:10									
NEFA solvable 10:45	.90	13	.0005	.95	12	.0005	.93	25	.0005
NEFA solvable 11:00	.90	14	.0005	.93	12	.0005	.89	26	.0005
NEFA unsolvable 10:45	.59	14	.025	.77	12	.005	.69	26	.0005
NEFA unsolvable 12:10	.74	13	.005	.84	12	.0005	.78	25	.0005
NEFA scan 6	.85	5	.05	.78	7	.025	.80	12	.005
NEFA solvable 3:30									
Cooperation interview	−.90	5	.025	−.91	5	.025	−.89	10	.0005
NEFA solvable 11:30									
Denial: anxiety	−.96	4	.025	−1.00	3	.0005	−.89	7	.005
NEFA unsolvable 7:30									
None									
NEFA unsolvable 10:45									
NEFA solvable 10:45	.47	14	.05	.77	18	.0005	.63	32	.0005
NEFA solvable 11:00	.55	15	.025	.88	18	.0005	.72	33	.0005
NEFA solvable 12:10	.59	14	.025	.77	12	.005	.69	26	.0005
NEFA unsolvable 11:00	.53	19	.01	45	21	.025	.44	40	.005
NEFA unsolvable 12:10	.58	14	.025	.64	12	.025	.59	26	.005
NEFA scan 4	.98	7	.0005	1.00	7	.0005	.99	14	.0005
NEFA scan 7	1.00	5	.0005	.99	9	.0005	1.00	14	.0005
NEFA scan 8	.99	3	.05	1.00	3	.0005	.99	6	.0005
Exercycle									
Participation	.38	60	.005	.42	60	.0005	.40	120	.0005
NEFA unsolvable 11:00									
Cardiac information test	.51	15	.025	.44	19	.05	.41	34	.01
NEFA solvable 10:45	.90	14	.0005	.63	18	.005	.67	32	.0005
NEFA unsolvable 11:00	.53	19	.01	.45	21	.025	.44	40	.005
NEFA unsolvable 12:10	.72	14	.005	.85	12	.005	.83	26	.0005
NEFA scan 1	.99	3	.05	.90	4	.05	.92	7	.005
NEFA scan 7	.98	5	.005	.60	9	.05	.65	14	.01
NEFA unsolvable 12:10									
Cardiac information test	.78	10	.005	.68	10	.025	.64	20	.005
NEFA solvable 10:45	.70	12	.01	.93	12	.0005	.82	24	.0005
NEFA solvable 11:00	.76	13	.005	.87	12	.0005	.84	25	.0005
NEFA solvable 12:10	.74	13	.005	.84	12	.0005	.78	25	.0005
NEFA unsolvable 10:45	.58	14	.025	.64	12	.025	.59	26	.005
NEFA unsolvable 11:00	.72	14	.005	.85	12	.0005	.83	26	.0005
NEFA unsolvable 3:30									
None									
NEFA unsolvable 11:30									
None									

Table K-1. Significant correlations in split-half samples and total sample
for MI patients—cont'd

Variable	Sample 1			Sample 2			Total sample		
	r	N	p	r	N	p	r	N	p
NEFA scan 1									
Mood II: social affection	−.77	7	.025	−.84	5	.05	−.76	12	.005
NEFA unsolvable 11:00	.99	3	.05	.90	4	.05	.92	7	.005
NEFA scan 2									
Mood I: concentration	−.63	9	.05	−.85	7	.01	−.76	16	.0005
LDH	.74	8	.025	.71	7	.05	.74	15	.005
Denial: dependence	.72	10	.01	.89	6	.01	.65	16	.005
NEFA scan 3									
None									
NEFA scan 4									
NEFA unsolvable 10:45	.98	7	.0005	1.00	7	.0005	.99	14	.0005
NEFA scan 5									
Total sleep	.80	8	.01	.68	7	.05	.66	15	.005
NEFA scan 6									
NEFA solvable 10:45	.73	6	.05	.81	13	.0005	.80	19	.0005
NEFA solvable 12:10	.85	5	.05	.78	7	.025	.80	12	.005
NEFA scan 7									
Mood II: social affection	−1.00	4	.0005	−.73	8	.025	−.76	12	.005
NEFA unsolvable 10:45	1.00	5	.0005	.99	9	.0005	1.00	14	.0005
NEFA unsolvable 11:00	.98	5	.005	.60	9	.05	.65	14	.01
NEFA scan 8									
NEFA unsolvable 10:45	.99	3	.05	1.00	3	.0005	.99	6	.0005

Table K-2. Significant correlations in split-half samples and total sample for on-ward non-MI patients

Variable	Sample 1			Sample 2			Total sample		
	r	N	p	r	N	p	r	N	p
Locus of control (LC)									
None									
Repression-sensitization (R-S)									
Mood I: anxiety	−.27	38	.05	−.39	40	.01	−.33	78	.005
Mood I: sadness	−.34	38	.025	−.41	40	.005	−.37	78	.0005
Mood II: anxiety	−.46	29	.01	−.66	20	.005	−.57	49	.0005
Mood II: social affection	−.36	29	.05	−.42	20	.05	−.38	49	.005
Mood II: sadness	−.31	29	.05	−.61	20	.005	−.43	49	.005
Mood II: skepticism	−.30	29	.05	−.48	20	.025	−.39	49	.005
Denial: dissatisfaction	.47	42	.005	.51	39	.0005	.49	81	.0005
Denial: anxiety	.54	42	.0005	.46	39	.005	.50	81	.0005
Coronary Proneness (CP) Scale I, R-S	−.37	43	.01	−.41	43	.005	−.39	86	.0005
Total CP scale	−.35	43	.025	−.47	43	.005	−.40	86	.0005
Depression change	−.33	28	.05	−.52	20	.01	−.41	48	.005
Size estimation (SE)									
None									
Sex									
Mood I: anxiety	.35	44	.01	.26	46	.05	.30	90	.005
Mood I: vigor	−.24	44	.05	−.28	46	.05	−.25	90	.01
Mood II: anxiety	.53	30	.005	.57	20	.005	.55	50	.0005
Denial: anxiety	−.34	42	.025	−.26	39	.05	−.29	81	.005
Phenothiazines	.24	49	.05	.23	48	.05	.20	97	.025
Analgesics	.32	49	.025	.26	48	.05	.31	97	.005
Temperature change	−.24	49	.05	−.28	49	.05	−.22	98	.025
NEFA scan 2	.87	9	.005	.75	8	.025	.58	17	.01
Age									
None									
Education									
Mood I: concentration	−.36	34	.025	−.40	34	.01	−.39	68	.0005
Mood II: social affection	−.36	27	.05	−.58	18	.01	−.41	45	.005
Religion									
None									
Salary									
None									
Hours TV									
None									
Information test									
None									
Familial heart disease (FHD)									
None									
Previous MIs									
None									
False alarms									
None									
Lie score									
Denial: self-interest	.45	42	.005	.66	39	.0005	.52	81	.0005
Denial: dissatisfaction	.32	42	.025	.44	39	.005	.40	81	.0005
Denial: hostility	.37	42	.01	.69	39	.0005	.52	81	.0005

Table K-2. Significant correlations in split-half samples and total sample for on-ward non-MI patients—cont'd

Variable	Sample 1			Sample 2			Total sample		
	r	N	p	r	N	p	r	N	p
Days CCU									
Days hospital	.59	49	.0005	.33	49	.01	.44	98	.0005
Days before testing	.23	49	.05	.27	49	.05	.25	98	.01
Severity II	.58	12	.025	.53	14	.025	.52	26	.005
Lactate dehydrogenase (LDH)	.29	47	.025	.52	48	.0005	.46	95	.0005
Days hospital									
Days CCU	.59	49	.0005	.33	49	.01	.44	98	.0005
Mood I: social affection	.31	44	.025	.26	46	.05	.29	90	.005
Anticoagulants	.24	49	.05	.47	48	.0005	.39	97	.0005
Heart history									
None									
Days before testing									
Days CCU	.23	49	.05	.27	49	.05	.25	98	.01
Severity II	.65	12	.025	.49	14	.05	.55	26	.005
Severity total	.53	12	.05	.49	14	.05	.52	26	.005
Comfort interview									
None									
Cooperation interview									
Denial: hostility	.33	26	.05	.41	19	.05	.37	45	.01
Relatives CP V, exercise	.84	7	.01	.99	3	.05	.90	10	.0005
Relatives CP VI, overeating	−.69	7	.05	−.99	3	.05	−.49	10	>.05
Nurses' cooperation									
NEFA scan 3	.79	7	.025	.79	7	.025	.68	14	.005
Severity I									
Severity II	.92	12	.0005	1.00	14	.0005	.95	26	.0005
Severity total	.97	12	.0005	1.00	14	.0005	.99	26	.0005
Severity II									
Days CCU	.58	12	.025	.53	14	.025	.52	26	.005
Days before testing	.65	12	.025	.49	14	.05	.55	26	.005
Severity I	.92	12	.0005	1.00	14	.0005	.95	26	.0005
Severity total	.98	12	.0005	1.00	14	.0005	.99	26	.0005
Depression I									
Depression II	.87	28	.0005	.82	20	.0005	.85	48	.0005
Mood I: surgency	−.27	42	.05	−.25	43	.05	−.27	85	.01
Mood I: vigor	−.50	42	.0005	−.26	43	.05	−.36	85	.0005
Depression II									
Depression I	.87	28	.0005	.82	20	.0005	.85	48	.0005
Mood II: fatigue	.42	29	.025	.46	20	.025	.43	49	.005
CP scale II, scanning	−.43	30	.01	−.53	20	.01	−.42	50	.005
Low alarms									
None									
High alarms									
Relatives CP IV, control of self	−.94	6	.0005	−1.00	3	.0005	−.92	9	.0005
Mood I: aggression									
17-OH-CS solvable 12:10	.57	14	.025	.49	18	.025	.52	32	.005
17-OH-CS unsolvable 12:10	.56	13	.025	.58	16	.01	.51	29	.005
17-OH-CS unsolvable 11:30	.56	11	.05	.83	8	.005	.71	19	.0005
Mood I: anxiety									
Repression-sensitization	−.27	38	.05	−.39	40	.01	−.33	78	.005

Continued.

Table K-2. Significant correlations in split-half samples and total sample for on-ward non-MI patients—cont'd

Variable	Sample 1			Sample 2			Total sample		
	r	N	p	r	N	p	r	N	p
Sex	.35	44	.01	.26	46	.05	.30	90	.005
Mood I: fatigue	.47	44	.005	.44	46	.005	.45	90	.0005
Mood I: sadness	.53	44	.0005	.47	46	.0005	.50	90	.0005
Mood II: anxiety	.49	28	.005	.73	20	.0005	.59	48	.0005
CP Scale IV, control of self	.33	38	.025	.38	40	.01	.35	78	.005
Total CP scale	.28	38	.05	.29	40	.05	.28	78	.01
Cards wrong	.48	18	.025	.52	15	.025	.46	33	.005
Mood I: surgency									
Depression I	−.27	42	.05	−.25	43	.05	−.27	85	.01
Mood I: elation	.63	44	.0005	.62	46	.0005	.63	90	.0005
Mood I: social affection	.44	44	.005	.37	46	.005	.39	90	.0005
Mood I: vigor	.58	44	.0005	.51	46	.0005	.54	90	.0005
Mood I: elation									
Mood I: surgency	.63	44	.0005	.62	46	.0005	.63	90	.0005
Mood I: social affection	.47	44	.005	.24	46	.05	.35	90	.0005
Mood I: concentration									
Education	−.36	34	.025	−.40	34	.01	−.39	68	.0005
Mood I: social affection	.36	44	.01	.32	46	.025	.32	90	.005
Mood II: concentration	.73	28	.0005	.44	20	.025	.56	48	.0005
Mood II: social affection	.50	28	.005	.42	20	.05	.45	48	.005
Mood II: vigor	.30	28	.05	.38	20	.05	.34	48	.01
Mood I: fatigue									
Mood I: anxiety	.47	44	.005	.44	46	.005	.45	90	.0005
Mood I: sadness	.30	44	.025	.40	46	.005	.35	90	.0005
Mood II: fatigue	.52	28	.005	.44	20	.025	.48	48	.0005
Mood I: social affection									
Days hospital	.31	44	.025	.26	46	.05	.29	90	.005
Mood I: surgency	.44	44	.005	.37	46	.005	.39	90	.0005
Mood I: elation	.47	44	.005	.24	46	.05	.35	90	.0005
Mood I: concentration	.36	44	.01	.32	46	.025	.32	90	.005
Mood II: social affection	.59	28	.0005	.53	20	.01	.58	48	.0005
Mood II: skepticism	.34	28	.05	.48	20	.025	.42	48	.005
NEFA scan 3	.61	10	.05	.61	11	.025	.54	21	.01
Mood I: sadness									
Repression-sensitization	−.34	38	.025	−.41	40	.005	−.37	78	.0005
Mood I: anxiety	.53	44	.0005	.47	46	.0005	.50	90	.0005
Mood I: fatigue	.30	44	.025	.40	46	.005	.35	90	.0005
Mood I: skepticism	.26	44	.05	.42	46	.005	.34	90	.005
CP Scale IV, control of self	.29	38	.05	.29	40	.05	.29	78	.005
Mood I: skepticism									
Mood I: sadness	.26	44	.05	.42	46	.005	.34	90	.005
Mood I: egotism	.29	44	.05	.50	46	.0005	.43	90	.0005
Mood II: skepticism	.43	28	.025	.47	20	.025	.46	48	.005
CP scale IV, control of self	.32	38	.025	.27	40	.05	.28	78	.01
Cards turned, unsolvable	.56	17	.01	.61	14	.01	.58	31	.005
NEFA solvable 11:00	−.53	12	.05	−.50	12	.05	−.50	24	.01
Mood I: egotism									
Mood I: skepticism	.29	44	.05	.50	46	.0005	.43	90	.0005
Mood II: egotism	.49	28	.005	.38	20	.05	.43	48	.005

Table K-2. Significant correlations in split-half samples and total sample
for on-ward non-MI patients—cont'd

Variable	Sample 1			Sample 2			Total sample		
	r	N	p	r	N	p	r	N	p
Mood I: vigor									
Sex	−.24	44	.05	−.28	46	.05	−.25	90	.01
Depression I	−.50	42	.0005	−.26	43	.05	−.36	85	.0005
Mood I: surgency	.58	44	.0005	.51	46	.0005	.54	90	.0005
Mood II: concentration	.31	28	.05	.48	20	.025	.33	48	.025
Sedimentation rate	−.35	37	.025	−.27	40	.05	−.30	77	.005
Mood II: aggression									
Relatives CP V, exercise	−.91	7	.005	−1.00	3	.0005	−.94	10	.0005
Mood II: anxiety									
Repression-sensitization	−.46	29	.01	−.66	20	.005	−.57	49	.0005
Sex	.53	30	.005	.57	20	.005	.55	50	.0005
Mood I: anxiety	.49	28	.005	.73	20	.0005	.59	48	.0005
Mood II: fatigue	.50	30	.005	.67	20	.005	.58	50	.0005
Mood II: sadness	.45	30	.01	.72	20	.0005	.56	50	.0005
Mood II: skepticism	.55	30	.005	.80	20	.0005	.68	50	.0005
Relatives CP VI, overeating	.84	7	.01	1.00	3	.0005	.56	10	.05
Analgesics	.33	30	.05	.43	20	.05	.37	50	.005
Mood II: surgency									
Mood II: elation	.67	30	.0005	.86	20	.0005	.76	50	.0005
Mood II: social affection	.38	30	.025	.47	20	.025	.42	50	.005
Mood II: skepticism	−.39	30	.025	−.38	20	.05	−.37	50	.005
Mood change	.60	28	.0005	.71	20	.0005	.64	48	.0005
Mood II: elation									
Mood II: surgency	.67	30	.0005	.86	20	.0005	.76	50	.0005
Mood II: social affection	.54	30	.005	.48	20	.025	.53	50	.0005
Mood II: vigor	.51	30	.005	.46	20	.025	.48	50	.0005
Mood change	.54	28	.005	.78	20	.0005	.63	48	.0005
Mood II: concentration									
Mood I: social affection	.73	28	.0005	.44	20	.025	.56	48	.0005
Mood I: vigor	.31	28	.05	.48	20	.025	.33	48	.05
Mood II: fatigue									
Depression II	.42	29	.025	.46	20	.025	.43	49	.005
Mood I: fatigue	.52	28	.005	.44	20	.025	.48	48	.0005
Mood II: anxiety	.50	30	.005	.67	20	.005	.58	50	.0005
Mood II: sadness	.36	30	.05	.61	20	.005	.45	50	.005
Mood II: skepticism	.59	30	.0005	.51	20	.025	.54	50	.0005
Mood II: vigor	−.34	30	.05	−.43	20	.05	−.38	50	.005
Relatives CP VI, overeating	.89	7	.005	1.00	3	.0005	.81	10	.005
Mood change	−.51	28	.005	−.63	20	.005	−.56	48	.0005
Mood II: social affection									
Repression-sensitization	−.36	29	.05	−.42	20	.05	−.38	49	.005
Education	−.36	27	.05	−.58	18	.01	−.41	45	.005
Mood I: concentration	.50	28	.005	.42	20	.05	.45	48	.005
Mood I: social affection	.59	28	.0005	.53	20	.01	.58	48	.0005
Mood II: surgency	.38	30	.025	.47	20	.025	.42	50	.005
Mood II: elation	.54	30	.005	.48	20	.025	.53	50	.0005
CP Scale IV, control of self	.49	29	.01	.40	20	.05	.42	49	.005
Mood II: sadness									
Repression-sensitization	−.31	29	.05	−.61	20	.005	−.43	49	.005

Continued.

Table K-2. Significant correlations in split-half samples and total sample for on-ward non-MI patients—cont'd

Variable	Sample 1			Sample 2			Total sample		
	r	*N*	*p*	*r*	*N*	*p*	*r*	*N*	*p*
Mood II: anxiety	.45	30	.01	.72	20	.0005	.56	50	.0005
Mood II: fatigue	.36	30	.05	.61	20	.005	.45	50	.005
Mood II: skepticism	.57	30	.005	.54	20	.01	.54	50	.0005
Mood II: skepticism									
Repression-sensitization	−.30	29	.05	−.48	20	.025	−.39	49	.005
Mood I: social affection	.34	28	.05	.48	20	.025	.42	48	.005
Mood I: skepticism	.43	28	.025	.41	20	.025	.46	48	.005
Mood II: anxiety	.55	30	.005	.80	20	.0005	.68	50	.0005
Mood II: surgency	−.39	30	.025	−.38	20	.05	−.37	50	.005
Mood II: fatigue	.59	30	.0005	.51	20	.025	.54	50	.0005
Mood II: sadness	.57	30	.005	.54	20	.01	.54	50	.0005
Relatives CP V, exercise	−.91	7	.005	−1.00	3	.0005	−.92	10	.0005
Analgesics	.39	30	.025	.40	20	.05	.40	50	.005
Mood change	−.31	28	.05	−.53	20	.01	−.40	48	.005
Mood II: egotism									
Mood I: egotism	.49	28	.005	.38	20	.05	.43	48	.005
Mood II: vigor									
Mood I: concentration	.30	28	.05	.38	20	.05	.34	48	.01
Mood II: elation	.51	30	.005	.46	20	.025	.48	50	.0005
Mood II: fatigue	−.34	30	.05	−.43	20	.05	−.38	50	.005
Mood change	.58	28	.005	.46	20	.025	.52	48	.0005
17-OH-CS scan 1									
17-OH-CS scan 2	.74	6	.05	.81	9	.005	.84	15	.0005
17-OH-CS scan 4	.99	3	.05	.99	4	.005	.99	7	.0005
17-OH-CS solvable 7:30	.95	4	.025	.80	5	.05	.90	9	.0005
17-OH-CS scan 2									
17-OH-CS scan 1	.74	6	.05	.81	9	.005	.84	15	.0005
17-OH-CS scan 4	.91	7	.005	.70	8	.05	.86	15	.0005
17-OH-CS solvable 10:45	.97	9	.0005	.61	11	.025	.83	20	.0005
17-OH-CS solvable 11:00	.81	9	.005	.65	11	.025	.80	20	.0005
17-OH-CS solvable 12:10	.86	9	.005	.62	11	.025	.75	20	.0005
17-OH-CS unsolvable 10:45	.92	9	.0005	.63	10	.025	.82	19	.0005
17-OH-CS scan 3									
17-OH-CS scan 4	.85	10	.005	.92	11	.0005	.90	21	.0005
17-OH-CS solvable 7:30	.76	9	.01	.73	11	.005	.77	20	.0005
17-OH-CS solvable 10:45	.88	11	.0005	.98	15	.0005	.95	26	.0005
17-OH-CS solvable 11:00	.81	11	.005	.97	15	.0005	.91	26	.0005
17-OH-CS solvable 12:10	.84	11	.005	.94	15	.0005	.91	26	.0005
17-OH-CS solvable 3:30	.69	11	.01	.84	12	.0005	.78	23	.0005
17-OH-CS solvable 11:30	.65	8	.05	.69	10	.025	.62	18	.005
17-OH-CS unsolvable 7:30	.89	10	.0005	.57	10	.05	.79	20	.0005
17-OH-CS unsolvable 10:45	.93	11	.0005	.81	13	.0005	.89	24	.0005
17-OH-CS unsolvable 11:00	.91	11	.0005	.76	13	.005	.85	24	.0005
17-OH-CS unsolvable 12:10	.81	10	.005	.76	13	.005	.81	23	.0005
17-OH-CS scan 4									
17-OH-CS scan 1	.99	3	.05	.99	4	.005	.99	7	.0005
17-OH-CS scan 2	.91	7	.005	.70	8	.05	.86	15	.0005
17-OH-CS scan 3	.85	10	.005	.92	11	.0005	.90	21	.0005
17-OH-CS scan 5	.94	5	.01	.88	6	.01	.88	11	.0005

Table K-2. Significant correlations in split-half samples and total sample for on-ward non-MI patients—cont'd

Variable	Sample 1			Sample 2			Total sample		
	r	N	p	r	N	p	r	N	p
17-OH-CS solvable 7:30	.96	8	.0005	.91	10	.0005	.94	18	.0005
17-OH-CS solvable 10:45	.95	10	.0005	.95	13	.0005	.96	23	.0005
17-OH-CS solvable 11:00	.88	10	.0005	.93	13	.0005	.89	23	.0005
17-OH-CS solvable 12:10	.88	9	.005	.95	13	.0005	.92	22	.0005
17-OH-CS solvable 3:30	.71	9	.025	.92	11	.0005	.84	20	.0005
17-OH-CS solvable 11:30	.75	8	.025	.71	10	.025	.72	18	.005
17-OH-CS unsolvable 7:30	.75	8	.025	.95	11	.0005	.87	19	.0005
17-OH-CS unsolvable 10:45	1.00	9	.0005	.97	13	.0005	.98	22	.0005
17-OH-CS unsolvable 11:00	.93	9	.0005	.96	12	.0005	.92	21	.0005
17-OH-CS unsolvable 12:10	.72	8	.025	.96	12	.0005	.83	20	.0005
17-OH-CS unsolvable 3:30	.88	8	.005	.95	9	.0005	.88	17	.0005
17-OH-CS unsolvable 11:30	.93	7	.005	.98	7	.0005	.93	14	.0005
17-OH-CS scan 4									
17-OH-CS scan 4	.94	5	.01	.88	6	.01	.88	11	.0005
17-OH-CS solvable 10:45	.99	6	.0005	.85	8	.005	.89	14	.0005
17-OH-CS solvable 11:00	.86	6	.025	.91	8	.005	.90	14	.0005
17-OH-CS solvable 12:10	.80	6	.05	.88	8	.005	.84	14	.0005
17-OH-CS solvable 3:30	.76	6	.05	.78	6	.05	.76	12	.005
17-OH-CS unsolvable 10:45	.99	6	.0005	.91	9	.0005	.93	15	.0005
17-OH-CS unsolvable 11:00	.80	6	.05	.90	8	.005	.87	14	.0005
17-OH-CS unsolvable 3:30	.85	6	.025	.92	4	.05	.88	10	.0005
17-OH-CS scan 6									
None									
17-OH-CS scan 7									
None									
17-OH-CS scan 8									
None									
Sedimentation rate									
Mood I: vigor	−.35	37	.025	−.27	40	.05	−.30	47	.025
Highest temperature	.42	42	.005	.41	43	.005	.43	85	.0005
Last temperature	.37	42	.01	.36	43	.01	.37	85	.0005
Uric acid									
Analgesics	−.34	41	.025	−.33	39	.025	−.35	80	.005
Cholesterol									
None									
SGOT									
LDH	.58	47	.0005	.30	48	.025	.37	95	.0005
Diversion	.27	38	.05	.32	33	.05	.29	71	.01
Blood pressure	.52	18	.025	.61	15	.01	.52	33	.005
LDH									
Days CCU	.29	47	.025	.52	48	.0005	.46	95	.0005
SGOT	.58	47	.0005	.30	48	.025	.37	95	.0005
WBC									
Highest temperature	.24	49	.05	.58	49	.0005	.48	98	.0005
Relatives Ullmann	.70	9	.025	.96	4	.025	.68	13	.005
Highest temperature									
Sedimentation rate	.42	42	.005	.41	43	.005	.43	85	.0005
WBC	.24	49	.05	.58	49	.0005	.48	98	.0005
First 4:00 temperature	.74	49	.0005	.45	49	.0005	.58	98	.0005

Continued.

Table K-2. Significant correlations in split-half samples and total sample for on-ward non-MI patients—cont'd

Variable	Sample 1			Sample 2			Total sample		
	r	*N*	*p*	*r*	*N*	*p*	*r*	*N*	*p*
Last 4:00 temperature	.64	49	.0005	.49	49	.0005	.55	98	.0005
First 4:00 temperature									
Highest temperature	.74	49	.0005	.45	49	.0005	.58	98	.0005
Last 4:00 temperature	.52	49	.0005	.58	49	.0005	.55	98	.0005
Temperature change	.73	49	.0005	.52	49	.0005	.63	98	.0005
Last 4:00 temperature									
Mood II: social affection	.38	30	.025	.46	20	.025	.37	50	.005
Sedimentation rate	.37	42	.01	.36	43	.01	.37	85	.0005
Highest temperature	.64	49	.0005	.49	49	.0005	.55	98	.0005
First 4:00 temperature	.52	49	.0005	.58	49	.0005	.55	98	.0005
Return to work									
None									
Subsequent hospitalization									
None									
Death									
None									
Denial: self-interest									
Lie score	.45	42	.005	.66	39	.0005	.52	81	.0005
Denial: dissatisfaction	.55	42	.0005	.47	39	.005	.49	81	.0005
Denial: hostility	.59	42	.0005	.69	39	.0005	.64	81	.0005
Denial: complacency	.35	42	.025	.42	39	.005	.39	81	.0005
Denial: sexuality	.46	42	.005	.60	39	.0005	.49	81	.0005
Denial: dissatisfaction									
Repression-sensitization	.47	42	.005	.51	39	.0005	.49	81	.0005
Lie score	.32	42	.025	.44	39	.005	.40	81	.0005
Denial: self-interest	.55	42	.0005	.47	39	.005	.49	81	.0005
Denial: hostility	.59	42	.0005	.72	39	.0005	.66	81	.0005
Denial: anxiety	.57	42	.0005	.60	39	.0005	.58	81	.0005
Denial: sexuality	.59	42	.0005	.56	39	.0005	.58	81	.0005
Denial: dependence									
None									
Denial: hostility									
Lie score	.37	42	.01	.69	39	.0005	.52	81	.0005
Cooperation interview	.33	26	.05	.41	19	.05	.37	45	.01
Denial: self-interest	.59	42	.0005	.69	39	.0005	.64	81	.0005
Denial: dissatisfaction	.59	42	.0005	.72	39	.0005	.66	81	.0005
Denial: anxiety	.28	42	.05	.40	39	.01	.34	81	.005
Denial: sexuality	.37	42	.01	.65	39	.0005	.50	81	.0005
Denial: anxiety									
Repression-sensitization	.54	42	.0005	.46	39	.005	.50	81	.0005
Sex	−.34	42	.025	−.26	39	.05	−.29	81	.005
Denial: dissatisfaction	.57	42	.0005	.60	39	.0005	.58	81	.0005
Denial: hostility	.28	42	.05	.40	39	.01	.34	81	.005
Denial: sexuality	.26	42	.05	.38	39	.01	.31	81	.005
17-OH-CS unsolvable 3:30	.50	15	.05	.72	9	.025	.58	24	.005
Denial: complacency									
Denial: self-interest	.35	42	.025	.42	39	.005	.39	81	.0005
CP Scale III, perfectionism	.33	42	.025	.62	39	.0005	.46	81	.0005
Total CP scale	.29	42	.05	.65	39	.0005	.47	81	.0005

Table K-2. Significant correlations in split-half samples and total sample
for on-ward non-MI patients—cont'd

Variable	Sample 1			Sample 2			Total sample		
	r	N	p	r	N	p	r	N	p
Denial: sexuality									
Denial: self-interest	.46	42	.005	.60	39	.0005	.49	81	.0005
Denial: dissatisfaction	.59	42	.0005	.56	39	.0005	.58	81	.0005
Denial: hostility	.37	42	.01	.65	39	.0005	.50	81	.0005
Denial: anxiety	.26	42	.05	.38	39	.01	.31	81	.005
CP Scale I, R-S									
None									
CP Scale II, scanning									
Depression II	−.43	30	.01	−.53	20	.01	−.42	50	.005
CP Scale III, perfectionism									
Denial: complacency	.33	42	.025	.62	39	.0005	.46	81	.0005
CP Scale IV, control of self	.44	43	.005	.51	43	.0005	.46	86	.0005
Total CP score	.68	43	.0005	.70	43	.0005	.69	86	.0005
CP Scale IV, control of self									
Repression-sensitization	−.37	43	.01	−.41	43	.005	−.39	86	.0005
Mood I: anxiety	.33	38	.025	.38	40	.01	.35	78	.005
Mood I: sadness	.29	38	.05	.29	40	.05	.29	78	.005
Mood I: skepticism	.32	38	.025	.27	40	.05	.28	78	.01
Mood II: social affection	.46	29	.01	.41	20	.05	.42	49	.005
CP Scale III, perfectionism	.44	43	.005	.51	43	.0005	.46	86	.0005
Total CP	.71	43	.0005	.61	43	.0005	.65	86	.0005
CP Scale V, exercise									
None									
CP Scale VI, overeating									
Total CP	.24	43	.05	.38	43	.01	.31	86	.005
Total CP									
Repression-sensitization	−.35	43	.025	−.47	43	.005	−.40	86	.0005
Mood I: anxiety	.28	38	.05	.29	40	.05	.28	78	.01
Denial: complacency	.29	42	.05	.65	39	.0005	.47	81	.0005
CP III, perfectionism	.68	43	.0005	.70	43	.0005	.69	86	.0005
CP Scale IV, control of self	.71	43	.0005	.61	43	.0005	.65	86	.0005
CP Scale VI, overeating	.24	43	.05	.38	43	.01	.31	86	.005
Relatives CP I, R-S									
None									
Relatives CP II, scanning									
None									
Relatives CP III, perfectionism									
None									
Relatives CP IV, control of self									
High alarms	−.94	6	.0005	−1.00	3	.0005	−.92	9	.0005
Relatives CP V, exercise									
Cooperation interview	.84	7	.01	.99	3	.05	.90	10	.0005
Mood II: aggression	−.91	7	.005	−1.00	3	.0005	−.94	10	.0005
Mood II: skepticism	−.91	7	.005	−1.00	3	.0005	−.92	10	.0005
Relatives CP VI, overeating									
Cooperation interview	−.69	7	.05	−.99	3	.05	−.49	10	>.05
Mood II: anxiety	.84	7	.01	1.00	3	.0005	.56	10	.05
Mood II: fatigue	.89	7	.005	1.00	3	.0005	.81	10	.005
Total relatives CP									
None									

Continued.

Table K-2. Significant correlations in split-half samples and total sample for on-ward non-MI patients—cont'd

Variable	Sample 1			Sample 2			Total sample		
	r	N	p	r	N	p	r	N	p
Relatives LC									
None									
Relatives Ullmann									
WBC	.70	9	.025	.96	4	.025	.68	13	.005
Relatives lie									
None									
Severity total									
Days before testing	.53	12	.05	.49	14	.05	.52	26	.005
Severity I	.97	12	.0005	1.00	14	.0005	.99	26	.0005
Severity II	.98	12	.0005	1.00	14	.0005	.99	26	.0005
Severity change									
None									
Phenothiazines									
Sex	.24	49	.05	.23	48	.05	.20	97	.025
Barbiturates									
None									
Anticoagulants									
Days hospital	.24	49	.05	.47	48	.0005	.39	97	.0005
Analgesics									
Sex	.32	49	.025	.26	48	.05	.31	97	.005
Mood II: anxiety	.33	30	.05	.43	20	.05	.37	50	.005
Mood II: skepticism	.39	30	.025	.40	20	.05	.40	50	.005
Uric acid	−.34	41	.025	−.33	39	.025	−.35	80	.005
Total sleep									
None									
Temperature change									
Sex	−.24	49	.05	−.28	49	.05	−.22	98	.025
First 4:00 temperature	.73	49	.0005	.52	49	.0005	.63	98	.0005
Depression change									
Repression-sensitization	−.33	28	.05	−.52	20	.01	−.41	48	.005
Mood change									
Mood II: surgency	.60	28	.0005	.71	20	.0005	.64	48	.0005
Mood II: elation	.54	28	.005	.78	20	.0005	.63	48	.0005
Mood II: fatigue	−.51	28	.005	−.63	20	.005	−.56	48	.0005
Mood II: skepticism	−.31	28	.05	−.53	20	.01	−.40	48	.005
Mood II: vigor	.58	28	.005	.46	20	.025	.52	48	.0005
Diversion									
SGOT	.27	38	.05	.32	33	.05	.29	71	.01
17-OH-CS unsolvable 7:30	−.61	13	.025	−.79	8	.01	−.45	21	.025
17-OH-CS unsolvable 10:45	−.48	14	.05	−.75	12	.005	−.55	26	.005
Participation									
None									
Information									
None									
Blood pressure									
SGOT	.52	18	.025	.61	15	.01	.52	33	.005
17-OH-CS solvable 7:30									
17-OH-CS scan 1	.95	4	.025	.80	5	.05	.90	9	.0005
17-OH-CS scan 3	.76	9	.01	.73	11	.005	.77	20	.0005

Table K-2. Significant correlations in split-half samples and total sample
for on-ward non-MI patients—cont'd

Variable	Sample 1			Sample 2			Total sample		
	r	N	p	r	N	p	r	N	p
17-OH-CS scan 4	.96	8	.0005	.91	10	.0005	.94	18	.0005
17-OH-CS solvable 10:45	.92	11	.0005	.82	13	.0005	.87	24	.0005
17-OH-CS solvable 11:00	.74	11	.005	.78	13	.005	.77	24	.0005
17-OH-CS solvable 12:10	.87	11	.0005	.87	13	.0005	.87	24	.0005
17-OH-CS solvable 3:30	.72	11	.01	.86	13	.0005	.80	24	.0005
17-OH-CS solvable 11:30	.80	12	.005	.68	12	.01	.71	24	.0005
17-OH-CS unsolvable 7:30	.92	12	.0005	.92	12	.0005	.91	24	.0005
17-OH-CS unsolvable 10:45	.86	12	.0005	.91	12	.0005	.87	24	.0005
17-OH-CS unsolvable 11:00	.85	12	.0005	.87	11	.0005	.87	23	.0005
17-OH-CS unsolvable 12:10	.80	11	.005	.94	11	.0005	.87	22	.0005
17-OH-CS unsolvable 3:30	.84	12	.0005	.87	9	.005	.87	21	.0005
17-OH-CS unsolvable 11:30	.85	10	.005	.96	7	.0005	.88	17	.0005
17-OH-CS solvable 10:45									
17-OH-CS scan 2	.97	9	.0005	.61	11	.025	.83	20	.0005
17-OH-CS scan 3	.88	11	.0005	.98	15	.0005	.95	26	.0005
17-OH-CS scan 4	.94	10	.0005	.95	13	.0005	.96	23	.0005
17-OH-CS scan 5	.99	6	.0005	.85	8	.005	.89	14	.0005
17-OH-CS solvable 7:30	.92	11	.0005	.82	13	.0005	.87	24	.0005
17-OH-CS solvable 11:00	.79	15	.0005	.94	18	.0005	.90	33	.0005
17-OH-CS solvable 12:10	.80	14	.0005	.96	18	.0005	.90	32	.0005
17-OH-CS solvable 3:30	.78	14	.0005	.91	15	.0005	.83	29	.0005
17-OH-CS solvable 11:30	.70	11	.01	.73	13	.005	.72	24	.0005
17-OH-CS unsolvable 7:30	.77	12	.005	.86	13	.0005	.82	25	.0005
17-OH-CS unsolvable 10:45	.94	13	.0005	.89	16	.0005	.91	29	.0005
17-OH-CS unsolvable 11:00	.85	13	.0005	.87	15	.0005	.86	28	.0005
17-OH-CS unsolvable 12:10	.73	13	.005	.89	15	.0005	.80	28	.0005
17-OH-CS unsolvable 3:30	.80	13	.0005	.94	11	.0005	.88	24	.0005
17-OH-CS unsolvable 11:30	.88	10	.0005	.84	8	.005	.84	18	.0005
17-OH-CS solvable 11:00									
17-OH-CS scan 2	.81	9	.005	.65	11	.025	.80	20	.0005
17-OH-CS scan 3	.81	11	.005	.97	15	.0005	.91	26	.0005
17-OH-CS scan 4	.88	10	.0005	.93	13	.0005	.89	23	.0005
17-OH-CS scan 5	.86	6	.025	.91	8	.005	.90	14	.0005
17-OH-CS solvable 7:30	.74	11	.005	.78	13	.005	.77	24	.0005
17-OH-CS solvable 10:45	.79	15	.0005	.94	18	.0005	.90	33	.0005
17-OH-CS solvable 12:10	.89	14	.0005	.95	18	.0005	.92	32	.0005
17-OH-CS solvable 3:30	.76	14	.005	.84	15	.0005	.78	29	.0005
17-OH-CS solvable 11:30	.87	11	.0005	.72	13	.005	.77	24	.0005
17-OH-CS unsolvable 7:30	.78	12	.005	.88	13	.0005	.84	25	.0005
17-OH-CS unsolvable 10:45	.89	13	.0005	.92	16	.0005	.91	29	.0005
17-OH-CS unsolvable 11:00	.78	13	.005	.92	15	.0005	.89	28	.0005
17-OH-CS unsolvable 12:10	.85	13	.0005	.93	15	.0005	.85	28	.0005
17-OH-CS unsolvable 3:30	.72	13	.005	.99	11	.0005	.91	24	.0005
17-OH-CS unsolvable 11:00	.97	10	.0005	.87	8	.005	.90	18	.0005
17-OH-CS solvable 12:10									
Mood I: aggression	.57	14	.025	.49	18	.025	.52	32	.005
17-OH-CS scan 2	.86	9	.005	.62	11	.025	.75	20	.0005
17-OH-CS scan 3	.84	11	.005	.94	15	.0005	.91	26	.0005
17-OH-CS scan 4	.88	9	.005	.95	12	.0005	.92	22	.0005

Continued.

Table K-2. Significant correlations in split-half samples and total sample for on-ward non-MI patients—cont'd

Variable	Sample 1			Sample 2			Total sample		
	r	*N*	*p*	*r*	*N*	*p*	*r*	*N*	*p*
17-OH-CS scan 5	.80	6	.05	.88	8	.005	.84	14	.0005
17-OH-CS solvable 7:30	.87	11	.005	.87	13	.0005	.87	24	.0005
17-OH-CS solvable 10:45	.80	14	.0005	.96	18	.0005	.90	32	.0005
17-OH-CS solvable 11:00	.89	14	.0005	.95	18	.0005	.92	32	.0005
17-OH-CS solvable 3:30	.80	14	.0005	.94	15	.0005	.86	29	.0005
17-OH-CS solvable 11:30	.94	11	.0005	.78	13	.005	.85	24	.0005
17-OH-CS unsolvable 7:30	.91	12	.0005	.91	13	.0005	.90	25	.0005
17-OH-CS unsolvable 10:45	.81	13	.0005	.92	16	.0005	.88	29	.0005
17-OH-CS unsolvable 11:00	.69	13	.005	.94	15	.0005	.83	28	.0005
17-OH-CS unsolvable 12:10	.89	13	.0005	.94	15	.0005	.91	28	.0005
17-OH-CS unsolvable 3:30	.73	13	.005	.95	11	.0005	.84	24	.0005
17-OH-CS unsolvable 11:30	.90	10	.0005	.89	8	.005	.88	18	.0005
17-OH-CS solvable 3:30									
17-OH-CS scan 3	.69	11	.01	.84	12	.0005	.78	23	.0005
17-OH-CS scan 4	.71	9	.025	.92	11	.0005	.84	20	.0005
17-OH-CS scan 5	.76	6	.05	.78	6	.05	.76	12	.005
17-OH-CS solvable 7:30	.72	11	.01	.86	13	.0005	.80	24	.0005
17-OH-CS solvable 10:45	.78	14	.0005	.91	15	.0005	.83	29	.0005
17-OH-CS solvable 11:00	.76	14	.005	.84	15	.0005	.78	29	.0005
17-OH-CS solvable 12:10	.80	14	.0005	.94	15	.0005	.86	29	.0005
17-OH-CS solvable 11:30	.87	11	.0005	.64	13	.01	.76	24	.0005
17-OH-CS unsolvable 7:30	.89	12	.0005	.92	13	.0005	.89	25	.0005
17-OH-CS unsolvable 10:45	.76	13	.005	.88	14	.0005	.81	27	.0005
17-OH-CS unsolvable 11:00	.61	13	.025	.90	13	.0005	.71	26	.0005
17-OH-CS unsolvable 12:10	.83	13	.0005	.89	13	.0005	.85	26	.0005
17-OH-CS unsolvable 3:30	.65	13	.01	.94	11	.0005	.72	24	.0005
17-OH-CS unsolvable 11:30	.84	10	.005	.92	8	.0005	.83	18	.0005
17-OH-CS solvable 11:30									
17-OH-CS scan 3	.65	8	.05	.69	10	.025	.62	18	.005
17-OH-CS scan 4	.75	8	.025	.71	10	.025	.72	18	.0005
17-OH-CS solvable 7:30	.80	12	.005	.68	12	.01	.71	24	.0005
17-OH-CS solvable 10:45	.70	11	.01	.73	13	.005	.72	24	.0005
17-OH-CS solvable 11:00	.87	11	.0005	.72	13	.005	.77	24	.0005
17-OH-CS solvable 12:10	.94	11	.0005	.78	13	.005	.85	24	.0005
17-OH-CS solvable 3:30	.87	11	.0005	.64	13	.01	.76	24	.0005
17-OH-CS unsolvable 7:30	.92	12	.0005	.63	12	.025	.76	24	.0005
17-OH-CS unsolvable 10:45	.71	12	.005	.70	12	.01	.71	24	.0005
17-OH-CS unsolvable 11:00	.61	12	.025	.77	11	.005	.70	23	.0005
17-OH-CS unsolvable 12:10	.95	11	.0005	.82	11	.005	.88	22	.0005
17-OH-CS unsolvable 3:30	.69	12	.01	.65	10	.025	.63	22	.005
17-OH-CS unsolvable 11:30	.88	11	.0005	.72	8	.025	.80	19	.0005
17-OH-CS unsolvable 7:30									
17-OH-CS scan 3	.89	10	.0005	.57	10	.05	.79	20	.0005
17-OH-CS scan 4	.75	8	.025	.95	11	.0005	.87	19	.0005
Diversion	−.61	13	.025	−.79	8	.01	−.45	21	.025
17-OH-CS solvable 7:30	.92	12	.0005	.92	12	.0005	.91	24	.0005
17-OH-CS solvable 10:45	.77	12	.005	.86	13	.0005	.82	25	.0005
17-OH-CS solvable 11:00	.78	12	.005	.88	13	.0005	.84	25	.0005
17-OH-CS solvable 12:10	.91	12	.0005	.91	13	.0005	.90	25	.0005

Table K-2. Significant correlations in split-half samples and total sample
for on-ward non-MI patients—cont'd

Variable	Sample 1			Sample 2			Total sample		
	r	N	p	r	N	p	r	N	p
17-OH-CS solvable 3:30	.89	12	.0005	.92	13	.0005	.89	25	.0005
17-OH-CS solvable 11:30	.92	12	.0005	.63	12	.025	.76	24	.0005
17-OH-CS unsolvable 10:45	.75	14	.005	.96	13	.0005	.87	27	.0005
17-OH-CS unsolvable 11:00	.47	14	.05	.95	12	.0005	.75	26	.0005
17-OH-CS unsolvable 12:10	.91	13	.0005	.93	12	.0005	.91	25	.0005
17-OH-CS unsolvable 3:30	.63	14	.01	.97	10	.0005	.81	24	.0005
17-OH-CS unsolvable 11:30	.75	12	.005	.96	8	.0005	.85	20	.0005
17-OH-CS unsolvable 10:45									
17-OH-CS scan 2	.92	9	.0005	.63	10	.025	.82	19	.0005
17-OH-CS scan 3	.93	11	.0005	.81	13	.0005	.89	24	.0005
17-OH-CS scan 4	1.00	9	.0005	.97	13	.0005	.98	22	.0005
17-OH-CS scan 5	.99	6	.0005	.91	9	.0005	.93	15	.0005
Diversion	−.48	14	.05	−.75	12	.005	−.55	26	.005
17-OH-CS solvable 7:30	.86	12	.0005	.91	12	.0005	.87	24	.0005
17-OH-CS solvable 10:45	.94	13	.0005	.89	16	.0005	.91	29	.0005
17-OH-CS solvable 11:00	.89	13	.0005	.92	16	.0005	.91	29	.0005
17-OH-CS solvable 12:10	.81	13	.0005	.92	16	.0005	.88	29	.0005
17-OH-CS solvable 3:30	.76	13	.005	.88	14	.0005	.81	27	.0005
17-OH-CS solvable 11:30	.71	12	.005	.70	12	.01	.71	24	.0005
17-OH-CS unsolvable 7:30	.75	14	.005	.96	13	.0005	.87	27	.0005
17-OH-CS unsolvable 11:00	.73	16	.005	.97	17	.0005	.88	33	.0005
17-OH-CS unsolvable 12:10	.71	14	.005	.84	17	.0005	.76	31	.0005
17-OH-CS unsolvable 3:30	.73	14	.005	.97	11	.0005	.87	25	.0005
17-OH-CS unsolvable 11:30	.75	11	.005	.96	8	.0005	.86	19	.0005
17-OH-CS unsolvable 11:00									
17-OH-CS scan 3	.91	11	.0005	.76	13	.005	.85	24	.0005
17-OH-CS scan 4	.93	9	.0005	.96	12	.0005	.92	21	.0005
17-OH-CS scan 5	.80	6	.05	.90	8	.005	.87	14	.0005
17-OH-CS solvable 11:30	.85	12	.0005	.87	11	.0005	.87	23	.0005
17-OH-CS solvable 10:45	.85	13	.0005	.87	15	.0005	.86	28	.0005
17-OH-CS solvable 11:00	.78	13	.005	.92	15	.0005	.89	28	.0005
17-OH-CS solvable 12:10	.69	13	.005	.94	15	.0005	.83	28	.0005
17-OH-CS solvable 3:30	.61	13	.025	.90	13	.0005	.71	26	.0005
17-OH-CS solvable 11:30	.61	12	.025	.77	11	.005	.70	23	.0005
17-OH-CS unsolvable 7:30	.47	14	.05	.95	12	.0005	.75	26	.0005
17-OH-CS unsolvable 10:45	.73	16	.005	.97	17	.0005	.88	33	.0005
17-OH-CS unsolvable 12:10	.54	14	.025	.89	17	.0005	.70	31	.0005
17-OH-CS unsolvable 3:30	.67	14	.005	.95	11	.0005	.88	25	.0005
17-OH-CS unsolvable 11:30	.85	11	.0005	.96	8	.0005	.89	19	.0005
17-OH-CS unsolvable 12:10									
Mood I: aggression	.56	13	.025	.58	16	.01	.51	29	.005
17-OH-CS scan 3	.81	10	.005	.76	13	.005	.81	23	.0005
17-OH-CS scan 4	.72	8	.025	.96	12	.0005	.83	20	.0005
17-OH-CS solvable 7:30	.80	11	.005	.94	11	.0005	.87	22	.0005
17-OH-CS solvable 10:45	.73	13	.005	.89	15	.0005	.80	28	.0005
17-OH-CS solvable 11:00	.85	13	.0005	.93	15	.0005	.85	28	.0005
17-OH-CS solvable 12:10	.89	13	.0005	.94	15	.0005	.91	28	.0005
17-OH-CS solvable 3:30	.83	13	.0005	.89	13	.0005	.85	26	.0005
17-OH-CS solvable 11:30	.95	11	.0005	.82	11	.005	.88	22	.0005

Continued.

Table K-2. Significant correlations in split-half samples and total sample for on-ward non-MI patients—cont'd

Variable	Sample 1			Sample 2			Total sample		
	r	*N*	*p*	*r*	*N*	*p*	*r*	*N*	*p*
17-OH-CS unsolvable 7:30	.91	13	.0005	.93	12	.0005	.91	25	.0005
17-OH-CS unsolvable 10:45	.71	14	.005	.84	17	.0005	.76	31	.0005
17-OH-CS unsolvable 11:00	.54	14	.025	.89	17	.0005	.70	31	.0005
17-OH-CS unsolvable 3:30	.53	14	.025	.94	11	.0005	.70	25	.0005
17-OH-CS unsolvable 11:30	.80	11	.005	.97	8	.0005	.84	19	.0005
17-OH-CS unsolvable 3:30									
17-OH-CS scan 3	.73	10	.01	.97	9	.0005	.86	19	.0005
17-OH-CS scan 4	.88	8	.005	.95	9	.0005	.88	17	.0005
17-OH-CS scan 5	.85	6	.025	.92	4	.05	.88	10	.0005
Denial: anxiety	.50	15	.05	.71	9	.025	.58	24	.005
17-OH-CS solvable 7:30	.84	12	.0005	.87	9	.005	.87	21	.0005
17-OH-CS solvable 10:45	.80	13	.0005	.94	11	.0005	.88	24	.0005
17-OH-CS solvable 11:00	.72	13	.005	.99	11	.0005	.91	24	.0005
17-OH-CS solvable 12:10	.73	13	.005	.95	11	.0005	.84	24	.0005
17-OH-CS solvable 3:30	.65	13	.01	.94	11	.0005	.72	24	.0005
17-OH-CS solvable 11:30	.69	12	.01	.65	10	.025	.63	22	.005
17-OH-CS unsolvable 7:30	.63	14	.01	.97	10	.0005	.81	24	.0005
17-OH-CS unsolvable 10:45	.73	14	.005	.97	11	.0005	.87	25	.0005
17-OH-CS unsolvable 11:00	.67	14	.005	.95	11	.0005	.88	25	.0005
17-OH-CS unsolvable 12:10	.53	14	.025	.94	11	.0005	.70	25	.0005
17-OH-CS unsolvable 11:30	.88	12	.0005	.96	7	.0005	.89	19	.0005
17-OH-CS unsolvable 11:30									
Mood I: aggression	.56	11	.05	.83	8	.005	.71	19	.0005
17-OH-CS scan 4	.93	7	.005	.98	7	.0005	.93	14	.0005
17-OH-CS solvable 7:30	.85	10	.005	.96	7	.0005	.88	17	.0005
17-OH-CS solvable 10:45	.88	10	.0005	.84	8	.005	.84	18	.0005
17-OH-CS solvable 11:00	.97	10	.0005	.87	8	.005	.90	18	.0005
17-OH-CS solvable 12:10	.90	10	.0005	.89	8	.005	.88	18	.0005
17-OH-CS solvable 3:30	.84	10	.005	.92	8	.0005	.83	18	.0005
17-OH-CS solvable 11:30	.88	10	.0005	.72	8	.025	.80	18	.0005
17-OH-CS unsolvable 7:30	.75	12	.005	.96	8	.0005	.85	20	.0005
17-OH-CS unsolvable 10:45	.75	11	.005	.96	8	.0005	.86	19	.0005
17-OH-CS unsolvable 11:00	.85	11	.0005	.96	8	.0005	.89	19	.0005
17-OH-CS unsolvable 12:10	.80	11	.005	.97	8	.0005	.84	19	.0005
17-OH-CS unsolvable 3:30	.88	12	.0005	.96	7	.0005	.89	19	.0005
Nonesterized fatty acids (NEFA) solvable 7:30									
None									
NEFA solvable 10:45									
NEFA solvable 11:00	.79	12	.005	.94	9	.0005	.88	21	.0005
NEFA scan 3	.80	8	.01	.65	8	.05	.66	16	.005
NEFA solvable 11:00									
Mood I: skepticism	−.53	12	.05	−.50	12	.05	−.50	24	.01
NEFA solvable 10:45	.79	12	.005	.94	9	.0005	.88	21	.0005
NEFA unsolvable 10:45	.70	10	.025	.64	9	.05	.66	19	.005
NEFA solvable 12:10									
NEFA unsolvable 10:45	.81	8	.01	.87	7	.005	.86	15	.0005
NEFA solvable 3:30									
None									

Table K-2. Significant correlations in split-half samples and total sample for on-ward non-MI patients—cont'd

Variable	Sample 1			Sample 2			Total sample		
	r	*N*	*p*	*r*	*N*	*p*	*r*	*N*	*p*
NEFA solvable 11:30									
None									
NEFA unsolvable 7:30									
None									
NEFA unsolvable 10:45									
NEFA solvable 11:00	.70	10	.025	.64	9	.05	.66	19	.005
NEFA solvable 12:10	.81	8	.01	.87	7	.005	.86	15	.0005
NEFA unsolvable 11:00	.64	10	.025	.77	9	.01	.75	19	.0005
NEFA scan 4	.87	5	.05	.98	7	.0005	.98	12	.0005
NEFA unsolvable 11:00									
NEFA unsolvable 10:45	.64	10	.025	.77	9	.01	.75	19	.0005
NEFA unsolvable 12:10									
None									
NEFA unsolvable 3:30									
None									
NEFA unsolvable 11:30									
None									
NEFA scan 1									
None									
NEFA scan 2									
Sex	.87	9	.005	.75	8	.025	.58	17	.01
NEFA scan 3									
Nurses' cooperation	.79	7	.025	.79	7	.025	.68	14	.005
Mood I: social affection	.61	10	.05	.61	11	.025	.54	21	.01
NEFA solvable 10:45	.80	8	.01	.65	8	.05	.66	16	.005
NEFA scan 4									
NEFA unsolvable 10:45	.87	5	.05	.98	7	.0005	.98	12	.0005
NEFA scan 5									
None									
NEFA scan 6									
None									
NEFA scan 7									
None									
NEFA scan 8									
None									

Table K-3. Significant correlations in split-half samples and total sample for off-ward non-MI patients·

Variable	Sample 1			Sample 2			Total sample		
	r	N	p	r	N	p	r	N	p
Locus of control (LC)									
Days hospital	−.38	39	.01	−.26	40	.05	−.31	79	.005
Denial: dissatisfaction	−.40	37	.01	−.27	39	.05	−.33	76	.005
Denial: anxiety	−.30	37	.05	−.35	39	.025	−.32	76	.005
Repression-sensitization (R-S)									
Education	.55	35	.0005	.29	35	.05	.42	70	.0005
Depression I	−.41	40	.01	−.32	39	.025	−.39	79	.0005
Denial: self-interest	.49	37	.005	.42	39	.005	.45	76	.0005
Denial: dissatisfaction	.68	37	.0005	.53	39	.0005	.60	76	.0005
Denial: hostility	.37	37	.025	.60	39	.0005	.50	76	.0005
Denial: anxiety	.51	37	.005	.52	39	.0005	.49	76	.0005
Size estimation (SE)									
Days ICU	.85	8	.005	.61	11	.025	.66	19	.005
Sex									
Denial: self-interest	.28	37	.05	.27	39	.05	.27	76	.01
Age									
None									
Education									
Repression-sensitization	.55	35	.0005	.29	35	.05	.42	70	.0005
Salary	.43	34	.01	.33	25	.05	.39	59	.005
Religion									
None									
Salary									
Education	.43	34	.01	.33	35	.05	.39	69	.0005
Denial: self-interest	−.28	33	.05	−.36	34	.025	−.30	67	.01
Lie score									
Denial: self-interest	.62	37	.0005	.47	39	.005	.53	76	.0005
Denial: dissatisfaction	.33	37	.025	.39	39	.01	.35	76	.005
Denial: hostility	.46	37	.005	.57	39	.0005	.51	76	.0005
Days ICU									
Size estimation	.85	8	.005	.61	11	.025	.66	19	.005
Days hospital	.68	10	.025	.60	12	.025	.64	22	.005
Days hospital									
Locus of control	−.38	39	.01	−.26	40	.05	−.31	79	.005
Days ICU	.68	10	.025	.60	12	.025	.64	22	.005
Days before testing	.63	40	.0005	.36	40	.025	.52	80	.0005
Nonesterized fatty acids (NEFA) unsolvable 12:10	−.54	11	.05	−.85	6	.025	−.62	17	.005
Days before testing									
Days hospital	.63	40	.0005	.36	40	.025	.52	80	.0005
Depression I									
Repression-sensitization	−.41	40	.01	−.32	39	.025	−.39	79	.0005
Denial: dissatisfaction	−.32	37	.025	−.40	38	.01	−.37	75	.005
Denial: anxiety	−.45	37	.005	−.48	38	.005	−.45	75	.0005
NEFA solvable 12:10	−.66	11	.025	−.74	6	.05	−.66	17	.005
NEFA unsolvable 12:10	−.53	11	.05	−.90	6	.01	−.62	17	.005
17-OH-CS scan 1									
None									
17-OH-CS scan 2									
NEFA unsolvable 11:00	−.83	5	.05	−.99	3	.05	−.63	8	.05

Table K-3. Significant correlations in split-half samples and total sample
for off-ward non-MI patients—cont'd

Variable	Sample 1			Sample 2			Total sample		
	r	N	p	r	N	p	r	N	p
17-OH-CS scan 3									
17-OH-CS solvable 7:30	.88	5	.025	.89	7	.005	.88	12	.0005
17-OH-CS solvable 10:45	.67	8	.05	.99	7	.0005	.89	15	.0005
17-OH-CS scan 4									
17-OH-CS unsolvable 11:00	.69	7	.05	.99	4	.005	.91	11	.0005
17-OH-CS scan 5									
17-OH-CS solvable 12:10	.98	5	.005	.99	3	.05	.93	8	.0005
17-OH-CS scan 6									
None									
17-OH-CS scan 7									
None									
17-OH-CS scan 8									
None									
Denial: self-interest									
Repression-sensitization	.49	37	.005	.42	39	.005	.45	76	.0005
Sex	.28	37	.05	.27	39	.05	.27	76	.01
Salary	−.28	33	.05	−.36	34	.025	−.30	67	.01
Lie score	.62	37	.0005	.47	39	.005	.53	76	.0005
Denial: dissatisfaction	.62	37	.0005	.50	39	.005	.56	76	.0005
Denial: hostility	.66	37	.0005	.75	39	.0005	.71	76	.0005
Denial: anxiety	.50	37	.005	.39	39	.01	.44	76	.0005
Denial: sexuality	.35	37	.025	.59	39	.0005	.48	76	.0005
Denial: dissatisfaction									
Locus of control	−.40	37	.01	−.27	39	.05	−.33	76	.005
Repression-sensitization	.68	37	.0005	.53	39	.0005	.60	76	.0005
Lie score	.33	37	.025	.39	39	.01	.35	76	.005
Depression I	−.32	37	.025	−.40	38	.01	−.37	75	.005
Denial: self-interest	.62	37	.0005	.50	39	.005	.56	76	.0005
Denial: hostility	.61	37	.0005	.59	39	.0005	.59	76	.0005
Denial: anxiety	.60	37	.0005	.45	39	.005	.53	76	.0005
Denial: dependence									
Denial: anxiety	.32	37	.025	.45	39	.005	.37	76	.005
Denial: complacency	.44	37	.005	.54	39	.0005	.46	76	.0005
Coronary proneness (CP) Scale III: perfectionism	.40	37	.01	.27	39	.05	.34	76	.005
Denial: hostility									
Repression-sensitization	.37	37	.025	.60	39	.0005	.50	76	.0005
Lie score	.46	37	.005	.57	39	.0005	.51	76	.0005
Denial: self-interest	.66	37	.0005	.75	39	.0005	.71	76	.0005
Denial: dissatisfaction	.61	37	.0005	.59	39	.0005	.59	76	.0005
Denial: anxiety	.53	37	.0005	.48	39	.005	.50	76	.0005
Denial: sexuality	.38	37	.01	.59	39	.0005	.50	76	.0005
Denial: anxiety									
Locus of control	−.30	37	.05	−.35	39	.025	−.32	76	.005
Repression-sensitization	.51	37	.005	.52	39	.0005	.49	76	.0005
Depression I	−.45	37	.005	−.48	38	.005	−.45	75	.0005
Denial: self-interest	.50	37	.005	.39	39	.01	.44	76	.0005
Denial: dissatisfaction	.60	37	.0005	.45	39	.005	.53	76	.0005
Denial: dependence	.32	37	.025	.45	39	.005	.37	76	.005
Denial: hostility	.53	37	.0005	.48	39	.005	.50	76	.0005

Continued.

Table K-3. Significant correlations in split-half samples and total sample for off-ward non-MI patients—cont'd

Variable	Sample 1			Sample 2			Total sample		
	r	N	p	r	N	p	r	N	p
Denial: complacency	.28	37	.05	.39	39	.01	.33	76	.005
Denial: complacency									
Denial: dependence	.44	37	.005	.54	39	.0005	.46	76	.0005
Denial: anxiety	.28	37	.05	.39	39	.01	.33	76	.005
CP Scale II, scanning	.28	37	.05	.32	39	.025	.31	76	.005
CP Scale III, perfectionism	.39	37	.01	.35	39	.025	.36	76	.005
17-OH-CS unsolvable 3:30	.63	9	.05	.78	10	.005	.68	19	.005
Denial: sexuality									
Denial: self-interest	.35	37	.025	.59	39	.0005	.48	76	.0005
Denial: hostility	.38	37	.01	.59	39	.0005	.50	76	.0005
CP Scale I, repression-sensitization									
None									
CP Scale II, scanning									
Denial: complacency	.28	37	.05	.32	39	.025	.31	76	.005
CP Scale IV, control of self	.32	40	.025	.53	40	.0005	.43	80	.0005
Total CP score	.40	40	.01	.51	40	.005	.46	80	.0005
CP Scale III, perfectionism									
Denial: dependence	.40	37	.01	.27	39	.05	.34	76	.005
Denial: complacency	.39	37	.01	.35	39	.025	.36	76	.005
CP Scale IV, control of self	.46	40	.005	.61	40	.0005	.53	80	.0005
Total CP	.73	40	.0005	.81	40	.0005	.77	80	.0005
CP Scale IV, control of self									
CP Scale II, scanning	.32	40	.025	.53	40	.0005	.43	80	.0005
CP Scale III, perfectionism	.46	40	.005	.61	40	.0005	.53	80	.0005
Total CP	.76	40	.0005	.74	40	.0005	.75	80	.0005
CP Scale V, exercise									
None									
CP Scale VI, overeating									
None									
Total CP scale									
CP Scale II, scanning	.40	40	.01	.51	40	.005	.46	80	.0005
CP Scale III, perfectionism	.73	40	.0005	.81	40	.0005	.77	80	.0005
CP Scale IV, control of self	.76	40	.0005	.74	40	.0005	.75	80	.0005
Blood pressure									
None									
17-OH-CS solvable 7:30									
17-OH-CS scan 3	.88	5	.025	.89	7	.005	.88	12	.0005
17-OH-CS unsolvable 10:45	.74	7	.05	.93	9	.0005	.83	16	.0005
17-OH-CS unsolvable 11:00	.80	7	.025	.84	9	.005	.79	16	.0005
17-OH-CS unsolvable 12:10	.87	7	.005	.94	9	.0005	.89	16	.0005
17-OH-CS solvable 10:45									
17-OH-CS scan 3	.88	5	.025	.99	7	.0005	.89	12	.0005
17-OH-CS solvable 11:00	.66	14	.005	.95	12	.0005	.89	26	.0005
17-OH-CS solvable 12:10	.62	13	.025	.96	9	.0005	.91	22	.0005
17-OH-CS unsolvable 10:45	.70	13	.005	.97	10	.0005	.89	23	.0005
17-OH-CS unsolvable 11:00	.59	13	.025	.96	10	.0005	.90	23	.0005
17-OH-CS solvable 11:00									
17-OH-CS solvable 10:45	.66	14	.005	.95	12	.0005	.89	26	.0005
17-OH-CS solvable 12:10	.47	14	.05	.97	9	.0005	.89	23	.0005

Table K-3. Significant correlations in split-half samples and total sample
for off-ward non-MI patients—cont'd

Variable	Sample 1			Sample 2			Total sample		
	r	N	p	r	N	p	r	N	p
17-OH-CS solvable 11:30	.64	9	.05	.93	8	.0005	.87	17	.0005
17-OH-CS unsolvable 10:45	.80	12	.005	.95	10	.0005	.92	22	.0005
17-OH-CS unsolvable 11:00	.78	12	.005	.96	10	.0005	.93	22	.0005
17-OH-CS solvable 12:10									
17-OH-CS scan 5	.98	5	.005	.99	3	.05	.93	8	.0005
17-OH-CS solvable 10:45	.62	13	.025	.96	9	.0005	.91	22	.0005
17-OH-CS solvable 11:00	.47	14	.05	.97	9	.0005	.89	23	.0005
17-OH-CS unsolvable 10:45	.58	12	.025	.99	8	.0005	.91	20	.0005
17-OH-CS unsolvable 11:00	.55	12	.05	.99	8	.0005	.91	20	.0005
17-OH-CS unsolvable 12:10	.62	12	.025	.99	8	.0005	.89	20	.0005
17-OH-CS unsolvable 11:30	.83	7	.01	.98	6	.0005	.96	13	.0005
NEFA solvable 12:10	−.62	11	.025	−.85	5	.05	−.63	16	.005
17-OH-CS solvable 3:30									
17-OH-CS unsolvable 7:30	.78	11	.005	.97	9	.0005	.86	20	.0005
17-OH-CS unsolvable 3:30	.66	10	.025	.97	10	.0005	.85	20	.0005
17-OH-CS solvable 11:30									
17-OH-CS solvable 11:00	.64	9	.05	.93	8	.0005	.87	17	.0005
17-OH-CS unsolvable 7:30	.67	10	.025	.78	9	.01	.73	19	.0005
17-OH-CS unsolvable 10:45	.74	10	.01	.83	9	.005	.79	19	.0005
17-OH-CS unsolvable 11:00	.73	10	.01	.90	9	.0005	.82	19	.0005
17-OH-CS unsolvable 3:30	.65	9	.05	.91	10	.0005	.88	19	.0005
17-OH-CS unsolvable 11:30	.82	8	.01	.98	9	.0005	.95	17	.0005
17-OH-CS unsolvable 7:30									
17-OH-CS solvable 3:30	.78	11	.005	.97	9	.0005	.86	20	.0005
17-OH-CS solvable 11:30	.67	10	.025	.78	9	.01	.73	19	.0005
17-OH-CS unsolvable 3:30	.70	10	.025	.91	9	.0005	.78	19	.0005
17-OH-CS unsolvable 10:45									
17-OH-CS solvable 7:30	.74	7	.05	.93	9	.0005	.83	16	.0005
17-OH-CS solvable 10:45	.70	13	.005	.97	10	.0005	.89	23	.0005
17-OH-CS solvable 11:00	.80	12	.005	.95	10	.0005	.92	22	.0005
17-OH-CS solvable 12:10	.58	12	.025	.99	8	.0005	.91	20	.0005
17-OH-CS solvable 11:30	.74	10	.01	.83	9	.005	.79	19	.0005
17-OH-CS solvable 11:00	.94	15	.0005	.98	12	.0005	.97	27	.0005
17-OH-CS solvable 12:10	.63	15	.01	.96	12	.0005	.81	27	.0005
17-OH-CS solvable 11:30	.85	8	.005	.80	8	.01	.80	16	.0005
17-OH-CS unsolvable 11:00									
17-OH-CS scan 4	.69	7	.05	.99	4	.005	.91	11	.0005
17-OH-CS solvable 7:30	.80	7	.025	.84	9	.005	.79	16	.0005
17-OH-CS solvable 10:45	.59	13	.025	.96	10	.0005	.90	23	.0005
17-OH-CS solvable 11:00	.78	12	.005	.96	10	.0005	.93	22	.0005
17-OH-CS solvable 12:10	.55	12	.05	.99	8	.0005	.91	20	.0005
17-OH-CS solvable 11:30	.73	10	.01	.90	9	.0005	.82	19	.0005
17-OH-CS unsolvable 10:45	.94	15	.0005	.98	12	.0005	.97	27	.0005
17-OH-CS unsolvable 12:10	.70	15	.005	.93	12	.0005	.82	27	.0005
17-OH-CS unsolvable 3:30	.89	8	.005	.88	8	.005	.86	16	.0005
17-OH-CS unsolvable 12:10									
17-OH-CS solvable 7:30	.87	7	.005	.94	9	.0005	.89	16	.0005
17-OH-CS solvable 12:10	.62	12	.025	.99	8	.0005	.89	20	.0005
17-OH-CS unsolvable 10:45	.63	15	.01	.96	12	.0005	.81	27	.0005

Continued.

Table K-3. Significant correlations in split-half samples and total sample for off-ward non-MI patients—cont'd

Variable	Sample 1			Sample 2			Total sample		
	r	N	p	r	N	p	r	N	p
17-OH-CS unsolvable 11:00	.70	15	.005	.93	12	.0005	.82	27	.0005
17-OH-CS unsolvable 11:30	.65	8	.05	.77	8	.025	.67	16	.005
NEFA solvable 12:10	−.52	11	.05	−.97	4	.025	−.63	15	.01
17-OH-CS unsolvable 3:30									
Denial: complacency	.63	9	.05	.78	10	.005	.68	19	.005
17-OH-CS solvable 3:30	.66	10	.025	.97	10	.0005	.85	20	.0005
17-OH-CS solvable 11:30	.65	9	.05	.91	20	.0005	.88	19	.0005
17-OH-CS unsolvable 7:30	.70	10	.025	.91	9	.0005	.78	19	.0005
NEFA solvable 12:10	−.59	9	.05	−.95	4	.025	−.65	13	.01
17-OH-CS unsolvable 11:30									
17-OH-CS solvable 12:10	.83	7	.01	.98	6	.0005	.96	13	.0005
17-OH-CS solvable 11:30	.82	8	.01	.98	9	.0005	.95	17	.0005
17-OH-CS unsolvable 10:45	.85	8	.005	.80	8	.01	.80	16	.0005
17-OH-CS unsolvable 11:00	.89	8	.005	.88	8	.005	.86	16	.0005
17-OH-CS unsolvable 12:10	.65	8	.05	.77	8	.025	.67	16	.005
NEFA solvable 7:30									
None									
NEFA solvable 10:45									
NEFA solvable 11:00	.93	11	.0005	.99	6	.0005	.95	17	.0005
NEFA unsolvable 10:45	.85	10	.005	.97	5	.005	.88	15	.0005
NEFA unsolvable 11:00	.84	10	.005	.85	5	.05	.80	15	.0005
NEFA solvable 11:00									
NEFA solvable 10:45	.93	11	.0005	.99	6	.0005	.95	17	.0005
NEFA solvable 12:10	.95	11	.0005	.80	6	.05	.87	17	.0005
NEFA unsolvable 10:45	.75	11	.005	.85	6	.025	.76	17	.0005
NEFA unsolvable 11:00	.81	11	.005	.90	6	.01	.78	17	.0005
NEFA scan 3	.85	6	.025	.92	4	.05	.87	10	.0005
NEFA solvable 12:10									
Depression I	−.66	11	.025	−.74	6	.05	−.66	17	.005
17-OH-CS solvable 12:10	−.62	11	.025	−.85	5	.05	−.63	16	.005
17-OH-CS unsolvable 12:10	−.52	11	.05	−.97	4	.025	−.63	15	.01
17-OH-CS unsolvable 3:30	−.59	9	.05	−.95	4	.025	−.65	13	.01
NEFA solvable 11:00	.95	11	.0005	.80	6	.05	.87	17	.0005
NEFA unsolvable 11:00	.89	11	.0005	.98	5	.005	.92	16	.0005
NEFA unsolvable 12:10	.70	11	.01	.92	5	.025	.74	16	.0005
NEFA solvable 3:30									
None									
NEFA solvable 11:30									
None									
NEFA unsolvable 7:30									
None									
NEFA unsolvable 10:45									
NEFA solvable 10:45	.85	10	.005	.97	5	.005	.88	15	.0005
NEFA solvable 11:00	.75	11	.005	.85	6	.025	.76	17	.0005
NEFA unsolvable 11:00	.92	11	.0005	.75	8	.025	.83	19	.0005
NEFA unsolvable 11:00									
17-OH-CS scan 2	−.83	5	.05	−.99	3	.05	−.63	8	.05
NEFA solvable 10:45	.84	10	.005	.85	5	.05	.80	15	.0005
NEFA solvable 11:00	.81	11	.005	.90	6	.01	.78	17	.0005

Table K-3. Significant correlations in split-half samples and total sample for off-ward non-MI patients—cont'd

Variable	Sample 1			Sample 2			Total sample		
	r	N	p	r	N	p	r	N	p
NEFA solvable 12:10	.89	11	.0005	.98	5	.005	.92	16	.0005
NEFA unsolvable 10:45	.92	11	.0005	.75	8	.025	.83	19	.0005
NEFA unsolvable 12:10	.89	11	.0005	.86	6	.025	.84	17	.0005
NEFA unsolvable 12:10									
Days hospital	−.54	11	.05	−.85	6	.025	−.62	17	.005
Depression I	−.53	11	.05	−.90	6	.01	−.62	17	.005
NEFA solvable 12:10	.70	11	.01	.92	5	.025	.74	16	.0005
NEFA unsolvable 11:00	.89	11	.0005	.86	6	.025	.84	17	.0005
NEFA unsolvable 3:30									
None									
NEFA unsolvable 11:30									
None									
NEFA scan 1									
None									
NEFA scan 2									
None									
NEFA scan 3									
NEFA solvable 11:00	.85	6	.025	.92	4	.05	.87	10	.0005
NEFA scan 4									
None									
NEFA scan 5									
None									
NEFA scan 6									
None									
NEFA scan 7									
None									
NEFA scan 8									
None									

Appendix L

CORONARY PRONENESS SCALE

Items in this scale are divided into the following categories:
- I. Repression (high score) versus sensitization
- II. Hyperscanning (high score) versus hyposcanning
- III. Perfectionism
- IV. Self-control
- V. Exercise
- VI. Overeating
- L. Lie score items

   Undesignated filler items

KEY: T = true = 1 point
  F = false = 1 point within each category

II		T	1. I like to travel because it gives me a chance to see a lot of different things.
III		T	2. I am a hard worker.
III		T	3. I am never late to an appointment.
I		T	4. When things are going badly for me, I just want to get away.
	(L)	F	5. I do not always tell the truth.
IV		T	6. Indecisive people bother me greatly.
	(L)	F	7. I do not read every editorial in the newspaper every day.
III		T	8. I get worked up over people who don't do a good job.
		F	9. I have not lived the right kind of life.
		F	10. I sometimes keep on at a thing until others lose their patience with me.
I		T	11. I never try to figure out why I get down in the dumps.
	(L)	F	12. I get angry sometimes.
		F	13. I am certainly lacking in self-confidence.
	(L)	F	14. Once in a while I put off until tomorrow what I ought to do today.
IV		T	15. I consider myself the boss in my home.
		F	16. I do many things which I regret afterwards (I regret things more or more often than others seem to).
	(L)	F	17. Sometimes when I am not feeling well I am cross.

210

III		T	18.	Once I start a job, I work at it until I finish.
IV		T	19.	If I'm not able to do things for myself I become very frustrated.
V		T	20.	I won't walk to a place when I can ride.
		F	21.	Someone has it in for me.
	(L)	F	22.	My table manners are not quite as good at home as when I am out in company.
I		T	23.	Nothing worries me.
III		T	24.	I hardly, if ever, make a mistake.
II		T	25.	People often refer to me as having a lot of curiosity.
	(L)	F	26.	I would rather win than lose in a game.
IV		T	27.	When I decide to do something, I do it.
	(L)	F	28.	I like to know some important people because it makes me feel important.
I		T	29.	It's not always good for people to be told what's going to happen to them.
		T	30.	I do not have a great fear of snakes.
IV		T	31.	I do not like to be rushed by others.
III		T	32.	At least some people call me a perfectionist.
	(L)	F	33.	I do not like everyone I know.
I		T	34.	People who are always asking questions bother me.
		F	35.	There is very little love and companionship in my family as compared to other homes.
V		T	36.	I believe that exercise, or the lack of exercise, had something to do with my present condition.
IV		T	37.	I consider myself a person of determination.
	(L)	F	38.	I gossip a little at times.
		F	39.	Once a week or oftener I become very excited.
III		T	40.	I am bothered by things not in their right place.
		F	41.	Once in a while I feel hate toward members of my family whom I usually love.
		F	42.	Life is a strain for me much of the time.
VI		T	43.	I tend to overeat at mealtime.
		F	44.	Even when I am with people I feel lonely much of the time.
I		F	45.	When I have a problem to solve, I try to get as much information about it as possible.
		F	46.	Bad words, often terrible words, come into my mind, and I cannot get rid of them.
V		T	47.	I typically do not enjoy vigorous exercise.
		T	48.	People say insulting and vulgar things about me.
		F	49.	I feel unable to tell anyone all about myself.
		F	50.	If given the chance, I could do some things that would be of great benefit to the world.
I		T	51.	No one has ever criticized me.
		F	52.	At times I think I am no good at all.
III		T	53.	I am always early to an appointment.
		F	54.	It makes me nervous to have to wait.
IV		T	55.	I live and work by the philosophy that there are not such words as "I can't."
I		F	56.	I wish my doctor would tell me more than he does.
III		T	57.	Everything I do is done very well.
		T	58.	I do not mind meeting strangers.
I		F	59.	The best way to solve a problem is to really think about it.

IV	T	60. It upsets me terribly when I'm trying to convince someone of something and they will not listen.
IV	T	61. Up until recently I made all the decisions in my family.
	F	62. I am afraid of finding myself in a closet or small enclosed place.
I	T	63. Most of the time when I get depressed I don't know why.
	F	64. I usually have to stop and think before I act, even in trifling matters.
V	F	65. I make it a point to set some formal exercise every day over and beyond the usual exercise I get from my job.
I	F	66. When someone has bad news to give me, I want to get it over with quickly rather than postponing it.
II	T	67. When I walk into a crowded room, I look around to see who is there rather than focus my attention on one individual.
II	T	68. When the car, TV, or radio is in disrepair, I like to find out as much about it as possible.
VI	T	69. I usually eat between meals.

Appendix M

DEPRESSION SCALE OF THE MINNESOTA MULTIPHASIC PERSONALITY INVENTORY (MMPI)*

T	71. I am easily awakened by noise.
F	72. My daily life is full of things that keep me interested.
F	77. At times I feel like swearing.
T	78. I find it hard to keep my mind on a task or job.
F	79. I seldom worry about my health.
T	81. I have had periods of days, weeks, or months when I couldn't take care of things because I couldn't "get going."
T	82. My sleep is fitful and disturbed.

INDEX